W9-CKI-296

374.012 BLA
Blake, Brett Elizabeth.
Literacy and learning :

JUL   2004

W 5/11
W 11/08   W 4/17
         W 4/14

WITHDRAWN

Literacy and Learning

●◆ A REFERENCE HANDBOOK

Other Titles in
ABC-CLIO's
CONTEMPORARY EDUCATION ISSUES
Series

African American Education, Cynthia L. Jackson
The Assessment Debate, Valerie J. Janesick
Bilingual Education, Rosa Castro Feinberg
Charter Schools, Danny Weil
Educational Leadership, Pat Williams-Boyd
Migrant Education, Judith A. Gowens
Special Education, Arlene Sacks
Student Rights, Patricia H. Hinchey
Teacher Training, David B. Pushkin

PROPERTY OF CLPL.

CONTEMPORARY EDUCATION ISSUES

Literacy and Learning

●◆ A REFERENCE HANDBOOK

Brett Elizabeth Blake and
Robert W. Blake

A B C ● C L I O

Santa Barbara, California • Denver, Colorado • Oxford, England

Copyright © 2002 by Brett Elizabeth Blake and Robert W. Blake

All rights reserved. No part of this publication may be reproduced, stored in a retrieval system, or transmitted, in any form or by any means, electronic, mechanical, photocopying, recording, or otherwise, except for the inclusion of brief quotations in a review, without prior permission in writing from the publishers.

Library of Congress Cataloging-in-Publication Data
Blake, Brett Elizabeth.
  Literacy and learning : a reference handbook / Brett Elizabeth Blake and Robert W. Blake.
      p.   cm. — (Contemporary education issues)
Includes bibliographical references and index.
   ISBN 1-57607-273-8 (hardcover : alk. paper)
   1. Literacy—United States—Handbooks, manuals, etc.   I. Blake, Robert W. (Robert William), 1930– II. Title. III. Series.

LC151 .B58 2002
302.2'244—dc21

                                                          2002014485

06   05   04   03   02   10 9 8 7 6 5 4 3 2 1

This book is also available on the World Wide Web as an e-book. Visit abc-clio.com for details.

ABC-CLIO, Inc.
130 Cremona Drive, P.O. Box 1911
Santa Barbara, California 93116–1911

This book is printed on acid-free paper ∞.
Manufactured in the United States of America

*To Robbie—my reader, writer, and
adolescent extraordinaire
and
To Carol, who was always there*

●← Contents

Series Editor's Preface   *xi*
Preface   *xiii*
Acknowledgments   *xvii*

Chapter One: The Meanings of Literacy   *1*

    Reasons for Literacy   *5*

        Literacy Is Good for the Individual   *5*
        Literacy Is Good for Economic Well-Being   *6*
        Literacy Is Good for Society   *6*
        Literacy Is Good for Political Stability   *6*
        Literacy Is Good for the Community   *7*
        *Literacy Is Good for the Economic Development
            of Countries*   *7*

    Definitions of Literacy: A Variety   *8*
    Evolution of the Terms   *10*
    Defining Functional Literacy   *11*
    Age and Functional Literacy   *12*
    The Skills of Literacy   *13*
    Measuring Literacy   *15*
    Critical Levels of Literacy   *15*
    How Literacy Has Changed over Time   *17*
    Literacy and the Nonnative Speaker   *18*
    Literacy Debates   *19*

        *Literacy/Illiteracy versus a Scale of Literacy
            Skills*   *19*
        A Single Literacy versus Many Literacies   *19*
        *High-Quantity Literacy Education versus
            High-Quality Literacy Education*   *21*

    Summary   *22*
    References   *23*

Chapter Two: Chronology   *25*

Chapter Three: The Foundations of Literacy   33

Speaking and Writing   33
Characteristics of Speech   34
The Development of Writing   35
The Alphabet versus the Syllabary   40
How the Alphabet Works   41
Results of the Invention of the Alphabet   42
Readership in Ancient Times   46
Summary   47
References   48

Chapter Four: The Consequences of Literacy   51

Homer's Poetry   52
The Birth of Prose in Western Thought and Language   56
Fundamental Consequences of the Alphabet   60
Early Modern Consequences of Literacy   62
Summary   70
References   71

Chapter Five: Reading: How We Learned to Read   73

What We Do as We Read   73
How We First Read: Texts with No Word
Separation   78
The Birth and Evolution of Modern Reading   82
Reading at the Beginning of the Early Modern Era   83
Summary   99
References   101

Chapter Six: Reading Literature: Literature as a Way of Knowing   103

Literature as a Way of Knowing   104
Summary   121
References   122

Chapter Seven: Reading Literature: New Criticism—Theory to Practice   125

Reading Literature: Background   128

New Criticism: Theory *135*

   Principles of New Critical Theory *142*

New Criticism: Practice *143*

Summary *152*

   *How We Read Literature Using Principles of
   New Criticism* *153*

References *154*

*Chapter Eight: Reading Literature: Reader Response—
Theory to Practice* *157*

Reader Response: Theory *159*

   The Submissive Reader *166*
   The Active Reader *168*
   The Semiotic Reader *170*
   The Subjective Reader *170*
   The Psychoanalytic Reader *173*
   The Interpretive Community Reader *176*
   Principles of Reader Response Theory *180*

Reader Response: Practice *182*

   *Why Reader Response Practice Has Evolved
   So Slowly* *185*

Classroom Reader Response: Practical Models *201*

   *Assumptions Underlying Classroom Reader
   Response* *203*
   *Classroom Reader Response Program for
   Secondary Students* *205*
   *Classroom Reader Response Program for
   Elementary Students* *211*

Summary *215*
References *217*

Chapter Nine: Literacy among Diverse Learners *221*

Who Are Today's Diverse Learners? *222*
Two Scenarios: English Language Learners in
Diverse Settings *223*
Where Do I Begin? *226*

   Second Language Acquisition Theories *226*
   Reading and Second Language *228*

Literacy and Diverse Learners   *229*
Five Assumptions   *229*
Classroom Examples   *230*
Standards and Accountability: Role of School versus "Local Literacies"   *235*
Summary and Implications   *236*
References   *237*

Chapter Ten: Organizations and Educational Associations   *239*

Organizations   *239*
Educational Associations   *245*

Chapter Eleven: Selected Print and Nonprint Resources   *247*

Print Sources   *247*
Nonprint Sources   *249*
General Interest   *249*
Lesson Plans and Teaching Resources   *250*
Literacy Research   *251*

Index   *253*
About the Authors   *267*

❧ Series Editor's Preface

The Contemporary Education Issues series is dedicated to providing readers with an up-to-date exploration of the central issues in education today. Books in the series will examine such controversial topics as home schooling, charter schools, privatization of public schools, Native American education, African American education, literacy, curriculum development, and many others. The series is national in scope and is intended to encourage research by anyone interested in the field.

Because education is undergoing radical if not revolutionary change, the series is particularly concerned with how contemporary controversies in education affect both the organization of schools and the content and delivery of curriculum. Authors will endeavor to provide a balanced understanding of the issues and their effects on teachers, students, parents, administrators, and policymakers. The aim of the Contemporary Education Issues series is to publish excellent research on today's educational concerns by some of the finest scholar/practitioners in the field while pointing to new directions. The series promises to offer important analyses of some of the most controversial issues facing society today.

☙ Preface

When we started this book—a quest for answers to the questions What is literacy? and How do we achieve it?—we had little idea of where our search would lead us. We both were of the mind, however, that literacy learning was the single most significant challenge not only facing our country but confronting peoples all over the globe.

As with all quests, we allowed the idea of literacy to lead us where it would. At this stage of the book's development—the work is not finished; we're just letting it go—we have arrived at two major conclusions about literacy: First, the invention of alphabetic writing, the foundation of popular literacy, was perhaps the most notable intellectual achievement by human beings, comparable only to the invention of language itself. Second, as a correlative to the discovery of alphabetic writing, with the invention of movable type and the printing press and the mass production of books in the vernaculars of many peoples, literacy was no longer the special province of a privileged few but became an activity available to all people.

In chapter 1, "The Meanings of Literacy," we explore the various interpretations of the word *literacy* as a necessary basis for analyzing and evaluating literary programs. In chapter 2, "Chronology," we present an arrangement of events in time—in many cases, the dates are only approximate—that are relevant to historical episodes in the book and that show—inadequately at best—the magnificent sweep of literacy throughout the Western world and in the United States.

In chapter 3, "The Foundations of Literacy," we attempt to explain in ordinary language a highly technical subject, that of alphabetic writing. Our contention is that unless we understand alphabetic writing—a phenomenon mostly below the level of our consciousness—we cannot indeed comprehend literacy. With chapter 4, "The Consequences of Literacy," we describe how the combination of alphabetic writing and movable type and the printing press literally shaped all aspects of Western thought and life and allowed us to enter the modern era. In chapter 5, "How We Learned to Read," we follow the glacially slow evolution of reading matter from a time in which we read pages chiefly in Latin with no spaces between words and without any of the aids to reading we now take for granted to a time when we read books in vernacular tongues with all the reading aids we now enjoy without thought.

In chapter 6, "Reading Literature—Literature as a Way of Knowing," we examine in detail the notion that there are two kinds of knowing and therefore two kinds of reading: what some call rational, scientific reading and literary reading. We pursue this topic because we contend that rational prose is ascendant in our culture and that literary reading—often considered a frill in our highly technical society—is not only a crucial aspect of knowing but should be afforded equal importance in our culture.

In chapter 7, "Reading Literature—New Criticism, Theory to Practice" and chapter 8, "Reading Literature—Reader Response, Theory to Practice," we present a thumbnail sketch of what we perceive as the evolution of how we have viewed reading literature during the twentieth century, from a focus on the author's intent—"Old Criticism"—to a focus on the literary text qua text—"New Criticism"—and finally to a focus on the individual's personal, intuitive response to a work of literature—"Reader Response." We find a major shift from criticizing literature as an activity for an educated few, to reading and responding to literature for all, if you will, to democratizing the reading of literature.

In chapter 9, "Literacy among Diverse Learners," we first explore the processes of language acquisition, especially as they relate to literacy learning. Here, we emphasize that the true challenge to successful literacy learning in today's world, among peoples of widely diverse ethnic backgrounds, cultures, linguistic heritages, and languages, is to be able to respect and appreciate the "local" literacies of all students: their many texts, voices, and ways in which they engage with language both in school and out of school. We also emphasize that language and literacy learning is always political, and thus is inextricably shaped by powerful institutions like governments and schools.

In chapter 10, "Organizations and Educational Associations," we list organizations that have a direct interest in literacy learning as a broad category. In chapter 11, "Selected Print and Nonprint Resources," in order to present a balanced portrait, we list print sources not already cited at the end of each chapter, including both popular and scholarly books and articles as well as selected presentations at professional conferences.

In this era of "one size fits all" quick fixes and cookbook recipes for "good" literacy learning, we offer ideas in this book from what we believe is a fresh perspective, a view that dares to look not only at where we've come, but also, perhaps most frighteningly, at where we're going. In our quest to define, explain, and explore the field of literacy, we have found ourselves surrounded with potentially dangerous conversations about literacy; questions and statements that have included, "whose literacy," "that's not language/that's not correct English," "there is only one way to teach literacy," or even "they don't deserve it."

From our explorations, however, we are confident that the notion of "literacy for all" will survive in our society just as it has done for thousands of years. We are reminded of how the Irish monks copied and transcribed the Bible, risking having their hands cut off or worse, in their brave efforts to bring vernacular English to the people, or how the slaves in pre–Civil War America taught themselves to read and write in the still of the night because being caught learning to read and write was punishable by death, or how the French hid books and other works of art from the Nazis during World War II so that future generations could read, interpret, and imagine another time and place.

No one government, society, school system, university professor, middle school teacher, or neighbor should have the power to decide whose literacy is most desirable, or what one tried-and-true method will best teach literacy, or most importantly that someone's language use is better than another's. We urge you the reader to join us in our quest: to read, to write, to learn; to engage your students in literacy learning, but most of all to question and to challenge. That, perhaps, is the greatest legacy modern literacy has given us.

☙ Acknowledgments

A warm thank you to Shirley Steinberg, who got us into this series, and this book in particular (not bad for a redhead); my former colleagues Josephine, Rob, and Devin; and my new colleagues Joanne, Lindamichelle, and Grace, who always believed I could write even though I had become a "teaching machine"; my family, and, of course, my Dad, with whom I finally got a chance to write a book. Those late night conversations over GlenKinchie paid off!

—BEB

No book can ever be completed without help—direct or indirect—from countless people, whose influence we still sense.

I thank my Interlibrary Loan team at the State University of New York College at Brockport, Drake Memorial Library, Paula Stull and Bob Gilliam. I was constantly amazed by and grateful for their ability to find for me *any* book on the face of the earth within a few days.

I've worked with a few editors in my time, but I have never had a better editorial group than the people at ABC-CLIO. Danny Weil, this series's editor, is a no-nonsense guy but a person who gave us much-appreciated support over a long period of writing. Alicia Merritt, the senior acquisitions editor, was efficient but always gracious. Anna Kaltenbach, production editor, was patient beyond all expectations but, in an amazingly understated way, kept us *almost* on schedule. And Kathy Delfosse, our copy editor, was virtually always right in her editing. As the saying goes, any errors that remain are not Kathy's but ours.

As a person who affected me beyond his knowledge, Philip L. Gerber, former university professor of English at the SUNY College at Brockport, was first my mentor and then became a dear friend.

What a wonderful opportunity this has been for me to work with my now grown-up daughter, Brett Elizabeth, on a task of this scope. I've come to appreciate her intelligence, wide knowledge, and impervious humanistic spirit. She may be my daughter, but she's undeniably her own person.

And finally I thank my wife, Carol, for allowing me to spend so much precious time writing this book.

—RWB

Chapter One

✎ The Meanings of Literacy

Literacy is at the heart of world development and human
rights. Its importance lies in what precedes literacy: the
words that are the expression of human thought. Its
importance lies equally in what can then be done with the
written word, which conveys thought across time and
across space and makes the reader a "co-author" and
active interpreter of the text. An oral society relies on mem-
ory to transmit its history, literature, laws, or music,
whereas the written word allows infinite possibilities of
transmission and therefore of active participation in com-
munication. These possibilities are what makes the goal of
universal literacy so important.
    —Federico Mayor, director general, UNESCO

As Federico Mayor points out in his eloquent epigraph, literacy is
indeed "at the heart of world development and human rights." The goal
of worldwide literacy is probably the most important one we face today.
We know that people who cannot read and write may be intelligent and
worthy, but if they are not literate in our present-day technological,
global society, they are at a dismaying disadvantage.

How then do we approach the overwhelmingly complex problem
of literacy? If we are to improve literacy even in the United States—
which enjoys a fairly high literacy rate among its citizens—first we need
to address questions like these: What precisely is literacy? What are the
fundamental skills of reading and writing? How do we measure these
skills once we have identified them? And how do we speak to such striking contemporary difficulties when we attempt to teach people to read
and write? Should we use the stark terms "literate" and "illiterate" to
label people, or should we use words on a scale from least important to
most crucial to designate stages of literacy? Is there a single, global
"autonomous" literacy, or are there many different but valuable "literacies"? And should we provide widespread but short-range, low-cost,
"quantity" literacy programs, which, from the evidence, we know are
minimally successful, or should we concentrate our efforts on long-

range, informed, and strenuous programs, which, on the other hand, have lasting, positive effects?

In this chapter, we speak to these questions and attempt to provide information necessary for arriving at informed answers.

In a recent article in the *New York Times,* reporter Peter Kilborn describes the effects of "illiteracy" on some people living in rural Kentucky. One mother of four, the daughter of a coal miner, is what statisticians call "functionally illiterate." "With the national economy bubbling along, soaking up workers and spreading wealth, she and much of Appalachia live not only in poverty and unemployment but also with the humiliation of being taken for ignorant" (Kilborn 2000, A1).

At this point in time, the operational definition for "functionally illiterate" persons is as follows. They are able to read a recipe, follow a map, and work the keys of a McDonald's cash register. On the other hand, they have trouble filling out a job application, typing data into a computer, using standard punctuation in a paragraph, getting their checkbooks to balance, or taking a written test for a driver's license. It is no wonder that such individuals, in our modern technological society, believe themselves to be inferior to those who can read, write, and do simple arithmetic in a seemingly effortless manner.

The problem of those labeled "functionally illiterate" is one not only for people isolated in rural Appalachia. According to a survey conducted several years ago by the Educational Testing Service (ETS) for the U.S. Department of Education, "more than 1 in 5 adults 16 and older, 40 million people in the United States, could read and calculate at no better than the lowest levels of literacy, called Level 1" (Kilborn 2000, A16).

Of these 40 million people, about a quarter are non-English-speaking immigrants while the rest are native speakers of English. "Many are blacks," we are told, "who live in large cities and rural Southern communities. Several million others live in Appalachia, which is almost entirely white. The national survey, and one three years ago by the State of Kentucky, found that about 30 percent of the adults in Appalachia were functionally illiterate" (Kilborn 2000, A16).

The problem of literacy and illiteracy is not only a challenge for the United States but also a difficulty for all other industrialized nations of the world and markedly a problem for all developing countries. "Adult literacy statistics—both in developing or industrialized countries—remain shocking as we approach the end of the twentieth century" (Wagner 1999, 5). According to Daniel Wagner, the United Nations Educational, Scientific, and Cultural Organization (UNESCO) estimates that there are still about 1 billion adult illiterates in the world today, most of whom are to be found in the world's poorest countries. (The estimated number of 1 billion individuals equals the present total population of India, the second most populated country in the world.)

More than fifty years ago, most children in developing countries had never been to school of any kind. At that time, the United Nations broadcast as one of its central goals to achieve literacy throughout the world, and UNESCO was assigned the task of putting into practice worldwide literacy programs. At present, UNESCO's concern, according to Director-General Federico Mayor, is to make sure that children throughout the world become literate as well as numerate through universal education. It is presently estimated that 100 million children worldwide are not in school, and even though a major effort was launched for universal literacy in 1990 under the Basic Education for All initiative at the Jontien Conference, "in spite of the positive achievements in the past decade, the challenge of universal literacy remains immense" (Mayor 1999, xiii).

For adults, considering the economic advances of industrialized countries, the situation regarding literacy is, unfortunately, even more alarming. The International Adult Survey discovered that even in such highly industrialized countries as Germany, Great Britain, and the United States, large numbers of adults, perhaps as many as 25 percent, had deficient literacy skills. Even though scholars and policymakers use various definitions of literacy and employ differing ways for assessing literacy in contemporary societies, "many industrialized countries are aware that they have serious problems with adults who are not literate enough to function well in modern economies" (Wagner 1999, 5).

In sum, the word "literacy" evokes strong emotions, and it is a term with many different meanings. Even scholars and specialists fail to agree on what actually counts as literacy or what the implications are for those who are illiterate in any society.

The study of literacy is a complex one, combining some of the best thinking of researchers, scholars, and educators from a number of disciplines: psychology, linguistics, history, anthropology, and sociology. In addition, the study of literacy also includes both public policy and actual educational practices from childhood through adulthood.

Literacy is almost universally associated with the most positive aspects of civilization. Throughout history, languages, scripts, and printed matter have been a part of human conflict and change—military, social, and cultural. After William the Conqueror defeated King Harold and the English at the Battle of Hastings in 1066, he established French as the official language of the nobility and of the church as well as of the courts. Anglo-Saxon, the language of the defeated, went underground and as a result became an almost exclusively oral language for several centuries.

For a recent example of how literacy affects societies, we turn to a decision by the Republic of Tatarstan, a part of the Russian Federation, to switch from the Cyrillic alphabet used in Russia to the Roman alphabet used in the West (reported in "Tatars to Drop Cyrillic Alphabet for Roman" in the *New York Times International* on August 31, 2000, A5). Since September 2000, children in a number of schools are now being taught to read the Tatar language using Roman rather than Cyrillic characters. For many centuries, Tatar, a Turkic language, was written in Arabic characters. In 1927, the Tatars had considered switching to the Roman alphabet, but in 1939 Stalin ordered that Cyrillic, with an additional six letters added, be used instead of the Roman alphabet. Many Tatars considered the Cyrillic alphabet a symbol of Stalinist tyranny. Officials in Tatarstan decided to switch to a Roman alphabet to celebrate ten years of self-rule following the collapse of the Soviet Union.

Another such example is found in a report of a government-financed television station in Ballinahown, Ireland, whose purpose is to promote and celebrate Gaelic, the ancient language of Ireland (Barry 2000, A6). Many individuals are determined to save Gaelic from the increased encroachments by the English language. Gaelic, once thought to be the language of the poor and uneducated, of those from the "back of beyond," now seems to symbolize the new spirit of those Irish who enjoy economic and cultural success.

There are many signs that Gaelic is enjoying new attention. Men named "Patrick" now spell their names in a Gaelic fashion, as "Padraig" (pronounced POH-rig), and women christened "Mary" have changed the spelling of their names to "Marie" (pronounced MOY-ra). As another sign of Gaelic's increased importance, Ireland now has fourteen all-Gaelic schools with more than 21,000 students, whereas thirty years ago there were barely thirty schools teaching Gaelic. Recently, in an event perhaps more significant than might appear at first sight, Gaelic was even used as an acceptable language of the courts: A witness in a corruption case in Ireland insisted on his right to respond in Gaelic to questions put to him in English (Barry 2000, A6).

Not everyone, however, is smitten by the recent movement to reinstall Gaelic as the national language of Ireland. Wrote Kevin Myers in the *Irish Times:* "Irish [Gaelic] will soon be spoken as Latin was in medieval Europe, a learned language of a cultural elite" (quoted in Barry 2000, A6). On the other hand, Gearoid O Tuathaigh, a professor of modern Irish history at the National University of Ireland, Galway, reported that he was encouraged by the resurgence of Gaelic study. He pointed out the special beauty of the language. Terms of endearment include *macushla*, "my colt," and *machree*, "my heart." The English phrase "I love you" translates literally in Gaellic as "I am melting for you." If one understands Gaelic, continues Professor O Tuathaigh, one is able to reconstruct Ireland's history by interpreting the names of villages and parishes in the country. The name of the village Geesala, for instance, in County Mayo, means literally "the breeze with salt upon it" (Barry 2000, A6).

Although literacy can be and has been used to maintain divisions between peoples, at the same time, it may be used to bring together people from diverse ethnic groups. As Daniel Wagner expresses it, "Thus, like all human endeavors, literacy often mirrors what is best (and worst), in human society" (Wagner 1999, 1).

REASONS FOR LITERACY

There have been many reasons over the centuries for establishing and encouraging literacy. The following are four of the most noteworthy:

Literacy Is Good for the Individual

As Wagner observes, "Literacy is often simply understood as something that is 'good' for the individual and society" (Wagner 1999, 2). Although virtually no one believes there should be less literacy, there is widespread disagreement about how literacy should be "increased." For example, bilingualism creates a significant question for increasing literacy: Should children be taught to read and write in their mother tongue or in a second language? Notwithstanding such questions relating literacy to the development of the individual, there appears to be little disagreement about the fact that primary education ought to be one of the chief educational goals of all nations. Even so, nonformal education (NFE) for children and methods for ensuring adult literacy vary a great deal from nation to nation.

Again, the ideal of universal literacy has been articulated by governmental agencies throughout the world. In 1990, at the World Conference on Education for All (WCEFA) sponsored by UNESCO, there was widespread agreement that there should be "literacy for all," as stated in the WCEFA's declaration (Wagner 1999, 2). In spite of this apparent consensus, however, there has been extended debate among countries over how this universal literacy is to be achieved.

Literacy Is Good for Economic Well-Being

There is little disagreement about the relation of literacy to economic progress. Very few countries are unaware that in order to become prosperous, their people must become skilled and literate. The direct cost of illiteracy to the United States, for example, has been estimated to be at $40 billion a year (Wagner 1999, 2).

Although anecdotal evidence suggests that workers' training for adults has value, there is little empirical research to substantiate this belief. New studies suggest, though, that what adults earn and how far they may advance in their jobs are strongly related to their literacy skills.

In summary, there is little "demonstrable empirical" research to suggest that adult literacy programs are enabling the unemployed to obtain new jobs or to make major career changes even though anecdotal claims abound (Wagner 1999, 3).

Literacy Is Good for Society

Literacy, especially for women, has important social consequences. The majority of illiterate or low-literate adults tend to be females, particularly in developing countries, and there is surprisingly strong empirical evidence for a relationship between a lack of literacy and infant mortality and even the fertility of mothers (Wagner 1999, 3). We are only now beginning to understand how a mother's level of education affects her children in many harmful ways. The social consequences of literacy, especially for illiterate women in developing countries, appear to be much more extensive than are merely direct economic results.

Literacy Is Good for Political Stability

There is a long tradition of language being used to unify the people of a country. One of the earliest examples was the campaign in Sweden in the 1500s to promote literacy for citizens, the primary goal being to spread a state religion through Bible study. Although the campaign's primary aim was to enable citizens to read the Bible and thus achieve religious solidarity, a secondary aim was to use literacy to create a unified nation. More modern examples of advancing literacy include the Francophone movement in Canada, where French-speaking people wish to make French the official language in the province of Quebec; the literacy work in the former USSR, in China, and in Cuba; and the efforts toward literacy in Europe, parts of Asia, and Africa. In the United States, speakers of Spanish have ensured that in some communities with heavy concentrations of Spanish speakers, signs in Spanish appear alongside signs in English. And the same Spanish speakers are outraged by efforts to have English named the official language of the country.

The reasons given for establishing a language as a nation's official one include the goals of achieving national solidarity, lowering social welfare costs, and providing greater economic productivity. In spite of the claims made by those who already speak the target language that implementing an official language will promote these goals, there are expected outcries by those who speak a minority language—such as Spanish in the United States—who deeply resent the imposition upon them of what they consider a foreign language and the loss of their native language and along with it their entire culture.

Literacy Is Good for the Community

There are strong pressures at the grassroots level, from churches, mosques, and other groups at the private, voluntary level, to provide literacy programs, mostly for adults. Such programs are on a small scale and are targeted for particular groups within the community: out-of-school adolescents, young mothers, the elderly, and the homeless. The government usually has no involvement in such community programs, in which the bulk of instruction is delivered by volunteer teachers and tutors.

The argument given in favor of such small-scale literacy programs is that community literacy promotes moral and social cohesion, thus providing a sense of community. We usually find these modest programs in industrialized countries, where the common governmental position is that illiteracy is so marginal that the government need not pay much attention or provide financial support to alleviating it.

Since the 1990s, however, the attitude of policymakers in industrialized countries toward community literacy programs has changed. The officials have found that community-based programs funded by nongovernmental organizations (NGOs) are often more effective than programs administered by the government.

Literacy Is Good for the Economic Development of Countries

Since the establishment of UN agencies after World War II, there have been growing pressures on developing nations to improve their performance in education and literacy. These external pressures are of two kinds.

First, lending agencies such as the World Bank tend to offer loans only if certain types of educational initiatives are promoted and literacy targets are met. At the same time, other UN agencies, such as UNESCO and the United Nations Children's Fund (UNICEF), have supplied considerable financial support for literacy programs in primary schools and for nonformal adult education programs (Wagner 1999, 4).

Second, certain countries that wish to be perceived as "progressive"—the "public appearance" notion—have promoted their efforts at literacy as a way of gaining international and national legitimacy in terms of social progress. Some developing countries, such as Zimbabwe, Tanzania, and Cuba, have advertised their literacy programs in order to gain international recognition as "progressive" countries. And among developed countries, Sweden currently publicizes its literacy efforts in terms of socialized welfare and educational benefits (Wagner 1999, 4).

DEFINITIONS OF LITERACY: A VARIETY

If we search for a single definition of the term "literacy" upon which most of us will agree, we shall be disappointed. It would be useful for us to agree on a set of standard definitions, which would then serve as the basis for policy decisions directed at the goal of achieving literacy. There are, however, no precise, neutral definitions that most observers will accept without debate and that will help us in the search for practical methods to strive for universal literacy.

The simplest and most straightforward definition—and at the same time, the one that causes the most discussion—is: "Literacy is the ability to read and write" (Goody 1999, 29).

Unfortunately, the term "illiteracy" is commonly associated with ignorance and poverty, with people who are thought to be of below-average intelligence or who are underprivileged. Although large numbers of people who cannot read or write and who live in poverty may be underprivileged and may indeed be illiterate, we need to emphasize that illiterate individuals are not somehow less intelligent or less worthy than those who are able to read and write. In chapter 3, we will discuss more fully the fact that "nonliterate" people, such as the ancient Greeks, developed highly sophisticated civilizations even though most of the population could not, and indeed had no need to, read or write.

As the classicist Eric Havelock argues, the terms "nonliterate" or "preliterate" should be more acceptable than the disparaging label "illiterate" (Havelock 1976). He refuted the commonly held myth that nonliterate people are barbaric, crude, or primitive. The evidence is irrefutable, points out Havelock, that from 1100 B.C. to 700 B.C., Greek culture was made up of totally nonliterate people who accomplished amazing social and cultural feats. They invented the Greek city-state, the *polis,* and all its essential features were in place by the tenth century B.C. During this time, the nonliterate Greeks created a technology for forging iron, learned how to navigate ships throughout the Mediterranean and Black Seas, and developed sophisticated modes of commerce. They constructed such magnificent edifices as the Parthenon, architectural marvels that still influence buildings across the globe. And most significantly, these nonliterate Greeks fostered the verbal art of Homer, who, we are told, created the enduring oral folk epics, the *Iliad* and the *Odyssey.* In summary, then, "a culture can somehow rely totally on oral communication and still be a culture" (Havelock 1976, 6).

In the Greek high classical period—the time of Pericles, Sophocles, Euripides, and Aristophanes—the Greeks did not speak of "illiterates," "nonliterates," or even "preliterates." Literacy and cultivation were not synonymous. As Havelock informs us, the Greeks used the terms "musical," "nonmusical," "educated," and "uneducated" to describe a person's level of cultural competence. Not until the fourth century B.C. do we find Greeks references to the *grammatikos,* a "man who could read." Later, the Romans used the term *litteratus* to designate the "man of letters" (Havelock 1976, 3). "In modern Western society," writes Havelock,

> "illiterate" is used to identify that proportion of the population which, because they cannot read or write, are presumed to be devoid of average intelligence, or else underprivileged. It is therefore pejorative, signifying those who have been left behind in the battle for life, mainly because they are not bright enough. (Havelock 1976, 3)

Although the term "illiterate" may be used today in a disparaging way, it should be noted that while nonliterate people are still worthwhile in spite of their lack of literacy, if they cannot read, write, and perform basic mathematical functions—we will not even address the matter of "computer literacy" here—they may indeed be "disadvantaged" in today's highly technological societies and in an increasing number of developing countries in this era of globalization.

In what follows, we outline a set of definitions, extended back to Roman times, and we analyze the precise meanings of concepts related to the word "literacy" and how those concepts affect present practices.

EVOLUTION OF THE TERMS

The most basic terms are the adjectives "literate" and "illiterate" and the nouns "literacy" and "illiteracy." These words derive from the Latin *litteratus,* which for Cicero meant a "learned person." In the Middle Ages, a *litteratus* was simply a person who could read Latin. The ability to write was not included in this definition because apparently literate people found it difficult to master the skill of using ink and quills to write on very scarce and precious parchment, a writing surface made from the skin of a sheep or goat (Venezky 1990, 3).

After A.D. 1300, a *litteratus* may have had only a minimal ability to read Latin, mainly because of the breakdown of learning during the Middle Ages. After the Reformation—the period during the sixteenth century in which there was an effort to reconstitute Western Christendom—with the spread of vernacular languages, literate persons became those who could both read and write in their native languages.

Although we do not find the word "literacy" in the English lexicon until the end of the nineteenth century, the actual ideas of "literate" and "illiterate" date from the last half of the sixteenth century. The classical definition of *litteratus* survived until at least 1740, the evidence of which is a quotation from Lord Chesterfield, as cited in the *Oxford English Dictionary (OED),* in which an "illiterate" is "ignorant of Greek and Latin" (Venezky 1990, 3).

Today, when the word "literate" is applied to those of advanced reading and writing abilities, the adjectives "advanced" or "high" are used. Lester Asheim, for instance, in a 1987 work, identifies those who are "highly literate" as those individuals who can read—and we assume make sense of—the novels of William Faulkner and the philosophy of Ludwig Wittgenstein (Asheim, quoted in Venezky 1990, 3).

The word "literate" is used today to refer to lower levels of reading and writing rather than to an above-average skill level. Another writer, discussing literacy in Anglo-Saxon England, used the term "pragmatic (practical) literacy" to refer to lower levels of literacy and the phrase "cultured literacy" to signify a higher than normal level of literacy (C. Patrick Wormald, quoted in Venezky 1990, 3).

As a first step in defining the word "literacy" for modern usage, we employ it to refer to a minimal or near-minimal level of skills, a meaning very distinct from the use of "literacy" in reference to a "high" or "advanced" category. At the same time, we use "literacy" for the ability of an individual to make sense of the material printed in most newspapers, which are commonly rated at the ninth-grade reading level and thus probably would exclude newspapers like the *New York Times,* whose "readability" is at a much higher level. The use of the word "literacy" implies that an individual can show at least a minimal ability both to read and to write. Even though at one time—and even today—"literacy" was applied to the ability to read only, it probably makes sense now to use "literacy" to mean the ability to read and as well to write.

A greater problem than agreeing on a precise definition of the word "literacy" is arriving at a consensus on a meaning for the word "illiteracy." Those who are labeled "illiterate" fall below some level, no matter how we define that level. For example, the label "illiterate" may be applied at the same time both to those who are able to read and write very simple prose and to those who are able to read or write not at all. In order to create a single definition of "illiteracy" for the purposes of discussion, we follow Richard Venezky in reserving the term "illiterate" "for those totally lacking reading/writing knowledge" (Venezky 1990, 4).

DEFINING FUNCTIONAL LITERACY

The next term to be defined is "functional literacy." It is interesting but of little practical value to note all the qualifying terms used to express the idea of functional literary: "conventional literacy," "survival literacy," "marginal literacy," and "functional adult literacy." Most writers, however, use the term "functional literacy" according to the definition first described by UNESCO in the 1950s: "In several seminal studies done by that agency, literacy was viewed as a continuum of skills, including both reading and writing" (Venezky 1990, 4). By this definition, literacy means "procedural knowledge": being able to do something. This is in opposition to "declarative knowledge": having knowledge "about" something. Such a distinction is analogous to being able to write an essay—actually writing—in opposition to being able to repeat definitions related to writing, like the terms "thesis" and "supporting details," that is, to knowing "about" writing. In the late 1950s, UNESCO proposed that the concept of literacy be divided into two levels: a minimal level, in which an individual demonstrates the ability to read and write a simple prose message, and a functional level, in which a person achieves a level of literacy high enough to be able to function in a social setting (Venezky 1990, 5).

Odd as it seems, some observers address the situation of a "nonfunctional" literacy. In the report "Survival Literacy Study," the result of a study carried out by Louis Harris and Associates in 1970 and reported to the U.S. House of Representatives, the study's authors distinguished between reading as a "survival technique" and reading as a nonpractical "academic pursuit" (cited in Venezky 1990, 5). It very well may be that a majority of people who distrust academics would support such a distinction between the practical literacy of the average person with "common sense" and the literacy of the highly schooled "educated fool." Since literacy is often correlated with levels of education and since one of the chief purposes of school is to provide individuals with opportunities to become increasingly numerate and literate, it is puzzling to find such a distinction persisting.

AGE AND FUNCTIONAL LITERACY

A crucial element in an adequate definition of functional literacy is its importance to performing in society. When we think about this element, it appears necessary to relate functional literacy to the ages of the individuals to which the term is applied. If functional literacy means successful literacy in various social situations, the individuals cannot be held accountable until they are able to practice these skills, at least until they near adulthood.

When we examine the practices of a number of social agencies in reporting functional literacy, we learn that logically young children cannot be held accountable for literacy skills. For instance, when the U.S. Census Bureau dealt with literacy statutes from 1870 through 1930, it reported the results only for children two years of age or older, whereas from 1959 to 1969, statistics were reported only for individuals fourteen and older (Venezky 1990, 5). In addition, the Division of Adult Basic Education of the U.S. Office of Education included in its data statistics only for persons sixteen and older. And finally, the UNESCO Expert Committee on Standardization of Educational Statistics recommended that reports on literacy should deal with persons of a minimum age of fifteen years (Venezky 1990, 5). If we think about the matter of age as related to literacy—and of the term "literacy" meaning the ability of a person to read and write—it would be ridiculous to label a five-year-old who was not literate as "illiterate."

So how do we arrive at an age—as arbitrary as the cutoff may be—when it seems reasonable to identify individuals as being able to use literacy skills to function in society (at work, for home management, for voting intelligently)? As indicators, we note that teenagers in most of the United States cannot receive work permits until they reach the age of sixteen, and they cannot vote until they are eighteen. Although using age as a criterion for identifying levels of literacy is convenient, such a distinction fails to take into account the exceptions; the idea of an "age range" at which a person may use literacy skills makes more sense. What is more significant than a person's arbitrary age is his or her ability to use literacy in the following ways: to drive responsibly; to be successful in the workplace; to be conscious of local, regional, national, and now of global politics and economics; to take part in social and recreational activities; and to make decisions on his or her own about what educational paths to follow. As Venezky summarizes his position: "It seems reasonable to continue to use literacy as a referent for adult or near-adult abilities and to avoid such compounds as 'functional adult literacy' and 'functional child literacy'" (Venezky 1990, 6). We are therefore on firm ground when we use the term "functional literacy" to mean an acceptable grasp of the skills of reading and writing for functioning in society as a young adult.

THE SKILLS OF LITERACY

If we accept that the phrase "functional literacy" refers to a minimal level of literacy and view "literacy" as an overall term for a set of higher literacy skills, what are the necessary skills in these categories? We find one scheme for defining these skills in the research done by the National Assessment of Educational Progress (NAEP) Adult Work Skills and Knowledge Assessment, done in 1973–1974, and in the Adult Performance Level Functional Literacy Test, also developed in the 1970s: literacy skills for occupational, civic, community, and personal functioning (Venezky 1990, 7). Other surveys usually include these broad categories of literacy skills: reading, writing, numeracy, and document processing. Though the skill of reading is present in all surveys, there continues to be widespread disagreement on the levels or types of reading necessary for functional literacy. For assessing literacy skills in school, tests usually include reading selections, of both exposition and fiction, with multiple-choice questions that test vocabulary and prose comprehension. Even though the test results are reported for grade levels, most experts maintain that the grade-level scores tell us little about the literacy of adults and give us little information about the wide range of literacy abilities for schoolchildren at single grade levels.

Most knowledgeable persons include numeracy in the broad skills of overall literacy, but again, as we might anticipate, there is little agreement on what precisely is meant by numerate literacy. One position for establishing numerate literacy holds that any skills beyond simple addition and subtraction are too difficult to be included in a definition of basic numeracy. This position argues that if we include higher numeracy skills such as multiplication and division—not to mention algebra, trigonometry, and calculus—we leave out a sizable population from the ranks of those who are numerately literate.

In order to decide what numeracy skills should be included in such a definition, we must await in-depth analyses of the skills necessary for functioning in a highly technological society. Or we might better "confine functional literacy to those numeric operations that are critical for ordinary meaning of print: basic addition and subtraction, comparisons (greater than, less than), dates, times, and perhaps a few others" (Venezky 1990, 5). Such an array of numeracy skills is minimal indeed for our present-day, highly technological society.

The fourth major category of functional literacy, document knowledge, as we might suspect, is also difficult to define precisely because of the small amount of systematic inquiry into or research on the topic. "Document knowledge," writes Venezky, "is usually defined as the ability to cope with document formats, such as job entry forms, tax schedules, television schedules, advertisements, and labels on products" (Venezky 1990, 9). It is not enough, however, simply to list the various types of documents persons must "read" and make sense of. We need critically to somehow identify the skills used in document processing and to describe in detail the psychological demands required of individuals who successfully negotiate the various kinds of documents we encounter in modern living, from the simplest, such as an advertisement, to the most complex, such as a modern tax form, for instance.

In summary, however we describe the broad categories of "functional literacy," we are left with an obvious conclusion: The ability to read is the overarching skill of literacy. Although writing, numeracy, and document processing are important elements of functional literacy, each of these skills is highly dependent upon reading. If by "functional writing" we mean making shopping lists, writing down messages, and even making notes on what has been read, then writing becomes a "craft" skill: that of merely copying words, a skill like that performed by medieval copyists. At the same time, persons who cannot read will obviously have to perform numerate skills "in their heads" and will be able only to react to documents orally. If they cannot read, then, even persons who are able to perform basic math skills or fill out documents are severely disadvantaged in our society. On the one hand, persons who can read at a basic level—and who can use a calculator and computer—

but who possess low-level numeracy skills may be able to function quite respectably. On the other hand, those persons who cannot read at a basic level, even if they are skilled in arithmetic and in working their way through documents—usually with the help of individuals who are able to read at least on a functional level—and even if they are intelligent, hardworking, and highly motivated, will be frustrated with their lack of opportunities to succeed in a highly technological society.

MEASURING LITERACY

Although we acknowledge there are differing needs at various levels of literacy in the various regions of the United States as well as differing needs for literacy levels according to different social levels and different levels of involvement in society, we need to design a single set of criteria for measuring literacy throughout the nation. A policy that set criteria for literacy in one region different from those in another region would not only make official the differences among people in our country but, in effect, perpetuate these differences. Therefore, what is desirable is a national literacy policy structured in terms of the general areas of literacy, the complex of skills within each of these overall components, and the generally agreed-upon criteria by which these literacy skills can be assessed. As Venezky rightly points out, "as long as literacy remains a national concern, it is incumbent upon the government to strive for an understanding of the general literacy needs of work, citizenship, housekeeping, and private life; to seek effective means for assessing these needs; and to encourage assistance to those who fall below minimal levels of performance, no matter how arbitrarily set" (Venezky 1990, 10).

CRITICAL LEVELS OF LITERACY

We are aware that literacy abilities for persons in our society range from being actually unable to read or write to having literacy skills right off any scale used to measure them. How, then, are we to indicate minimal literacy? We may take the suggestion made by UNESCO in 1957 to report two levels of literacy: minimal literacy and functional literacy.

With respect to reading literacy, we now have evidence of the complex of skills necessary for effective reading, and particularly for reading alphabetic script and print systems. On the basis of analyses of the common core of psychological abilities necessary for reading, we can identify the crucial skills essential for reading, we can have children learn and practice these core reading skills, and we can assess how well children perform these skills and thus have proof of their ability to read. Such abilities include developing the competence to recognize instantaneously the relationship between the sounds of speech and the written symbols used to represent them and then to move from syllables to single words to groups of words in longer and longer phrases and clauses. Finally, neophyte readers need to learn such skills as making sense of unfamiliar words by the context and by deferring comprehension until a good deal of material has been "read." (We shall discuss in more detail "how we read" in chapter 5.)

A minimal level of reading ability is generally described as the beginning level of reading required for individuals to continue on their own in the further development of reading skills. We assume this minimal reading stage is normally achieved after four to five years of formal schooling, including home instruction.

Since the 1960s, there has been much research, observation, analysis, and speculation dealing with the creative writing process and with the teaching of writing. From this significant body of information, we are now in a much better position to name and describe the skills required for composing material from simple messages to expository prose to written responses to literature. To reflect this increased knowledge about writing, most experts term this new approach "process writing," by which one follows a series of at least four recursive stages: prewriting, first-draft writing, revising, and editing. Just as we are now able to devise realistic criteria for measuring reading skills, we are also able to assess the writing skills essential for effective and worthwhile writing.

If we are similarly able to define the skills vital for achieving numerate literacy and document literacy—and it seems evident that computer literacy may be added to the preceding elements of literacy—then we may be able to define three levels of literacy in these areas:

> "basic literacy," which applies to the level that allows self-sustained development in literacy; "required literacy," which applies to the level that allows self-sustained, independent development in literacy; and "advanced literacy," which is the literacy level required for any given social context and which might, therefore, change over time, place and social condition. (Venezky 1990, 11)

It is important to note that serious students of literacy would not accept grade-level equivalents as proof of literacy levels. One drawback of applying grade-level performance to the literacy levels is the fact that although writing skills—including writing whole essays as well as responding to multiple-choice items about writing—are not a staple of most literacy instruments, reading is still the primary activity for measuring literacy. There remains much work to be done to determine what exactly we shall label as numeracy, document processing, and (it appears inevitable) computer literacy.

The other major drawback to using grade levels to justify literacy levels is that the grade levels are based on what school-aged children can do and therefore are not appropriate for measuring adult literacy. For instance, research has shown—and it is only common sense to recognize this—that we read subject matter about which we already know a great deal more easily than we read unfamiliar material. Adults, because of their life experiences, may be much more successful at reading than would be children, who have less experience to fall back on.

Related to the matter of skill in reading familiar material is the problem of reading various kinds of printed matter. A person who is accustomed to reading exposition may read with ease essays and books dealing with scientific matters but nevertheless may have considerable trouble reading fiction, poetry, and especially plays because he or she has little experience reading literature. Even though school tests of literacy frequently include questions dealing with fiction and poetry, virtually none of the discussion of literacy includes the skills of reading literature. It almost seems as if there is an unwritten agreement that reading literature is not necessary for becoming literate, that reading literature is an unnecessary "frill" for a literate person. With the advent of a rather recent movement called Classroom Reader Response, we may come to recognize that reading literature, although it employs a set of skills radically different from those employed in reading exposition, is a unique way of knowing and an integral element of literacy (Blake 1996).

HOW LITERACY HAS CHANGED OVER TIME

If we are concerned with the level of functional literacy skills for those in our workforce, we recognize that literacy demands have changed drastically over the centuries and, of course, have changed at a dizzying pace in recent times. Some researchers maintain that the complexity of grammar and the difficulty of vocabulary have not changed for legal documents, newspapers, and public announcements over the past century and may even have become simpler than they were a hundred years ago. But though the complexity of functional reading matter has not changed, the sheer quantity of print has increased. As a result, we all have to read more material and read it faster than we once did.

Another problem with changing literacy requirements is relating them to the changing labor demands in our rapidly expanding technological society. Future literacy needs for workers will change in ways we find difficult to anticipate. In any event, we need to be aware of these changes in job requirements and of the resulting alterations in our notions about literacy, and we need to make the necessary adjustments to teaching reading and writing and to assessing these literacy skills. As Venezky suggests, "perhaps we need a literacy index, equivalent to the consumer price index, to register yearly shifts in functional literacy requirements. With or without such codification of change, an adequate definition of literacy must incorporate changing literacy demands in some meaningful way" (Venezky 1990, 13).

LITERACY AND THE NONNATIVE SPEAKER

Nonnative speakers of English present other problems with literacy, which we treat in detail in chapter 9. Although the issue of bilingualism is found in all cultures, our concern here is with literacy among nonnative speakers of English, specifically in the United States. Three groups of nonnative speakers of English face challenges with literacy in English.

First, there are nonnative speakers of English who are able to read and write, at least to some extent, in their native language. It is not reasonable to identify such individuals as "illiterate." Since they are already literate in their native tongue—whether it is Spanish, Russian, Chinese, Korean, or Japanese—they may be able to become literate in English fairly easily.

Second, there are nonnative speakers of English who, although they may speak English, are not literate in their native tongue. These individuals may be labeled "illiterate," since they are unable to read and write even in their native language. Such people, whether children or adults, face several obstacles. They need help to become literate first in their native language before attempts are made to teach them to become literate in English.

Third, there are nonspeakers of English who not only speak little or no English but also cannot read or write in their own tongue. Such persons face the most formidable barriers to acquiring literacy in our culture. It is generally agreed that such individuals will probably profit from intensive instruction in spoken English—as well as instruction in their native language—before they can become literate in English.

LITERACY DEBATES

The future of literacy depends on the ability of researchers, teachers, and policymakers to come to agreement not only on definitions of literacy but also on descriptions of the elements of reading and writing and on the standards required for literacy in these two major areas.

Literacy/Illiteracy versus a Scale of Literacy Skills

Before World War II, it was common to make a distinction between those who had some schooling and those who did not as a basis for measuring literacy. This was particularly true in developing countries. By the end of the twentieth century, this situation had changed strikingly. Although there are still millions who have had no schooling, even in the poorest countries most of the youngest generations—up to the age of forty—are usually reported as having had some formal education. In the light of this information, it would seem that a more finely tuned method of measuring degrees of literacy than simply "schooled" or "not schooled" is needed.

A remaining difficulty with developing a more accurate method for measuring literacy is the evidence that many countries continue to report on literacy using the simple opposition "literate/illiterate." As a result, literacy statistics from these countries are grossly inaccurate and therefore virtually meaningless. Learning achievement data—test results—would provide much more sophisticated ways of measuring actual literacy. Wagner succinctly describes the issue this way: "The point here is the previous dichotomy is not only inaccurate and of little use today but is also misleading in terms of the types of policies that need to be put into place. Yet it is a dichotomy that is dying a relatively slow death, though it seems likely that this situation will change as we move toward 2000" (Wagner 1999, 5).

A Single Literacy versus Many Literacies

One aspect of the debate over a single literacy versus many literacies involves the tendency to list "literacies" other than reading and writing, such as "computer literacy," "geographical literacy," "historical literacy," and "scientific literacy." Since it is the responsibility of the varied disciplines represented by these subjects to define their respective "literacies," we believe it is our obligation here to deal with "literacy" only as it relates to reading and writing.

The notion of a single literacy, a set of global skills related to read-ing and writing, unrelated to any social context, is known as the "autonomous" model of literacy. The sociologist Brian Street defines this conception of literacy thus: "It [literacy] is treated as 'autonomous' in the sense that it has its own characteristics, irrespective of the time and place in which it occurs and also in the sense that it has consequences for society and for cognition that can be derived from its distinctive and intrinsic character" (Street 1999, 35).

Many authors in the field of literacy, we are informed by Street, have used the term "autonomous literacy," in the sense that print is dif-ferent from oral language because "it is, at least potentially, 'an autonomous mode of communication.'" Street continues:

> Writing is closely connected to, "fosters," or even "enforces" the devel-
> opment of logic, the distinction of myth from history, the elaboration of
> bureaucracy, the shift from "little communities" to complex cultures,
> the emergence of scientific thought and institutions, and the growth of
> democratic political processes. . . . We can be detached, critical, reflec-
> tive only because writing allows us to express ourselves outside of the
> constraints of ordinary everyday intercourse. (Street 1999, 35)

Even though other writers have argued against the position that the distinction between oral discourse and literacy is overstated, some extend the debate about the autonomous nature of literacy to law, bureaucratic organizations, and even to economic development. With the advent of literacy, so the argument goes, courts relied on the written word rather than on notoriously unreliable oral testimony. Writing pro-motes the autonomy of bureaucracies, since writing allows them to keep written records in order to develop a body of procedures (e.g., the U.S. Constitution, constitutional amendments, and U.S. Supreme Court decisions) and to educate those who specialize in creating and main-taining organizations.

Other writers have attempted to modify the idea of an autonomous literacy. David R. Olson, for one, has softened his earlier position that literacy is indeed autonomous. Rather than stating that there is a single, autonomous model of literacy for all peoples through-out the world, Olson now argues that literacy, by bringing language into our consciousness, not only aids our memory but also, on a deeper level, changes our conception of knowledge: "The differences between speech and writing and the complex relations between them make writ-ing a powerful tool of cognition, a tool central to cultural development in the West and elsewhere as well" (Olson 1999, 132). In effect, literacy changes the way we think, believes Olson, and it "gives us the ability to step into, and on occasion to step out again, from this new world, the world on paper" (Olson 1994, 18).

The idea of "many literacies" is most prominently advanced by sociologist Brian Street, who has labeled this concept "social literacies" (Street 1995). For Street, it is obvious that literacy is always practiced in social situations. What is not so apparent is that this truism has important ramifications for an accepted definition of literacy as well as implications for how literacy is taught. Expanding on the topic of "social literacies" and "literacy practices," some scholars now speak of "multiple literacies," such as "social," "community," and "individual" literacies.

Even within a given culture, this argument goes, there may be numerous literacies, including all examples of reading and writing, both inside formal educational institutions and beyond school walls.

> From this perspective one may ask what are the literacy practices at home of children whose schooled practices are judged problematic or inadequate? From the school's point of view, those home practices may represent simply inferior attempts at the real thing; from the researcher's point of view these home practices represent as important a part of the repertoire as different languages or language varieties. (Street 1999, 38)

High-Quantity Literacy Education versus High-Quality Literacy Education

The problem of quantity versus quality is especially troublesome for literacy education, particularly in adult education. The question relates directly to the definition of "literate." When does an "illiterate" person become "literate"? If it is a simple matter to make a person "literate," then campaigns such as Literacy Volunteers of America or literacy teachers' corps should be successful. Volunteers do not need extensive training, the periods of instruction for students need not be extensive, and therefore such popular programs should be quick and cheap ways to make large numbers of students literate.

A close look at such programs reveal they do not deliver as much as they promise. Volunteers seldom stay long enough to become expert instructors, and decisions about what language is to be the target language (e.g., in Quebec, French or English?) are usually determined by political forces rather than by careful study of which language would be more desirable for the people to be taught (Wagner 1999, 6).

SUMMARY

Although people who are not literate are worthwhile and may have achieved magnificent cultures, in this present era of technology and globalization, people who are illiterate are simply at a disadvantage. The reasons for people to become literate are individual (personal development and fulfillment), economic, social, and political.

The fact that distinctions such as "preliterate," "nonliterate," "highly literate," and "marginally literate" abound is a sign of the chaotic nature of the study of literacy. The most commonly used distinctions are "literate," "illiterate," and "functionally literate," although the range of meanings applied to these terms is enormously wide.

The most pressing literacy problems to be addressed in the future are the following: literacy versus illiteracy; a single literacy versus many literacies; and quality versus quantity literacy education.

For the future, there are a number of new directions for literacy research. First, we need to move away from simplistic distinctions between "literacy" and "illiteracy," which suggest that the problem of literacy is a simple one. As Wagner phrases it, such simplistic distinctions are based on a belief "that literacy is like a 'light bulb'" that simply needs to be "turned on" to make a person literate or that literacy is merely a matter of political will (Wagner 1999, 7).

Second, we need to recognize that there is not one "literacy" for all occasions and that literacy is a human rights issue, an educational right, and at the same time, a legitimate aspect of national and global efforts to improve education, individual development and well-being, and self-respect. In spite of the widespread notion that literacy may be relatively easy to accomplish, serious students of literacy now realize that literacy is a much more intricate matter than first believed, even when we agree—which we seldom do—on what literacy is.

As a sign of the increased interest in all aspects of literacy, we are seeing researchers from many fields, including history, linguistics, psycholinguistics, sociolinguistics, and education, making significant contributions to our understanding of literacy. As a result, we may see the development of accurate indices of literacy, a new base for literacy study, and recently discovered methods—based upon research and extensive practical applications of that research to teaching reading and writing—all in the pursuit of the admirable but possibly unattainable goal of universal literacy.

REFERENCES

Barry, Dan. 2000. "Gaelic Comes Back on Ireland's Byways and Airways." *New York Times International,* July 25, A6.

Blake, Robert W. 1996. "Reader Response: Toward an Evolving Model for Teaching Literature in the Elementary Grades." *Language and Literacy Spectrum* 6 (Spring): 39–44.

Goody, Jack. 1999. "The Implications of Literacy." In *Literacy: An International Handbook,* ed. Daniel A. Wagner, Richard L. Venezky, and Brian V. Street. Boulder, CO: Westview Press.

Havelock, Eric A. 1976. *Origins of Western Literacy.* Toronto, Ontario: Institute for Studies in Education.

Kilborn, Peter T. 2000. "Illiteracy Pulls Appalachia Back, and Efforts to Overcome It Grow." *New York Times,* July 27, A1, A16.

Mayor, Federico. 1999. Forward to *Literacy: An International Handbook,* ed. Daniel W. Wagner, Richard L. Venezky, and Brian V. Street. Boulder, CO: Westview Press.

Olson, David R. 1999. "Literacy and Language Development." In *Literacy: An International Handbook,* ed. Daniel A. Wagner, Richard L. Venezky, and Brian V. Street. Boulder, CO: Westview Press.

———. 1994. *The World on Paper: The Conceptual and Cognitive Implications of Writing and Reading.* New York: Cambridge University Press.

Street, Brian V. 1999. "The Meanings of Literacy." In *Literacy: An International Handbook,* ed. Daniel A. Wagner, Richard L Venezky, and Brian V. Street. Boulder, CO: Westview Press.

———. 1995. *Critical Approaches in Development, Ethnography, and Education.* New York: Longmans.

Venezky, Richard L. 1990. "Defining Literacy." In *Toward Defining Literacy,* ed. Richard L. Venezky. Newark, DE: International Reading Association.

Wagner, Daniel A. 1999. "Rationales, Debates, and New Directions: An Introduction." In *Literacy: An International Handbook,* ed. Daniel A. Wagner, Richard L. Venezky, and Brian V. Street. Boulder, CO: Westview Press.

Chapter Two

⚫◆ Chronology

This chronology cannot, of course, be complete and exact. It can only be a list of dates and approximate periods of time that are relevant to the historical episodes referred to in the main text.

CA. 3200 B.C.

The earliest attempts to represent speech through logographic scripts occur, according to the evidence of discovered artifacts. Logographic writing represents words by individual visual signs, the total number—unlike the twenty-six letters in the English alphabet—being very large. Logographic scripts appear in the deltas of Egypt and Mesopotamia.

CA. 1100–700 B.C.

Greeks are totally nonliterate, but in these centuries Greece invents the first forms of the government and artistic achievement that become her glory, irrefutable proof that a nonliterate people are not lacking in intelligence or creativity but are able to create vigorous, sophisticated societies.

CA. 900 B.C.

In Greece, the great oral epics, the *Iliad* and *Odyssey,* are believed to have been composed.

CA. 750 B.C.

The first truly alphabetic system of writing is invented. An alphabetic system is made up not of logographs, symbols for whole words, but of separate, meaningful symbols for two major categories of sounds, consonants and vowels, which make up the speech sounds of a language, its phonemes.

650–600 B.C.

Ancient Greece is "craft-literate," that is, only those persons are literate who are especially trained and whose life work is reading and writing.

600–400 B.C.

Ancient Greece, scholars maintain, moves through three periods of literacy. In the first period, a period of "semiliteracy," only a small number of people are able to read and write. In the second, some persons are "recitation-literate"; that is, they can "read" only texts they have memorized. And in the third, some persons, whose occupation is reading and writing, have "scriptorial literacy"; that is, they can read unfamiliar texts.

403 B.C.

Greek letters used in writing texts of ancient works are standardized in Athens, by decree, as the "East Ionic," official language.

400–300 B.C.

This is Greece's golden age, in which Athenian democracy blossoms. It is the era of such Greek philosophers and playwrights as Plato, Sophocles, and Euripides, whose writings are saved in alphabetic script.

70 B.C.–A.D. 14

This is Rome's golden age, when such Roman authors as Cicero, Horace, Virgil, and Ovid are writing in Latin.

CA. A.D. 50

During the first century A.D., the alphabet of the Etruscans, the original inhabitants of what is now Italy, is adapted by the Romans and eventually becomes the Latin language.

A.D. 400–1100

The early part of the Middle Ages, the entire period of classical civilization to the retrieval of learning in the West, is called the "Dark Ages" because so little writing of the era survived.

400

Germanic runic script is brought from Europe to England by the Anglo-Saxons, possibly as early as the fifth century A.D.

476–1453

In European history, the period between antiquity and the Renaissance stretches from 476, when Romulus Augustulus, the last emperor of the western Roman empire, is deposed, to 1453, when the Turks conquer Constantinople.

597

When Saint Augustine arrives in England at the end of the sixth century A.D., a few Anglo-Saxons are probably able to write in runic script, a written language made up of angular letters to be carved in wood or in stone. The letters are used by ancient Germanic peoples, especially Scandinavians and Anglo-Saxons. At this time, Anglo-Saxon is not written down; rather, it is the language spoken by the native, preliterate people.

600–700

At the end of the seventh century A.D., Celtic (Irish) scribes first use word separation and syntactic punctuation in transcribing Latin and Greek texts and Syriac Gospels. Formerly, Latin texts were written in *scriptura continua,* a script in which words were not separated by spaces and there were no punctuation marks or other graphic aids to reading.

650–LATE 900s

The oral English epic poem *Beowulf* is composed not in Latin but in the vernacular, the indigenous language known as Anglo-Saxon or Old English.

CA. 690s

Toward the end of the seventh century A.D., Old English (Anglo-Saxon) is written in a variant of the Roman alphabet.

800s

In the ninth century A.D., Saint Cyril (after whom the Cyrillic alphabet is named) and his brother Saint Methodius translate the Bible into Slavonic, adapting the Greek alphabet and adding characters as needed.

900s

During the tenth century A.D., word-separated texts, first introduced by Celtic scribes—whose writing is unknown outside Ireland and England—first appears on the Continent, most strikingly at the Abbey of Saint Gall in Switzerland.

CA. 1100

So-called Arabic numerals, which perhaps are really Indian in origin, appear on the European scene, making modern calculation possible.

EARLY 1100s

By the beginning of the twelfth century, modern pages of word separation and syntactical punctuation have spread across most of western Europe.

1200s–1300s

First in Italy in the thirteenth century and then in France in the fourteenth century, standardized spelling, word separation, and a highly legible cursive script are used, not only in Latin texts for scholastics but also for laypersons in such vernacular languages as Italian, French, and German.

1200s–1400s

An era usually known as the Late Middle Ages.

1300s–1500s

The Renaissance—roughly, the humanistic revival of classical art, literature, and learning—originates in Italy in the fourteenth century and spreads throughout the rest of Europe during the fifteenth and sixteenth centuries.

CA. 1390–1468

Johannes Gutenberg, the German inventor of movable type and of the printing press, is alive.

1455

Gutenberg's Latin Bible, the first complete book to be typeset, is produced at Mainz.

1475–1500

After about 1475, printing exponentially increases the production of books so that by 1500, moderately priced books are available for readers from London to Warsaw.

1500s ON

A system of notation is invented and used in written musical scores, particularly for modern polyphonic music.

1600s–1900s

Teaching reading tends to follow the two-stage model in which the first stage is concerned with letters and the sounds they represent and the second stage is then concerned with meaning.

CA. 1820

Sequoyah, a Cherokee who was not literate in English, invented a Cherokee syllabary, borrowing freely from Roman, Cyrillic, and Greek scripts to devise a set of symbols that could be used for writing.

1920s–1960s

Reading is generally viewed as a one-stage process, as a direct connection between print and meaning, and little or no preliminary instruction is offered in the relationship between letters and the sounds they represent. The "sight" or "whole word" methods— all one-stage models of the reading process—are widely accepted from the 1920s through the 1960s.

1930s

I. A. Richards, a Cambridge don, advocates the close reading of literary texts. In his important book *Practical Criticism: A Study of Literary Judgment* (1929), he isolates the now notorious ten "difficulties" that adults, mostly university students, have with criticizing and evaluating a wide range of poems. This monumental work is considered a major influence on U.S. New Criticism.

1940s–1950s

New Criticism achieves prominence in literary theory. Such respected university scholars as John Crowe Ransom, René

Wellek, Austin Warren, W. K. Wimsatt, and Monroe C. Beardsley advocate a literary criticism based on the assumptions that readers essentially "find" an inherent meaning within a literary text and that methods of literary criticism should be technically precise, objective, and more "scientific" than was previously the case.

1950s

Spearheaded by a best-selling book by Rudolph Flesch, *Why Johnny Can't Read* (1955), there is a clamorous movement toward teaching reading chiefly by a systematic teaching of "phonics." In this system, children are taught to read by first learning the "names" of letters and of the sounds they "make."

1960s

Reader Response literary criticism arises, usually viewed as a reaction to New Criticism. Although there is no single, unified theory of Reader Response, the general position taken by most Reader Response theorists is that reading literature involves a relationship—a "transaction"—between a reader and a text in which the reader participates in the course of reading a text. For the most part, the theorists are university professors, and their views are seldom based upon research with actual students. Reader Response theories have little impact on secondary school English teaching and even less influence on elementary school English language arts teaching methods.

1960s–1980s

The psycholinguistic approach to reading is most prominently articulated in Frank Smith's book *Understanding Reading: A Psycholinguistic Analysis of Reading and Learning to Read* (first published in 1971). Smith argues that to read with comprehension, children must focus primarily on the meaning of a text, not on its letters (phonics) or even on individual words.

Smith's psycholinguistic theory of reading—that children should learn how to read by immediately interacting with "whole" books written by real authors rather than by working in basals written by committees of reading experts—is supported by the sociolinguistic theories of M. A. K. Halliday and blossoms into an elaborate instructional philosophy and educational movement known as "whole language." The "whole language" movement represents another example of a one-stage model of the reading process.

1970s–1980s

There is sustained interest in the idea of comprehending reading texts in terms of underlying structures. Researchers study the organizations of narratives and of expository prose and argue that readers can read narration and exposition more effectively by first studying their configurations. D. E. Rumelhart is a significant figure in this field.

1980s

Another influential structure of reading comprehension is that of "schema theory," a model of human knowledge based upon how we remember. Schema theory has been particularly influential in compelling us to focus on the notion that we read texts more effectively if they deal with subjects about which we already know a great deal than if they contain material completely new to us. In other words, we need to recognize the importance of background knowledge in text comprehension.

1990s

On the basis of the most recent research, best exemplified by Marilyn Adams's book *Beginning to Read: Thinking and Learning* (1991), the most popular contemporary view toward teaching beginning reading is that no single method—not phonics nor the whole word—is appropriate for teaching reading. The key to models of reading is not the dominance of one form over another but the coordination and cooperation of all elements with each other, including instruction in sound-symbol correspondences, reading whole books, writing, spelling, and all kinds of language exploration.

1994

The fourth edition of *Theoretical Models and Processes of Reading* is published. It is a crucial work written by the most respected leaders in the field of reading. The book presents the current views toward the value of the respective one- or two-step models of the reading process, explaining how children first acquire the skills of reading and how their reading skills are developed.

1996

The second edition of Jeanne Chall's *Stages of Reading Development* is published. Its paradigm of reading development becomes one of the most influential of the multiple-stage theories of reading development. Chall's model has been used in teacher education, curriculum development and assessment, and adult literacy, and it has been adapted for the diagnosis and treatment of reading disabilities.

Chapter Three

☙ The Foundations of Literacy

The development of a full Greek alphabet, expressing single sounds, is the last important step in the history of writing. From the Greek period up to the present, nothing new has happened in the inner structural development of writing. Generally speaking, we write consonants and vowels in the same way as the ancient Greeks.
—*I. Gelb*, A Study of Writing

Why should we be concerned with the foundations of literacy? If we can read and write passably well, is that not enough? Should we bother to learn where reading and writing come from? In what ways is writing different from speech? What is the story of the development over many centuries of reading and writing, and what is the precise nature of the kind of reading and writing we presently use? What are the conditions necessary for large numbers of people—not just a select elite—to be able to read and write? How has this radical, technological invention—for that is what reading is, a human invention—come literally, in the most amazing way, to change the way we think?

In this chapter, we shall deal with questions like these about literacy. Most of the time, we do not bother to think much about how we speak, read, and write because such activities come so naturally to most of us that they are usually below the level of our consciousness. As we become more sophisticated, though, in our ability to use language, we may feel the need to adjust our language to differing social situations and for various purposes. In short, we may arrive at an understanding of how reading literally changes the workings of our minds.

SPEAKING AND WRITING

Why study speech when our concern is with reading and writing, with literacy? Because inscribed signs—"inscribed" meaning carved and engraved on clay tablets, stone, and wood, as well as written on paper—are attempts to represent first objects and even ideas as well as sounds on relatively permanent surfaces. If we can imagine our world without print, how would we use symbols to show what we see or hear in language? We can draw pictures of things and of fairly concrete ideas such as numbers; for example, we might draw pictures of two cats or of a new moon or of a house. But how would we show the word "love"? And how would we use signs rather than pictures to show these sounds or objects?

We have a long history of using writing for many purposes—a history during which we invented several writing systems and eventually arrived at the magical invention of the alphabetic system of writing.

CHARACTERISTICS OF SPEECH

How is speech different from reading or writing? First of all, we need to accept the fact that speech comes first in language. Human beings, we might say, are biologically—as well as mentally—"programmed" for speech.

No other creature on earth, contrary to what is argued for chimpanzees' or gorillas' ability to "speak," has the physical apparatus for speech. We explain the physical process of speaking here because through this knowledge, we come to comprehend how speech is physically divided into what we term consonants and vowels. It was the discovery of these speech elements that led to the invention of the alphabet, which in turn provides the foundation of literacy.

How, physically, do humans make speech? First we send air from our lungs up through the windpipe, or "trachea." Now how do we turn that column of air into speech? As the air is sent through the windpipe, it meets the vocal bands, or "glottis," which can be open or closed. If the bands are open, we have an "unvoiced" sound, such as the first sound in the word "thin." If the vocal bands are constricted, we make a "voiced" noise, such as the initial sound in the word "then."

How else can we alter this column of air into distinctly different sounds? Primarily, we modify the air so that it becomes one of the two fundamental sounds, either a consonant or a vowel. We can do that first through the "resonating cavities": the "pharyngeal cavity," the area way in the back of the throat; the "nasal cavity"; and the "oral cavity." In speech, we change the shape and open or close off these cavities to alter the sounds produced.

Next, we can change sounds by moving parts of the mouth, the "articulators": the lower lip, the tongue, and the uvula, the little flap that hangs down in the back of the mouth.

Finally, we change sounds by placing the movable parts against the fixed parts of the mouth, the "points of articulation": the upper lip, the upper teeth, the alveolar ridge (the bony ridge toward the front of the roof of the mouth), the palate (the soft part of the upper mouth), and the velum (the part of the upper mouth in the back).

Now, back to the vibration of air in the throat. After being modified by the vocal bands, the air is then sent past the pharynx and through either the mouth or the nose, where we make one of two choices. If we modify this vibration in some way so that it is "unobstructed," we call that sound a "vowel." Different vowels are produced by shaping the resonating cavities differently. But if we stop or start the vibrating air in some way, by moving the articulators against the points of articulation, the sounds produced we call "consonants."

"Although both 'vowel' and 'consonant' seek to describe sounds, they were coined only after the Greek alphabet made these sounds 'visually' recognizable as 'letters,' and strictly speaking vowel and consonant, though derived from the Latin, denote types of letters of the Greek alphabet" (Havelock 1976, 29). So, contrary to the belief still held by many in our print-saturated culture, that writing is the primary mode of language, speech comes first. The use of scripts is a comparatively late technological invention, but alphabetic writing—which is generally acknowledged as the only genuine writing—was invented around 750 B.C. by the Greeks.

THE DEVELOPMENT OF WRITING

Literacy, essentially reading and writing, has spread historically "through communication between people who possessed written languages and those who did not" (Bernard 1999, 22). People from different cultures came in contact chiefly through trade, religion, and schooling. The contact through schooling generally came about because a dominant people forced their own language upon a conquered people.

Scholars estimate that 3,000 years ago there were some 500,000 bands, tribes, and states—all independent groups of people—who spoke mutually unintelligible languages. Today, we are told, there are people in some 200 countries who speak—and sometimes write—approximately 6,000 different languages. These peoples, and their languages, therefore, because of increased methods of communication, are in contact more than ever were ancient peoples (Bernard 1999, 22).

The generally accepted view now is that people invented writing independently of each other in the New World as well as in Europe and the Middle East. Early writing systems were invented in the Old World in ancient Mesopotamia around 3200 B.C. and spread throughout this region through cultural contact. The writing system first used in the ancient Indus civilization, for example, may very well have been spread by traders from the Middle East. Others, who argue that writing originated in Mesopotamia, believe that writing was initially developed in what is now Iraq, Egypt, India, or even as far east as China.

Wherever and whenever a type of writing was first invented in the Old World, there is now general agreement that writing was also invented—without any influence from the Old World—in the New World in what is now Mexico. The Olmecs, according to the evidence of inscriptions, developed a writing system of some 180 glyphs. (A glyph is an inscribed symbolic figure representing a figure or object. The prefix "hiero-" comes from the Greek *hieros*, "sacred," and thus, the word "hieroglyphic," used for Egyptian religious carved symbols, refers to ancient Egyptian sacred writings.) The Olmec system was used throughout parts of present-day Mexico around 600 B.C. It is estimated that there may have been as many as fifteen different writing systems in pre-Columbian Mexico. Unfortunately, the Europeans who arrived in Mexico in the sixteenth century stopped all instruction in the original languages and also destroyed all existing manuscripts. Since 1521, natives in Mexico and throughout Latin America have continued writing their indigenous languages, not in the original glyphs, however, but in the alphabetic script that the conquerors brought from Europe (Bernard 1999, 22).

Most scholars break scripts—writing systems—into roughly three categories.

First, in *logographic scripts,* the earliest of scripts, signs and symbols represent entire words, such as the symbol "$" for "dollar" and the letter "e" for "energy" in physics. (The word "logographic" is based on the Greek *logos,* "word," and *graphos,* "written," joined, meaning "to write a word.") Each logograph is a single visual sign that stands for an individual word. The number of different logographs for the major words in a language, as we might imagine, can be very large. A major drawback with logographic writing is simply memorizing the daunting number of symbols.

Second are *syllabic scripts.* As we can surmise, such scripts use symbols to represent not words but syllables. Such a script generally uses some three hundred signs per language and presents problems not only with memorizing all the syllables but also with remembering which symbol stands for which syllable.

Third are *alphabetic scripts*. Alphabetic scripts, it is argued, are the only full-fledged scripts and are the most efficient of scripts. They use symbols to represent the basic elements of speech, the "phonemes." But what is a phoneme? A phoneme is the smallest unit of meaningful sound in any language. It is important to understand this concept if we are to understand alphabetic writing.

The words "run" and "pun," for instance, begin with the different sounds: /r/ and /p/. (The slashes show the representation of phonemes to differentiate them from letters in "conventional orthography," the term for writing in ordinary written language.) These sounds are significantly "different" for speakers of English—that is, as speakers of English we hear them as different sounds—and therefore they are different phonemes in English. The letter "u" in the two words represents the same sound and therefore indicates the same phoneme.

But there is more to this business of a phoneme. Consider the words "pin" and "spin." The sound for "p" in the word "pin" is actually different from the sound for "p" in the word "spin." If you don't believe it, try this experiment. While holding a lighted match a few inches from your mouth, repeat the word "spin" several times: "spin, spin, spin." The flame wavers but does not go out. Now say "pin, pin, pin." With the first "pin," the flame is extinguished. The "p" in "pin" is pronounced with a slight puff of air. Although the sound for "p" in "pin" and the sound for the "p" in "spin" are *acoustically* different, they are not different in a meaningful way to a speaker of English. We interpret them as the same sound. Both sounds, therefore, represent the same phoneme in English: /p/.

There is no difference, though, in sound between the two initial written symbols in the words "cite" and "sight," although the written letters are different. Thus, though there is a written difference—a "graphemic" difference—between the two letters, there is no phonemic difference between the sounds represented in this case by the letters "c" and "s."

If the alphabetic script invented by the Greeks in the eighth century B.C. is the only full-fledged script, if it was a radical invention that is responsible for literacy as we know it, why is this so? Why are the other types of scripts, using symbols to represent either words or syllables, not just as good as the alphabetic script? There are several reasons.

We may assume that the more readers there are in proportion to the whole population, the more literate the population is. So the quantitative aspect of literacy depends upon how many persons out of a population can read and write. Sheer numbers are an important factor in full literacy. Those who can read by either a logographic or syllabic script, however, number comparatively few in any population. Only those persons who are specially trained, almost always those whose full-time occupation is reading and writing, are able to enjoy the luxury of literacy. Such a situation we call "craft literacy."

What about the qualitative aspects of a script? What makes a particular script efficient? "Efficiency" refers to how easily a person can read a script. What features of a script allow a large percentage of the people of any ethnic, religious, or racial group to read it swiftly and effortlessly?

It must be granted that especially gifted persons can, by arduous training, make sense of virtually any script. If large numbers of people are to learn to read, however, they must learn to recognize the shapes of the written language and match them with the sounds they are designed to represent. Furthermore, if they are to read well, they must match signs with sounds almost instantaneously and virtually below the level of consciousness. With alphabetic reading, the written shapes are meaningless in themselves. The signs are not meant to represent objects or ideas. Those who read alphabetically, although they realize that the shapes have no inherent meaning, have learned a process that is not really a skill, or even a set of skills, but, rather, is a process that models language and thinking.

The primary act of reading, if it is to be enjoyed by large numbers of people, must be an easy, swift, and unconscious act. (Interpretation, finding the meaning of what one reads, is a different matter. We may say that interpreting meaning in writing is determining the difference between "what is written" and "what is meant." We address the issue of interpreting literature in chapters 7 and 8.)

What, then, are the conditions necessary if a script is to fulfill the requirements for large numbers of persons to read easily and swiftly, often below the level of consciousness? First, ideally, the symbols used to represent the sounds of a language should be *exhaustive;* that is, the written shapes should cover all the sounds of the language. The visible shapes must be sufficient in number to trigger the reader's memory of every distinctive sound—each phoneme—of the language. Amazingly, all the sounds of any language can be described and reduced to a fairly small number of phonemes, one phoneme for one sound. If a system of writing were perfect, there would be no exceptions. No writing system is ideal, however, especially not that of English.

When we read the English word "knight," for instance, we have learned by listening to the way others say the word that it is pronounced "nite," not "kuh-nik-ta," as it was pronounced hundreds of years ago. The letters "-ght," represent a sound technically called a "velar fricative."

(The velar fricative is a made with the back of the tongue on or near the soft palate. The sound is popularly known as a "guttural." Although the sound is prominent in German, it is no longer heard in English, except in Scottish dialects, as in the word "loch.")

The English writing system, therefore, is not perfect. But the script, which has only twenty-six symbols, is able in some fashion to account for all the sounds of the language. These twenty-six symbols—or letters—sometimes must represent more than one sound, though; for example, the "c" must stand for the "soft" sound at the beginning of "censure" as well as the "hard" sound at the beginning of "cat" or "catalog."

Second, again ideally, for a script to be efficient, there should be no question as to what sound the shape represents; that is, the shapes should be *unambiguous.* In other words, each sign should trigger in the memory of the reader—which is what reading is all about—one sound, and one sound only. Again, if the system of writing were flawless, there would be no exceptions to the sound-symbol correspondences. There should be no times when the reader must guess at how to read a word or determine how to read it by how it is used in relation to other words. How do we know, for instance, how to say the word "bass"? Only when we see it with other words, in context. The word "bass" is read one way if it refers to a musical instrument, another way if it signifies a fish.

Third, the total number of signs for the phonemes of the language must be *small enough* that any reader can memorize all of them and be able to relate them to all the sounds of the language. It is no wonder that only a few specially trained or gifted individuals can read a logographic script, in which symbols represent the words of the language. In English, even discounting many compound and scientific words, there are estimated to be some 500,000 words. Think of trying to memorize only a small number of the symbols for all the possible words in English!

It is not enough for us simply to remember the twenty-six shapes in the English alphabet. Once we learn our ABCs, we must associate these symbols with the sounds they stand for. Furthermore, in order to read fluently, we need to recognize these myriad sound-symbol connections, not in the neat, constant letters of the alphabet, an "abecedarium," but in the potentially limitless, irregular combinations of words and sentences. "The brain has been biologically encoded to contain a memory of these varieties as they occur acoustically in a spoken tongue. It has not been encoded to manage a corresponding variety of shapes" (Havelock 1976, 23). When we think of reading from this perspective, we can only marvel at what an intellectual feat the process of reading actually is.

So for reading to be within the reach of a great many people in a community, a script must necessarily be *exhaustive,* covering all distinctive sounds of the language; it must be *unambiguous,* ideally, with each sound of the language being represented by one symbol only; and the number of signs standing for the sounds of the language must be *small enough*—generally between twenty and thirty—so that the human brain can memorize and process all the potentially infinite combinations of signs that make up words and sentences.

Are these three conditions all that is necessary for literacy? Not quite. Full literacy, not craft literacy, is possible only when a fourth condition exists: an *early systematic reading instruction program,* and this program must be of a special kind. Instruction in reading must begin early enough that the child is able to internalize the process of connecting the sounds of a language with the symbols representing them. This recognition of sound-symbol correspondences apparently must occur while the brain is plastic and has not fully concluded its growth, that is, before puberty. This habit of recognizing sound-symbol connections evidently must occur at the same time the brain is developing oral language, for which it is biologically programmed. The codes of speaking and reading have to blend at a time when the child's brain is still in a formative stage. This is the optimum time for a child to learn how to read so that the act of reading becomes a virtually unconscious reflex.

The early systematic reading instruction program is thus the fourth condition for full literacy. "In short, a population is rendered literate when an educational apparatus can be brought into being which is able to teach reading to very young children before they have been introduced to other skills. The adult who learns to read after his oral vocabulary is completed rarely if ever becomes as fluent" (Havelock 1976, 24).

THE ALPHABET VERSUS THE SYLLABARY

Why are the logographic and syllabic scripts not as well suited for widespread literacy as is the alphabetic script, according to the criteria established for an efficient script: clear (unambiguous), comprehensive, and small in number?

We can immediately see that the logographic scripts are unsuited, because if we use a specific symbol for each word in a language we end up with far too many symbols to remember. We are either restricted to a very simple vocabulary, or if we do use a fairly large number of symbols for many words, only those elite, especially talented, or highly trained people who continually study and memorize the symbols will be able to read anything but the simplest of messages.

There were many attempts to develop scripts before the Greeks devised a complete alphabetic script that represented both vowels and consonants. The Phoenicians invented a syllabic script, and so did the North Semitic tribes, from whose languages Persian, Sanskrit, Aramaic, Hebrew, and Arabic have evolved. But the term "alphabet"—a word simply made up of the names for the first two letters of the Greek alphabet—should be applied only to the Greek system and to those scripts derived from it, the Roman and Cyrillic.

Why is the Greek system superior to the Phoenician syllabic system and the syllabaries descended from it? The answer lies in the script's ability to represent the two fundamental sounds of speech by written signs. Basically, scripts that use symbols for consonants only have no vowels and are thus "unvocalized."

If we represent the sounds of a language by syllables and these syllables by consonants only, we have scripts that are very difficult to make sense of. We, who have been brought up from childhood with the ideas of "vowels" and "consonants," may find it incomprehensible that these two concepts had to be invented. What was the result of the perception that speech was made up of two basic kinds of sounds and that these sounds could be represented in alphabetic writing?

As we "read" the syllables in a syllabary, we have to guess at the missing vowels. Or, on the basis of prior teaching, we supply the missing vowels to make words. So we are right back where we started from, with ambiguous symbols. Such a situation does not make for fluent reading. Rather, reading becomes a difficult, often puzzling, and laborious task.

As the Greeks divided speech sounds into the two written elements of vowels and consonants and reduced each sound into its basic acoustic element—the phoneme—they invented the alphabetic script, a writing system obviously far more useful than the cumbersome logographic and syllabic scripts. "In short, non-vocalized syllabaries require a little more effort, a little more time, on the part of the reader who deciphers accurately, than does the Greek system. To that extent, even at their best they are less efficient reading instruments" (Havelock 1976, 32).

HOW THE ALPHABET WORKS

If we are truly to comprehend our writing system, we need to look more closely at the alphabet and discover how it works. It is important to do so because, according to Eric Havelock, the new form of script represented by the Greek alphabet may have in fact in the long run changed the content of the human mind (Havelock 1976, 46).

The problem of an efficient script is that it must be at the same time both acoustic (we hear the sounds of language) and visual (we must be able to match letters with the sounds they stand for). To show the difference between an unvocalized script, in which there are no vowels, and an alphabetic script, which uses both consonants and vowels, we reproduce the first three words of the familiar nursery rhyme, "Jack and Jill went up the hill . . ." in both scripts (Havelock 1976, 39–43).

First, we show an alphabetic script representation of the first three words to the nursery rhyme:

1. JAK AND JIL

Notice that in this phonemic version, we have omitted the unnecessary "c" from the word "Jack" and the superfluous "l" from the double consonant in the word "Jill." Remember, this is a phonemic rendering of the oral phrase; it is not the way we write it in "conventional orthography." For all of us who grew up with this nursery rhyme, who have mastered the English alphabet, and who have learned how to read, these symbols are instantly meaningful. Note that in this simple phrase, we have used nine symbols, of which only seven are different.

How do we write the same phrase, "Jack and Jill," using an unvocalized system, one that uses no vowels?

2. J K N D J L

First of all, if we did not know that these symbols stand for the phrase "Jack and Jill," could we read it? Not at all easily. But that is a major shortcoming with an unvocalized script. If we do not already know what the script says, we can make sense of it only with difficulty.

Now we can see quite clearly that this unvocalized phrase uses fewer signs than does the alphabetic phrase—only six symbols, of which five are unique. So it would appear that because the system uses fewer symbols, it is more efficient than the alphabetic phrase. But even though the unvocalized phrase is more economical than the alphabetic phrase by this measurement, the true test of a script's efficiency is how easily and unambiguously we can read it. The unvocalized script clearly fails this second criterion.

RESULTS OF THE INVENTION OF THE ALPHABET

So we now have at our disposal the invention of an efficient script—a technology as radical and influential as the printing press or the computer chip. This discovery, like all major inventions, was not fully developed overnight. It took literally hundreds of years for its full potential to be realized. We first used signs—carved, inscribed, and written—to represent objects and natural creatures and then to stand for complete words. Next, we used symbols to represent syllables. But both systems were too difficult and unwieldy for most people to read quickly and surely. Both the logographic and syllabic systems of writing failed to meet the criteria of an efficient writing system. The symbols of a logographic script could not cover all the possible words of a language (and a reader would not be able to not learn them all). The syllabic script could not account for all the syllables of a language in all their infinite combinations. These scripts, therefore, were not exhaustive.

Since the two pre-alphabetic scripts could not represent all the words of a language, specific signs had to stand for several sounds or words; the signs were therefore ambiguous. There were far more symbols for logographic scripts than the twenty to thirty signs a human brain can comfortably retain, and far too many to memorize. Although some syllabic scripts drastically cut down the number of signs for sounds—even fewer than the twenty-odd signs used in an alphabetic script—the remaining signs had to do double duty in representing the signs. Thus the signs were ambiguous.

What has happened to the Greek alphabet since its invention? How has it changed over the centuries? Is it still efficient?

There is no doubt that the original Greek alphabet has been altered since its invention. But if the original Greek alphabet was superior, why did it develop into the two other main phonemic alphabets, the Roman (or Latin) alphabet and the Cyrillic alphabet (used for Russian, Bulgarian, and certain other languages of the former Soviet Union)? Why, even in the modern Roman alphabet, do we have to add special marks to letters to show how to pronounce them?

In Spanish, for instance, we add a diacritical mark, the tilde (~) above the letter "n" to show how to pronounce a word like *señor* or *cañon*. In English, we may solve the problem by adding a letter, for example, spelling the English word that comes from *cañon* as "canyon." French places a diacritical mark, a cedilla, below the letter "c" to show that the sound is not the hard "k" sound but the soft, sibilant "s" sound, as in *garçon,* "boy."

We use other marks in addition to the letters themselves to indicate other aspects of pronunciation, such as accent marks. In French, for example, we use the *accent ague* to show the stress of a syllable, as in the word *cliché,* for instance.

And why is it that the North Semitic unvocalized scripts have held their own in representing existing languages like Arabic? Why did Turkish replace the Greek alphabet after the fall of Constantinople to the Turks? Why is it that the script now used to write Hebrew, a language derived from the North Semitic, has replaced the Roman alphabet in modern Israel?

The answer lies in the fact that no script is ideal; none provides perfect correspondences between the signs of its written language and the possible sounds it is supposed to represent. This situation we call the law of "residual ambiguity" (Havelock 1976, 53). All scripts, even those of the three major alphabetic systems, are to some degree ambiguous. There are several reasons for this.

First, the pronunciations of words may change over time, but the written signs for the words may not have changed. Thus, spelling often lags behind pronunciation. The English word "bright," for instance, was at one time pronounced as "brich-ta." We now pronounce this word as "brite," but we still spell it the way it was first spelled hundreds of years ago.

Also, the alphabet was originally devised by the Greeks to reflect the distinctive sounds in their language. Other languages, however, have sounds that do not exist in Greek. And likewise, languages other than English have sounds not found in English. German, for instance, has a sound in the word *Ich*—the velar fricative described above—that we do not have in English. In order to represent the sounds in their own languages, writers had to find new ways to symbolize the sounds by adding accent marks or diacritical marks; or they simply assumed readers would be taught how to pronounce these words. Furthermore, as efficient as the Greek alphabet was, it did not account even for all the sounds in Greek. Some residual ambiguities remained. Readers are required simply to learn from teachers how certain words are pronounced.

So the three major alphabetic systems—the Greek, Roman, and Cyrillic—all have exceptions no matter what particular language they are used for, but the alphabet was never devised to be perfect:

> The function of the original model [the Greek alphabet] was not to
> replace a prior knowledge of spoken speech but to trigger a recall of that
> knowledge. Its effective use depended upon the requirement that the
> oral vocabulary of the reader first be fluent and educated. The alphabet
> was and is an instrument of acoustic recognition, and only that. It hap-
> pens to be the most efficient so far devised by man. (Havelock 1976, 55)

In effect, the alphabet simply activates the memory of the reader to associate written symbols with certain speech sounds. In order for the reader to use the alphabet for this purpose, though, the reader must first have a fully developed command of oral language.

Even though the Greek alphabetic script was the most efficient yet invented, it did not represent all the dialects of Greek equally well. Why, among all Greek dialects at the time the alphabet was developing, did it come to represent the Athenian dialect? The Greek language, as spoken and written by the literate citizens of Athens, became dominant because this city-state was the most important cultural and political force in Greece. Although in Athens both the eastern and western pronunciations had been in competition, it was the Attic—or Athenian—pronunciation that prevailed. Because of the sheer quantity as well as the high quality of Athenian writing, the alphabet that best represented the Athenian dialect "became the alphabet of all literate Greeks. The end result was that a choice technological in character imposed itself through influences political and cultural" (Havelock 1976, 56, 57).

In short, the fact that the Greek alphabet was a marvelous technological invention was not the sole reason why the Athenian writing system became the standard. Rather, it was because the Attic alphabet was the writing system of the citizens of the most influential city in Greece, in terms of both its type of government, the "polis," and its cultural achievements in architecture, literature, and philosophy.

Just as the Athenian writing system became the preeminent script in the east for cultural and political reasons, so too the Latin writing system became the dominant system for similar historical reasons. Greeks colonized sections of what is now Italy, bringing, as might be assumed, the Greek writing system. Although some scholars believe that Latin speakers used an Etruscan version of the immigrant Greek system, this is not certain. It may be that the early speakers of Latin were preliterate, just as the Greeks themselves had been before 750 B.C., and that they had an oral, poetic tradition. In any event, the early Romans readily adopted the Greek alphabetic system.

The Roman alphabet was later adapted to represent the sounds of English. But new symbols had to be added to represent the sounds of Old English. The letter "c" came to stand for two sounds: the "hard c" and the "soft c," as in the modern words "call" and "censor," respectively. The letter "w"—or "double v"—was used by Norman scribes to provide a different sign for the sound represented by the letter "v." For the Old English version of the Roman alphabet, the symbols "Þ" ("thorn") and "ð" ("barred d") were created to stand for the unvoiced "th," the first sound in our modern word "thin," and the "voiced" "th," the first sound in our modern word "then."

We discuss such matters not to show that the Greek alphabet and its adaptations are so full of exceptions that they must be hopelessly inadequate to the task of efficiently representing speech in writing. Not at all. We point out these linguistics discrepancies simply to illustrate that no alphabet is perfect, that all languages exhibit residual ambiguity. No alphabet is able to depict all the sounds in a single language, much less to stand for language sounds not found in the original language. Furthermore, the choices made concerning alphabets are likely to be made not on the basis of rational linguistic considerations but, rather, as a result of political decisions.

As an example of residual ambiguity in a language, let us look at a sentence that demonstrates the sometimes irrational nature of written English: "These are the English shoes which are worn out quickly by Christian scholars" (Havelock 1976, 61).

First, the letter "e" in the words "these," "the," and "English" stands for three different sounds. We have learned how to pronounce these words simply because we have memorized the sounds in these very common words. Why do we know how to pronounce the sounds represented by the "o" in the words "shoe" and "worm"? Only because we learned how these letters are pronounced. Likewise, the sound for the "e" in "shoe" is an unusual use of the "e."

Why do letters not correspond perfectly on a one-to-one basis with the sounds of a language? Because languages change; the fact that letters do not always reproduce the sounds of the language they represent is often a historical matter. We must accept "that etymologies [the histories of words] are part of the history of sound, not of letters, even if, when examined by the literate scholar today, the letters take on the appearance of being a function of the language. The conventions of the script . . . are theoretically one thing: the behavior of the spoken tongue is something else altogether" (Havelock 1976, 62).

READERSHIP IN ANCIENT TIMES

The alphabet did not come into its own—full literacy was not possible—until movable type and the printing press were invented and until plentiful (and thus cheaper) paper was available. We explore this situation in some detail in chapter 4.

In early Greece, stone and baked clay were the earliest surfaces for writing. The Greek historian Herodotus noted that parchment—that is, cured animal skin—was available for writing, but, as we can imagine, it was scarce and expensive. The Egyptians used the other basic writing surface available: papyrus. From the available evidence, the Greeks used papyrus in Athens at least during the first half of the fifth century B.C. Waxed tablets for making notes were also used in writing.

There is no doubt that without the printing press and a cheap writing surface, writing was difficult and limited. The idea that there were "books"—in our present-day idea of bound pages—available for general readership during ancient times is misleading. The words *biblos* or *biblyos* refer not to our modern, many-page books but to papyrus. In order to create a surface for writing extended pieces, people would connect several sheets of papyrus by gumming them together at the edges. This made a continuous surface for written material that could conveniently be rolled up for carrying or for stuffing into a pigeonhole. Unfortunately, finding one's place after leaving off reading required unrolling the scroll of papyrus sheets until it appeared. Not exactly a "pocket book" that could be slipped into a toga. (Ironically, in order to find our place in a manuscript on a computer, we must again "scroll" back to find the section we want.)

As we can see, early reading was neither a simple nor an easy pastime. Rapid reading by a great number of people was simply not the reality at this time. Although the alphabet existed, the shortage of writing materials and the lack of standardization in writing and spelling, which was made possible by a printing press, led to a very limited readership indeed. It would be centuries before the potential of the alphabetic system was fully realized:

> Alphabetic literacy, in order to overcome these limitation of method and so achieve its full potential, had to await the invention of the printing press. The original achievement, the Greek one, had solved an empirical problem by applying abstract analysis. But the material means for maximizing the result required the assistance of further inventions and had to await a long time for it. . . . The energy of the alphabet . . . had to await the assistance provided by the dawning of scientific advance in Europe in order to be fully released. (Havelock 1976, 73)

SUMMARY

In order to comprehend the nature of literacy, we need to know the story of writing. For centuries, people engraved or wrote symbols to represent objects, creatures, and ideas. The logographic system of writing employs signs to stand for whole words. The syllabic system uses signs to represent syllables. Only the alphabetic system of writing uses symbols—the letters of an alphabet—to represent the meaningful sounds, the phonemes, of a language.

For a writing system to be efficient, it must meet three conditions: It must be comprehensive, it must be unambiguous, and it must employ relatively few—twenty to thirty—symbols. Although the alphabet, based upon the Greek invention from around 750 B.C., is the most efficient writing system yet devised, it is not perfect; its exceptions make it less than ideal and lead to the residual ambiguity of any written language. But the written symbols of an alphabetic writing system were intended to trigger a memory of the corresponding speech sounds for readers.

For a writing system to produce full literacy, though, a fourth condition is necessary: an education system that teaches children how to read and write while they are young enough and their brains are pliable enough to internalize the concept of written symbols corresponding to speech sounds.

Although alphabetic writing was conceived in the eighth century B.C. in Greece, many centuries would pass before the invention of movable type and the printing press allowed the full potential of writing to be released throughout the Western world.

REFERENCES

Bernard, H. Russell. 1999. "Language and Scripts in Contact: Historical Perspectives." In *Literacy: An International Handbook,* ed. Daniel A. Wagner, Richard L. Venezky, and Brian V. Street. Boulder, CO: Westview Press.

Eisenstein, Elizabeth L. 1983. *The Printing Revolution in Early Modern Europe.* Cambridge: Cambridge University Press.

———. 1979. *The Printing Press as an Agent of Change: Communications and Cultural Transformations in Early-Modern Europe.* 2 vols. Cambridge: Cambridge University Press.

Gelb, I. J. 1952. *A Study of Writing.* Chicago: University of Chicago Press.

Goody, Jack. 1999. "The Implications of Literacy." In *Literacy: An International Handbook,* ed. Daniel A. Wagner, Richard L. Venezky, and Brian V. Street. Boulder, CO: Westview Press.

———, 1986. *The Logic of Writing and the Organization of Society.* Cambridge: Cambridge University Press.

Goody, Jack, and Ian Watt. 1968. "The Consequences of Literacy." In *Literacy in Traditional Societies,* ed. Jack Goody. Cambridge: Cambridge University Press.

Havelock, Eric A. 1976. *Origins of Western Literacy.* Toronto, Ontario: Institute for Studies in Education.

Olson, David R. 1999. "Literacy and Language Development." In *Literacy: An International Handbook,* ed. Daniel A. Wagner, Richard L. Venezky, and Brian V. Street. Boulder, CO: Westview Press.

———. 1994. *The World on Paper. The Conceptual and Cognitive Implications of Writing and Reading.* New York: Cambridge University Press.

———. 1991. "Literacy and Objectivity: The Rise of Modern Science." In *Literacy and Orality,* ed. David R. Olson and Nancy Torrance. Cambridge: Cambridge University Press.

Chapter Four

⊷ The Consequences of Literacy

*Literacy makes an important and distinctive contribution
to language development. It contributes not only through
the access to information that readership provides, it
contributes by making language "opaque," that is, making
language an object of knowledge in its own right. This
knowledge about language—its sounds, words, and
meanings—provides the basis for a somewhat new and
distinctive mode of thought.*

*—David R. Olson, "Literacy and
Language Development"*

What were the long-range consequences of the invention of the alphabet and of the spread of literacy throughout the Western world? In what ways was full literacy—the ability of large numbers of people, not just an elite few, to read—destined, after many centuries, to permeate and influence every aspect of society: culture, religion, law, politics, science, and even government?

If we are to understand this transformation, though—a change in the very character of the Western mind—we need to review the background of this momentous alteration from an oral to a literate culture in the Western world.

We attribute the invention of the alphabet and the potential for full literacy to the ancient Greeks, but one man, the Greek philosopher Plato, as spokesman for a new kind of written, prosaic language—in direct opposition to the dominant oral poetic language of the day—almost single-handedly introduced a radically new way of using language. Particularly in *The Republic*, Plato makes a persuasive case for a rational, logical, and "scientific" discourse, one with novel elements of prose such as analysis, classification, cataloguing, and arguments from cause and effect.

HOMER'S POETRY

In what ways was a nonpoetic, rational language different from the oral, poetic narrative of Homer, which was ascendant before the invention of the alphabet? And how was it that writing was chiefly responsible for the invention of this novel, prosaic mind-set? In order for Plato to set in place this new style of language, he needed to supplant the old language, that of the orally transmitted, poetic Homeric epics, the *Iliad* and the *Odyssey*.

What were the characteristics of the Homeric epics—both of content and language—that Plato's language replaced? First of all and fundamentally, the Homeric epics were poetic. And they were transmitted orally. Furthermore, although the public presentations of the epics were entertaining, their primary purpose was to teach; that is, they were "didactic." We need to emphasize these elements because in present-day society, poetry does not have such a crucial role. Many people dismiss poetry as a "frill." Although some audiences may enjoy public poetry readings, the number of people in attendance is far fewer than the number at presentations of the epics or at the productions of Greek plays, such as *Antigone* and *Oedipus Rex*. Even though modern poetry may teach its readers and audiences, few poets would hold that the contemporary purpose of poetry was to educate. And certainly, the poems we do enjoy today are seldom long, narrative epics. The poetic epics of Homer's era had a much different place in society than does poetry today.

Because the Homeric epics were handed down orally, the minstrels who recited them and the people in the audience who memorized them needed a type of language they could easily recall. The ancient Greeks were totally nonliterate, or since they lived in an era before print, we might say they were preliterate. They had no texts of the epics or plays to turn to in order to refresh their memories about them.

Furthermore, oral epics were instructive: They were created primarily to pass on to the people a certain unique worldview, a common history they needed to share in order to survive as a cohesive people. But how was such a tradition passed on among people who could neither read nor write? A common core of beliefs can be handed down only through language in some kind of permanent and unalterable form. In a literate culture, such as ours, customs and usages are transmitted through formal education; through books, written laws, and decrees; and through libraries. But among preliterate people, like the ancient Greeks, since there was no writing system available, this practice of conveying written records was impossible.

The only recourse for the culture's preservation is through the living memories of human beings. But memorizing the whole body of a long epic like the *Iliad,* for instance, is an amazing feat. In Homer's time, the minstrel—the person who memorized the epic and presented it in performance—had to take advantage of the techniques for memorization, of the available mnemonic devices. We know it is easier to commit to memory a regular, rhyming poem than it is to memorize a long passage of prose. Just so with a long, poetic narrative.

What characteristics of long poems allowed the minstrels to memorize them? First of all, the poems contained many elements that are not necessarily part of the way we now present material to be learned. The epic was made up of continually recurring rhythms, images, and words. To reinforce the effects of the verse, musicians frequently accompanied the poetry with simple, repetitive rhythms produced on a popular musical instrument, the lyre. All these rhythmic elements—verbal and musical—contributed to make the poetic presentation pleasurable and, at the same time, more easily memorizable than would be prose passages. The whole production, we are told, was aimed at drawing the spectators into a highly emotional, psychologically satisfying experience. We might liken this participation to that at a highly emotional production of a TV program, movie, rock concert, or play. The rhythms and repetitive body movements of the minstrel had an emotional influence upon the members of the audience, providing a release from tension and anxiety. As a result, the performance often created a hypnotic effect, casting a virtual spell upon the members of the audience and creating an intimate linkage between the didactic purpose of the narrative and a complementary sensual experience.

If the performance produced strong feelings and helped the audience remember what was said and done in the epic, what were the mnemonic elements of the narrative poem? Since the epics needed to be memorized and understood not by just a gifted elite but by ordinary people, the body of the epic consisted not of abstract rules and prosaic statements—which are nearly impossible to memorize—but of a series of connected tales. We are all aware how much easier it is to remember narrative episodes with characters in dramatic events than it is to keep in mind expository statements. The epics consist of many connected episodes, all related in an overarching grand story. The characters do not think about their motives and behavior, as characters in modern prose fiction do; rather, they perform one action after another, without apparent conscious thought. And the primary characters—for example, the great warrior Achilles—are not just ordinary citizens. Since the primary aim of the epic was to educate, to teach the laws and customs of the culture, then the chief characters need to be outstanding persons in high offices whose actions are directly related to two basic kinds of laws of supreme importance to Greek culture: public law, the *nomos,* and family or private "law," the *ethos,* the Greek term from which we derive the modern word "ethics." In other words, the characters are "political" in the most fundamental sense of the word. These exemplary men and women, such as the Trojan hero Hector, perform passionate acts that are deeply felt by all members of the society. These political leaders have major roles in the epics "so the things they do will send out vibrations into the farthest confines of society, and the whole apparatus becomes alive and performs motions which are paradigmatic" (Havelock 1963, 168).

A great deal has been made of the fact that characters in the ancient Greek epics and plays are "highborn" and "noble." When Arthur Miller's American play *Death of a Salesman* was first produced, critics noted that because the chief character, Willy Loman, is not a "noble" hero but, rather, a "common man," the play technically—in the original Greek sense—could not be a tragedy. But the characters in the ancient Greek epics and plays were not chosen for snobbish reasons; they were chosen because their actions teach valuable lessons on how *not* to behave as well as on *how* to behave. "In sum, the saga [any long narrative] in order to do its job for the community and offer an effective paradigm of social law and custom, must deal with those acts which are conspicuous and political. And the actors who alone can furnish these paradigms in this kind of society we designate as 'heroes.' The reason for the heroic paradigm is in the last resort not romantic but functional and technical" (Havelock 1963, 168). We might make the concept of the tragic hero more meaningful in modern terms by reflecting on the lives and deaths of prominent political "heroes" such as Mahatma Gandhi, John F. Kennedy, and Martin Luther King Jr.

The heroes in the Greek oral epics and plays thus represented the mores of all the citizens. For these preliterate people, who learned these epics by heart, the heroes epitomized the most respected men and women in the society. The members of the audience observed the noble characters participating in an almost endless series of formal ceremonies surrounding births, marriages, great battles, deaths, and funerals. They saw how the highborn characters behave during these key rituals, and they themselves learned how to act at such conventional public events.

What is the purpose for this endless chronicle of short, episodic milestones in a heroic character's life? This narrative strategy is again necessary for ease of memorization. A single great story can only be remembered if it is made up of a number of related specific episodes. Therefore, the events in the oral poetic epic are all complete and satisfying in themselves. Action succeeds action in a seemingly unbroken chain, without any authorial generalizations (such as "Achilles was a great warrior"). In the epic, incident after incident deals with specific warriors—a great many are named—fighting in numerous battles. These events are presented without coordinate or subjunctive conjunctions (such grammatical forms were not used in the epics) in what is called a "paratactic" sentence structure: The basic structure in this oral story is shown by words and phrases like "next" and "and then."

Furthermore, the oral epic is made up of a great number of visual images, in contrast with the present-day practice in nonpoetic writing of using abstractions and generalizations. The reason for creating these elements in the epic—for stringing all the episodes together without general statements and making overwhelming use of concrete details and visual images—is to enable the audience to memorize the stories and, through an emotional, rhythmic, spellbinding performance, learn the political and family laws of the people. "Hence neither technical information [such as directions for navigating boats] nor moral judgment [such as pointing out that Achilles acts immaturely when he sulks in his tent and refuses to fight] can be presented reflectively in the saga as true generalization couched in the language of universals" (Havelock 1963, 181). Without the aid of written records, the ancient Greeks, although they could remember the exciting doings of great heroes, were not expected to memorize long, complex prose statements. Besides, we have no evidence of generalizations in Greek oral literature.

In short, the oral epic performance was like a dream: The audience came under the spell of the narrative as performed by the minstrel with his physical gestures and with musical accompaniment on a lyre. This spell contrasts vividly with prosaic language, which is reflective, rational, and analytic and which can be created only when people are literate, when they can write down information and think about it, when they no longer need mnemonic devices necessary for memorization. Poetic language obviously has its drawbacks, but before we are too quick to condemn it, we should acknowledge that it was preeminent in one area, which it did superbly well: teaching citizens public and private laws while at the same time supplying a complete emotional life. "It was a life without self-examination, but as a manipulation of the resources of the unconscious in harmony with the conscious it was unsurpassed" (Havelock 1963, 190).

THE BIRTH OF PROSE IN WESTERN THOUGHT AND LANGUAGE

Now we turn to a consideration of just how the invention of the Greek alphabet and full literacy, not the craft literacy of a few, created a revolution in language, literally changing the content, vocabulary, and syntax of the Greek language and indeed the mind-set of Western culture. The introduction of Greek letters in the eighth century B.C. was to alter forever the character of Western culture, creating a gulf between all alphabetic cultures and those of peoples who were not literate or who had a nonalphabetic script. "The Greeks did not just invent an alphabet; they invented literacy and the literate basis of modern thought" (Havelock 1976, 44).

Is this an extreme statement? Possibly not. But how long did it take for this revolution in language to occur? Was a single person responsible? And in what specific ways did this new language take the place of oral poetry in the Homeric epic, a kind of language so deeply embedded in the Greek culture that it had held sway literally for hundreds of years? That the Greek language eventually changed from a concrete, visual language to a rational, abstract, even "scientific" language is not an outlandish statement. The transformation did not happen overnight; it took more than three hundred years, from about 700 to 400 B.C., for the "new" Greek language to be fully developed.

No one person could be solely responsible for this change, but we generally acknowledge that the Greek philosopher Plato described in considerable detail the elements of this new language in *The Republic*, thus making his thoughts available to a wide range of sophisticated readers. Before Plato, a number of Greek philosophers had attempted to work out, step-by-step, these ideas about a kind of abstract language. These pioneering thinkers were the pre-Socratic philosophers and Socrates himself, the mentor of Plato. In *The Republic*, Plato himself spoke of this age-old debate between poetic language and the abstract language employed by philosophers: "There has been a quarrel between philosophy and poetry which goes back a long way" (quoted in Havelock 1963, 278). Although we usually credit Plato with most effectively articulating a new prose discourse, he was not the only advocate for rational, abstract thought; he was, however, undoubtedly the most significant. Plato was "one of those thinkers in whom seminal forces of a whole epoch sprang to life. Plato thinks the unconscious thoughts of his contemporaries. He gives to the intellectual currents of his age their direction and drive. He sought to create the current of intellectualism itself" (Havelock 1963, 277).

One of the most strikingly innovative discoveries contributing to this new thought appears to be the Greek acknowledgment of the "psyche," the entity that we might define as soul and have later called personality. By the end of the fifth century B.C., some Greek philosophers began to talk about their "souls," which they saw as autonomous and which had distinctive selves and personalities. The Greek word *psyche* may also be translated as "ghost," not the scary Halloween ghost of our culture but, rather, a "spirit who thinks." In this view, an individual psyche is not only separate from all other psyches, but it is also capable of "thinking" as well as acting. In the Greek oral epics, the characters did not think; they forthrightly acted and apparently did not think about their actions. Such thinking could only be accomplished through the statement of abstractions. But there was no abstract thinking in the Greek epics, certainly no thinking about thinking because this mental act and the words to describe it had not yet been devised. What we now call "metacognition," that is, "thinking about thinking," or "metalinguistics," that is, "thinking about language," were simply not present in the ancient Greek mind and therefore in the Greek language. So this psyche not only thinks, it must think about something, and this something was the result of "scientific" thought. Finally, this thinking psyche was infinitely precious, an essence absolutely unique in the whole realm of nature.

Thus, Plato's opposition to the poetic experience involved two assumptions: There is a psyche (personality) that thinks, and there is a body of knowledge that is not felt but, rather, thought about and knowable. How did this philosophic discovery of the individual self, the psyche, contribute to a new language? This individual psyche has the power to think, to cogitate, and to know. These mental powers are diametrically opposed to the poetic ability to see, to hear, and to feel. We see this separation in its clearest form in the dialectic method of Socrates. Very simply, Socrates asks questions that compel speakers to think about what they have said. But the questions are of a special kind. When Socrates asks questions, he urges his hearer to repeat what he has said and then to explain what he meant by his words. By being forced to repeat a statement and to explain what it means, the speaker is compelled to think about his words. By this process, Socrates arouses the speaker from an unsubstantiated emotional opinion, which is likened to the "dream state" of poetry. Socrates, by his use of the dialectic, in which he insists that the speaker think about what he has said, forces the speaker to think abstractly. For instance, instead of identifying emotionally with the great hero Achilles, Socrates' student is now asked to think about Achilles' behavior and made a general statement summarizing the great warrior's actions. Did he act childishly? Bravely?

As the speaker in the Socratic dialogue repeats what he has said and then thinks about his original statement, explaining what he meant, he is interpreting. The idea of "interpretation" is also new to Western thought. Socrates says to the speaker, "Tell me what you just said. Say it again." He is requiring the speaker to restate his original position. And this time, the speaker needs to say it in prosaic, rational, and abstract language. Aha! The clever teacher educates his pupil in how to think by using new language.

Thus is born "hermeneutics," the science and methodology of interpretation. And with it, the ability to think about language, literally to think "beyond language," which we now consider an extremely high-level abstract mental activity. In order to think this way with and about language, though, we need a fresh vocabulary. If we are to make a statement, to say that "something is ———," we need the verb "is." For example, if we want to make a general statement about Achilles, such as "Achilles is a great hero," then we are obliged to use the verb "is." In the ancient Greek language and in the oral epics, the verb "is" does not exist. Why is this fact significant? In oral poetry we know how heroes like Achilles and Hector behave by observing their actions through numerous episodes. Because the language used to recount the events is concrete, we can only think concretely, not abstractly. But if we want to make a general statement—which the language of the epic does not allow us to do—we need to use the verb "is": "The hero is brave." "He is compassionate." And "He is law-abiding." With the invention of the alphabet and writing, we are now able to draw from many examples and make a general statement. We have learned how to generalize. Instead of describing concrete objects and creatures poetically, we now have the option of constructing abstract statements about what we see and hear. With this radical idea of being able to see ourselves "outside" language and thus to think about language—rather than being passively moved by an emotionally overpowering, poetic performance—we are now able to think about a thing "per se," the thing "in itself." The phrase "per se," which literally means "by itself," is another element of this new prosaic language that allows us to think abstractly. Thinking about something per se is a new mental habit. Instead of showing characters in a number of episodes acting heroically, we can now say "Heroism 'per se' is a quality to be desired in a warrior."

At the heart of this linguistic revolution, however, is Plato's invention of the theory of forms: "Here is a new form of discourse and a new kind of vocabulary offered to the European mind" (Havelock 1963, 260). Plato's theory of the forms may best be explained by his own example in *The Republic* of the different levels of abstraction for the word "bed."

1. *The original, the form Bed.* At the first and highest level of abstraction, in the realm of pure essence, is the unique and eternal form Bed, corresponding to the word "bed." This form, however, is not what we call a generalization or concept, which we as humans are able to create. As human beings, we do not create forms. They already exist. We can only apprehend them through our intellect. "So the Forms are not the creation of the intellect, and this means that the 'objects' represented by such linguistic devices as 'the itself per se' are not the creations of the intellect either" (Havelock 1963, 263). Today, we commonly translate Plato's forms as "ideas," the notion that forms the basis of the branch of philosophy known as idealism.

2. *Secondhand copy of Bed by a craftsman.* The worker who makes a physical bed may create any of a number of kinds of beds— four posters, sleigh beds, rope beds, ad infinitum—but all are derived from the abstract form ("idea") Bed.

3. *Thirdhand copy of a copy of Bed by a poet or artist.* The artist, be it a poet, painter, or sculptor, copies the copy of the form Bed made by the craftsman. Thus, the poet deals with the essential form Bed at third hand, as a copy of a copy of the original form.

What is the result of this revolutionary concept of forms, the abstract essences of all creatures, things, and ideas? With the discovery of the abstract forms, we can now think about such matters, and we thus are able to create new words to describe these forms. We can think and write about such abstractions as "beautiful," "just," and "good" and about their opposites, "ugly," "unjust," and "evil." We can also think about ideas such as "double," "half," "great," "small," "light," and "heavy." We can think about numerical notions such as "odd," "even," "square," three types of "angles," "square" per se, and "diameter" per se. In other words, we can think about and describe the natural world by equations, laws, formulas, and categories. These ideas are timeless. They are completely different from the actions of characters in epics and plays, which occur during periods of time and are thus "time conditioned." For the first time, the theory of the forms "announced the arrival of a completely new level of discourse which as it became perfected was to create in turn a new kind of experience in the world—the reflective, the scientific, the technical, the theological, the analytic" (Havelock 1963, 267).

What do we call a person who is able to think abstractly? The word for a person able to employ fully this new discourse, so antithetical to the poetic language of the Homeric poetic epics, is "philosopher."

The word "philosopher" first appears in works from early in the fourth century B.C., but the verb "philosophize" is found in works from the last quarter of the fifth century B.C.; the best-known use of the word is by Pericles in his justly famous funeral speech: "We [Athenians] philosophize without effeminacy" (quoted in Havelock 1963, 288). It was, however, Plato who first used the word "philosopher," in *The Republic,* to describe the kind of person who epitomized the idea of a rational thinker "simply as a man who is prepared to challenge the concrete over the consciousness, and to substitute the abstract" (Havelock 1963, 281).

The modern etymology given for the word "philosopher," as literally meaning "one who loves wisdom," is not only insufficient but actually misleading. Working directly from the Greek, Havelock translates *phil-* not as "love" but as "psychic urge, drive, thirst, all consuming desire," and *sophia* not as "wisdom" but, rather, as "capacity for abstract thinking." A more accurate literal rendition for "philosopher," then, would be "one who has an unconquerable urge to deal with abstractions," that is, a person we now label—minus all the negative connotations—an "intellectual" (Havelock 1963, 282).

FUNDAMENTAL CONSEQUENCES
OF THE ALPHABET

After this examination of how Plato, because of the prior invention of the alphabet and of a written language, could reveal the vital existence of this new rational, abstract language, what can we say about the influence of the alphabet and literacy upon the cognition and psychology of the Western mind?

On the one hand, the invention of the alphabet may have actually transformed the makeup of mental processes in Western civilization. "What the new script may have done in the long run was to change somewhat the content of the human mind" (Havelock 1976, 46). The psychological effect of the Greek alphabet was that the twenty-odd symbols, once learned, were pushed down below the level of awareness and virtually forgotten. Once internalized, the symbols allowed persons to read easily and quickly. What of the psychological effects of the alphabet? With the Greek alphabet, the burden of remembering thousands of symbols—one for each word—was lifted. Now the energy once expended on memorizing symbols was made available for thinking about new thoughts and writing them down so they could be consulted again and again without worrying about remembering them. In the process, we gained the opportunity not just to memorize the same old stories, familiar myths, plays, and long narrative poems, without the aid of written records, but to contribute to the expansion of knowledge available to the human mind.

Although some scholars argue that the alphabet literally changed the cognitive and psychological processes of the Western mind, others believe that rather than actually altering minds, the alphabet and literacy provided novel "models" for thinking about language and ways of using language in writing as well as in speaking. In other words, through reading, we learn strikingly new ways of thinking, speaking, and writing, including thinking "about" language. "The magic of writing," states David Olson,

> arises not so much from the fact that writing serves as a new
> mnemonic device, an aid to memory, as from the fact that writing may
> serve an important epistemological function. Writing not only helps us
> remember what we thought and said but also invites us to see what was
> thought and said in a new way. It is a cliché to say that there is more to
> writing than the abc's and more to literacy than the ability to decode
> words and sentences. (Olson 1994, xv)

In sum, writing has either altered the human mind or, with the same result, opened the mind to new ways of thinking, speaking, and writing. Writing became a "technology of the intellect" (Goody 1986). Through writing, for instance, we can make lists of words and then group the words into certain categories, thus utilizing the language skills of classification and generalization. In ancient oral poetry, for instance, we find lists not as separate kinds of language but as language embedded within the poetic narrative, such as the list of warriors from different parts of Greece in the *Iliad*. The primitive classification, rather than being an integral part of the poetic epic, may have served as a forerunner of one part of the whole logical, specialized, and cumulative tradition of the Athenian prose of the sixth century B.C.

If we consider this notion that reading and writing serve as models for thinking, we can notice that writing is not simply speech written down word for word. All we have to do to recognize this fact is to tape-record friends chatting. When we play the conversation back, we should not be amazed at how unlike purposeful writing casual speech is—lacking in cohesion and full of repetitions and false starts. Rather than merely transcribing speech, then, writing serves as a tentative structure of language, showing us the infinite variety of sentences and words available. "Learning to read and write is, therefore," writes Olson, "learning to hear and think about one's language in a new way. Consequently, it may alter speech practices as well as report them. This is what makes learning to read both important and difficult" (Olson 1999, 132).

In short, writing and reading may very well provide models for more prosaic uses of language than are available with poetry, both for speaking and for writing. It may even be that reading actually changes the minds of those who read. Such a distinction is possibly too fine for our purposes, because in the end, the results are the same. Reading changes the way we think about and use language. Plato, standing on the shoulders of great thinkers before him, propagated the idea of knowledge as we now know it and established it as the proper study of an educational system, with these being the branches of study in classical antiquity: ethics, politics, psychology, physics, and metaphysics. Although Plato's student Aristotle brilliantly examined the subject of poetry in *The Poetics,* poetry, once the superior mode of discourse, lost the day to rational thought. The momentous shift from poetry's dominance as the sole kind of language to the preeminence of scientific thought had been accomplished. "Man's experience of his society, of himself, and of his environment was now given separate organized existence in the abstract word. . . . Europe still lives in their [Plato's and Aristotle's] shadow, using their language, accepting their dichotomies, and submitting to their discipline of the abstract as the chief vehicle of education, even to this day" (Havelock 1963, 305).

EARLY MODERN CONSEQUENCES OF LITERACY

One might say that the primary consequence of the development of the alphabet and literacy was to change Western thinking, to provide a model of perceiving and using language, a model destined to penetrate every aspect of early modern Western literacy. It was many centuries, however, before the invention in Europe of movable type and the printing press in the fifteenth century A.D. released the full power of the alphabet. For hundreds of years after the invention of the Greek alphabet, literate Greeks for the most part copied down manuscripts of oral Greek literature, such as the Homeric epics and Athenian plays. How could it be otherwise? Rational language had not yet been conceived.

The Romans adapted the Greek alphabet for their own use and with their own symbols, and Roman literature flourished until roughly the fall of the Roman Empire at about the end of the fifth century A.D. After this time, Western literacy became a craft literacy, and only those whose primary function was to copy over existing manuscripts or to use language for written purposes, typically monks, priests, and others in religious orders, were able to read and write.

It was only the invention of movable type and the letter-press printing press, "the iron-and-levers-and-roller-based rude mechanicals that enabled all to enjoy and savor the teachings of the ancients" (Winchester 2001, 8). The consequences of cheap and easy printing affected family life, communication, and education; it enabled the rapid expansion of libraries and other repositories of written language and the development of the English language and of modern science; and it even contributed to the idea of democracy in Great Britain, an idea that then spread to the American colonies and led to the creation of the United States.

A primary consequence of printing was its effect on family life. For the first time, the socialization of children—moral as well as educational—was removed from the family and handed over to persons who were not members of the children's immediate families. As we might imagine, this was a wrenching change. This practice grew until, in the nineteenth century, most of the children in Europe and in the United States who received schooling were in schools for "universal education, a profound and revolutionary move. . . . The development of writing, then, involved the establishment of schools, the training of teachers, [and] the emergence of specialist producers of knowledge" (Goody 1999, 30–31).

And as a result of "book learning," schooling became longer and more abstract. Children's education grew longer because after a fairly extended period of learning to read and write, children then had at least to be exposed to the literary canon of the culture, including essays and other works written in this new expository, "scientific" prose. Instruction became more and more removed from "real life" and increasingly abstract because pupils now learned about the world not at home or on the job but through books while squirming in classrooms. As we can appreciate from our present-day experiences in schools, education appeared to have little to do with the "real world." The chief complaint from students to this day is that school consists of sticking one's nose in books, listening to teachers lecture, and talking about impractical matters rather than actually doing anything in the world "out there." The implication is that schooling has little relevance to their lives. And the student has only the invention of the alphabet and printing press to thank for this brand of education.

The invention of printing also had a far-reaching effect on communications systems. We have only to look around us to see how completely the written word dominates our lives. Granted, a great deal of information is passed on to us orally through television, but even there, it is surprising how much of this information is either in print or is based upon print. In fact, we have been officially notified by the *New York Times* that, through what is known as the "Crawl" on cable news programs, "television has become a print medium" (Sella 2001, 66). Anyone who watches the major cable outlets—CNN, Fox News, and MSNBC— cannot help but notice the continuous, scrolling printed information across the bottom of the TV screen. The reason for the Crawl, we are informed, is that with the glut of "breaking news," the cable news channels believe it is impossible to channel "through a single televised human" all the information from all the events occurring throughout the world at this minute, and thus "the Crawl is multimedia's alternative to Babel." Possibly, though, the Crawl is "a favor to the younger generation of multitaskers." For others, the swiftly moving blurbs are, to say the least, distracting (Sella 2001, 66).

The Crawl may have been begun in 1980 by the Financial News Network, now extinct, when an unsung media genius first added a stock ticker—obviously transferred from the stock tickers of the nation's stock exchanges—to the program. Beyond this bit of evidence, no one in the news world appears willing to answer the question "Who first came up with the idea of transplanting the news ticker that pedestrians see every day in Time Square to the television screen?" (Sella 2001, 66).

Reading and writing also take up a great deal of time for literate people: in newspapers, in magazines, in mail, and on the computer, a technological invention that requires more, rather than less, reading and writing than ever before.

In addition, the invention of print has allowed us to accumulate and store information from all over the globe and from centuries long past. "As an agent of change, printing altered methods of data collection, storage, and retrieval systems and communication networks used by learned communities throughout Europe. It warrants special attention because it had special effects" (Eisenstein 1979, xvi). Modern storage and retrieval systems are marvelous developments. We are able to pull up past information in seconds, and we have the luxury—which we accept without thinking about it—of studying and analyzing printed information at our leisure and now, because of the computer, in our own homes. We can then skim and choose what material we wish to retain from the available print. Such an activity is impossible with oral language. "Documents give us a different sense of history, since we can readily retrieve the literature of our predecessors, their spoken word as well as their visual records" (Goody 1999, 31).

Now, however, the storage system may be a victim of its own success. Our libraries, so administrators report, are running out of room to store the plethora of printed matter produced in books, in periodicals, and especially in newspapers. Storing such materials on microfilm and microfiche has not solved the unanticipated and unwelcome problem. One interested "friend of the library," Nicholson Baker, in his aptly titled book *Double Fold: Libraries and the Assault on Paper* (2001), argues that there is no need for library officials to convert countless books and newspapers to microfilm, which in any case does not always preserve print, since often over years the print fades, develops spots and blemishes, and even suffers from fungal infections (Baker 2001, cited in Gates 2001, 8). Baker first spoke out in the San Francisco Library's auditorium in 1996 as a "library activist" against the library's practice of sending books to landfills because it had no room to store them. He also complains about the current library practice of "disbinding" books, in which librarians "guillotine" volumes—which had not been checked out for decades—along their spines and then throw them away. He feels so strongly about saving old newspapers, such as the *Chicago Tribune,* the *New York World,* and the *New York Times,* from destruction that he has started a nonprofit foundation for rescuing valuable old newspapers and is renting a decrepit warehouse in New Hampshire, where he stores thousands of volumes of old newspapers scheduled for destruction (Gates 2001, 8). Some librarians say that they cannot stop destroying priceless books and newspapers. "We simply can't save everything," they exclaim, literally and figuratively throwing up their hands. But Baker replies with these words: "Well, we're not asking them to save *everything.* We're not talking about airplane tickets or check stubs here. We're talking about the major newspapers that should be at the top of their lists of things to save" (Garner 2001, 9).

Modern political bureaucracies also owe their existence to the alphabet and the invention of printing. Only with writing can we retain the information that forms the basis of all such organizations: files, correspondence, and financial accounts as well as a country's evidence and records of all its interactions with other governments. Furthermore, no political bureaucracy can exist without legal codes, and writing drastically altered legal activities. Courts, in effect, began to depend on written records rather than on oral evidence and testimony for trials and other transactions. Written statutes and laws form the basis of a literate society. How can a legal system exist without lawyers and judges looking up what a previous ruling "said" for a precedent? Writing made it possible to save exact copies of contracts and laws rather than having lawyers rely on oral testimony. Even oral depositions and oral testimony are turned into written records to be later examined in solitude by lawyers and judges. No longer can a person only orally lay claim to a title for owning land; written records of all titles have become the standard.

The invention of the alphabet and later the printing press also profoundly influenced the progress of the Protestant Reformation and, some believe, may have at the same time led to the birth of modern science. Printing, according to this view, had a direct influence on how literate individuals perceived Scripture and on how scientists viewed the natural world (Eisenstein 1983; Olson 1999).

This is a bold position indeed, but let us examine how it is substantiated. The basic argument is this: Printing "fixed"—providing large numbers of identical copies—both Scripture and ancient "science" books, which dealt with the natural world. These fixed, original, and objective texts were then put into millions of hands (Olson 1991, 151). Print allowed a clear distinction between what was "observed" and the "interpretation" of what was seen as "fixed," "objective," and "permanent."

The core element of the religious reform movement of the sixteenth century in Europe was the "return to the book." Before the advent of printing, the Roman church's official view of interpretation was that expressed by Thomas Aquinas in his thirteenth-century *Summa Theologica:* Aquinas held that there are several levels of interpretation in Scripture, including literal, spiritual, and moral interpretations. All of these levels of meaning were inherent, "given," in the text.

Printing made an exact copy of Scripture available to anyone who could read and thus also made possible a new, personal way of interpreting the Bible. The Protestant reformer Martin Luther articulated the radically new viewpoint that there is a literal, historical meaning in the text of Scripture. Everything else attributed to Scripture, he held, is the result of tradition, of individuals attempting over time to "interpret" Scripture for those who were unlettered. Scripture—the exact, printed copy of the book—stands by itself, inviolate and autonomous, and needs no interpretation. All the rest is made up, a product of centuries of human explanation. If we accept this stance, we acknowledge the crucial distinction between the "given"—in this case, the "given" of the exact, faithful, printed copy of Scripture—and various "interpretations" of the everlasting, unchanging book made throughout the ages by a literate elite.

How did the invention of the printing press lead to the rise of modern science at the same time it was influencing theological thought? The connection between print and the interpretation of Scripture is analogous to the connection between print and a new interpretation of the natural world by early modern scientists, in which a special "scientific" language for observing the natural world, a "given," and for writing about the meaning of these observations, "interpretation," is now available.

During the Middle Ages, it was common to speak of two kinds of "books": Scripture as God's word and nature as God's work (Olson 1991, 154). Francis Bacon in 1620 wrote of "the book of God's word and the book of God's work" (quoted in Olson 1991, 154). Thomas Browne, a seventeenth-century cleric, talked of God's two great books, Scripture and nature (Olson 1991, 154). To make this view slightly more complex, Galileo maintained that the book of nature was written in the language of mathematics. Eric Havelock believes the modern scientific era did not depend solely on the printed page, important as it was "for the compilation and distribution of theoretic reasoning and empirical information"; he holds that "it relied also upon a revolution in the symbolization of quantitative measurement" (Havelock 1976, 78). Musical "literacy," in this view, should be added to linguistic and numerical literacy, to complete the picture of the three literacies that were responsible for the modern era. "Linguistic, numerical, and musical 'literacy,' so to speak, can be thought of as forming a tripartite foundation of Western culture, built upon three technologies each of which is designed to trigger mental operations with automatic rapidity by using the sense of visual recognition" (Havelock 1976, 81).

For those who created the modern scientific movement, the "given" of natural "facts"—analogous to the "given" word of Scripture—was the foundation upon which modern science was built. Everything else, the interpretation of nature, all the hypotheses, inferences, and "final causes," were invented by man. Even today, the nature of science is still founded on the distinction between "observation" and "inference." Observations of eternal nature are objective and reliable; inferences are made by humans and are merely theoretical interpretations of these observations. Although this distinction has undergone some revisions in modern times, present-day scientists still consistently and systematically separate observation from hypothesis. In short, centuries ago, reading the book of nature, that is, making scientific observations, was a new method of interpreting the facts of the natural world. This new science of interpretation, originally applied to Scripture, is hermeneutics, the science and methodology of interpretation.

In the process of creating a new way of viewing the natural world, print also was responsible for changing scientific language. Since scientists now read "perfect," exactly reproduced, printed books of observations and theoretical statements—what we now call primary sources—they had to devise a new language for writing about the book of nature. Early modern scientists could talk about novel ideas only if they coined new words to express these unfamiliar conceptions. For instance, early modern scientists arrived at such fundamental terms as "observation" and "inference," "fact" and "theory," and "evidence" and "claim." They also made up a whole set of related concepts, such as "hypothesis," "conclusion," "conjecture," "assertion," and "assumption" (Olson 1991, 155).

These early modern scientists also began to develop a new discourse for writing about science by writing not in the then-familiar flowery style but in a new, "plain" style. For instance, in 1667, the historian of the Royal Society of London, Thomas Sprat, described how members' writing should reflect the society's current attitudes toward Scripture and nature. The society was concerned "with the advancement of science and with the improvement of the English language as a medium of prose" (quoted in Olson 1991, 155, 156) and demanded a mathematical plainness in style, free from all "amplifications, digressions, and swellings of style" (quoted in Olson 1991, 156).

In short, it very well may be that the great changes of this period in religion and science were direct results of new ways of thinking about Scripture and the natural world, and this new thinking in turn changed scientific prose:

> Perhaps Luther, Galileo and Descartes shared a common but new way of reading—of relating what was said to what was meant by it! But even to pose such questions required some analysis of just what scripts and writing systems are, how they relate to speech, how they are read, how those ways of reading changed, how ways of reading called for new distinctions, new awareness and new modes of thinking . . . how the very structure of knowledge was altered by the attempts to represent the world on paper. (Olson 1994, xvii)

Finally, several scholars have focused on the influence of the printing press, via the publication of a single book, the King James Bible of 1611, on the English language and on the birth of popular government both in England and in the American colonies.

First, what was the impact of the publication of the King James Bible on the English language itself? "Many of the Semitic turns of phrase that have gained an accepted place in modern English," we are told by Alister McGrath, "can be traced directly to the King James Bible of the Old Testament" (McGrath 2002, 362). McGrath quotes William

Rosenau, from his 1978 book *Hebraisms in the Authorized Version of the Bible,* who stated flatly that the King James Bible "has been—it can be said without any fear of being charged with exaggeration—the most powerful factor in the history of English literature" (quoted in McGrath 2002, 263).

Here are examples of Hebraic idioms that have become a part of English usage: "sour grapes," "pride goes before a fall," "to put words in his mouth," and "like a lamb to slaughter" (McGrath 2002, 263). Other English phrases that have been adopted, with some minor changes, from Hebrew include these: "rise and shine," "to see the writing on the wall," "a fly in the ointment," and "a drop in the bucket" (McGrath 2002, 264).

The case has also been made that printing the various translations of the Bible, and especially the King James Bible, was responsible for creating popular government, a novel idea in both England and the American colonies in an era of kings and queens. As Simon Winchester reports, in his review of both Alister McGrath's 2002 book *In the Beginning* and Benson Bobrick's 2002 book *Wide as the Waters,* Bobrick's "case is that the very warp and woof of popular government was created by the democratization of translated Scripture—that the newly evangelized people won from the Bible's teachings a spiritual strength sufficient to help them overcome the tyranny of their arrogant and detached rulers" (Winchester 2001, 8). In the following quotation, Benson Bobrick presents his case for the unimaginable power of the King James Bible to affect all aspects of the era:

> The growth of independent thought in the interpretation of the Bible was symptomatic of a larger spirit of questioning and inquiry which marked the age. Traditional explanations of the physical universe were rapidly yielding to the revelations of astronomy and the New Science, even as continued exploration of the globe "stimulated imaginations in every walk of life." In politics, people began to insist on their right to a government that ruled with equity and justice, and in religion, on their right to worship as they pleased. . . .
>
> Their [the general public's] free discussions about the authority of Church and state fostered concepts of constitutional government in England, which in turn were the indispensable prerequisites for the American colonial revolt. Without the vernacular Bible—and the English Bible in particular, through its impact on the reformation of English politics—there could not have been democracy as we know it, or even what today we call the "Free World." In short, the English Bible,

with all that followed in its train, had sanctioned the right and capacity of the people to think for themselves. (Bobrick 2002, 268–269)

It does not really matter for our discussion here whether or not the newly printed Bible turned those who read it into Christians. What was important was that two ideas from the Bible formed the basis for popular government in the Western world: first, that each person was born with certain inalienable rights that could not be taken away, and second, that any government built upon this recognition was truly a government "by, for, and of the people" (Winchester 2001, 8).

SUMMARY

The invention of the alphabet and the subsequent invention of movable type and the printing press literally shaped Western thought and culture.

In a deeply fundamental way, the poetic language of the oral Homeric epics and Athenian plays was superseded by a new prose, propagated chiefly by the Greek philosopher Plato. Greek oral poetry was repetitive, rhythmic, imagistic, concrete, and didactic, all the mnemonic features contributing to people's ability to memorize oral works. The content of the poetic epics and plays consisted of familiar stories of heroes who were directly involved in actions reflecting the basic customs of the people. The epics and plays entertained but were also didactic because their primary purpose was to teach the public and family laws to a preliterate people.

Plato synthesized the thinking of his day about a new language: a rational, expository, abstract, and scientific discourse in direct opposition to Homeric poetry. The person epitomizing this new way of thinking and using language was the "philosopher king," a kind of individual we might call an "intellectual," one who is capable of and who has an overwhelming desire for abstract thinking.

The full effect of the invention of the alphabet was not realized, however, until the invention of movable type and the printing press in the fifteenth century in Germany by Johannes Gutenberg. When cheap and plentiful printed matter was available for all literate persons, the consequences were momentous and universal: All aspects of culture were affected—family life, education, mass communication, libraries and all other storage systems for print, bureaucracies, law, religion, science—and print was responsible for introducing a concept of government originally created by the ancient Greeks, democratic government.

REFERENCES

Baker, Nicholson. 2001. *Double Fold: Libraries and the Assault on Paper.* New York: Random House.

Bobrick, Benson. 2002. *Wide as the Waters: The Story of the English Bible and the Revolution It Inspired.* New York: Penguin.

Eisenstein, Elizabeth L. 1983. *The Printing Revolution in Early Modern Europe.* Cambridge: Cambridge University Press.

———. 1979. *The Printing Press as an Agent of Change: Communications and Cultural Transformations in Early-Modern Europe.* 2 vols. Cambridge: Cambridge University Press.

Garner, Dwight. 2001. "The Collector: Interview [with Nicholson Baker]." *New York Times Book Review,* April 15, 2001, 9.

Gates, Dates. 2001. "Paper Chase: Nicholson Baker Makes a Case for Saving Old Books and Newspapers." Review of *Double Fold: Libraries and the Assault on Paper* by Nicholson Baker. *New York Times Book Review,* April 15, 8.

Gelb, I. J. 1952. *A Study of Writing.* Chicago: University of Chicago Press.

Goody, Jack. 1999. "The Implications of Literacy." In *Literacy: An International Handbook,* ed. Daniel A. Wagner, Richard L. Venezky, and Brian V. Street. Boulder, CO: Westview Press.

———. 1986. *The Logic of Writing and the Organization of Society.* Cambridge: Cambridge University Press.

Goody, Jack, and Ian Watt. 1968. "The Consequences of Literacy." In *Literacy in Traditional Societies,* ed. Jack Goody. Cambridge: Cambridge University Press.

Havelock, Eric A. 1976. *Origins of Western Literacy.* Toronto, Ontario: Institute for Studies in Education.

———. 1963. *Preface to Plato.* Cambridge, MA: Harvard University Press.

McGrath, Alister. 2002. *In the Beginning: The Story of the King James Bible and How It Changed a Nation, a Language, and a Culture.* New York: Anchor.

Olson, David R. 1999. "Literacy and Language Development." In *Literacy: An International Handbook,* ed. Daniel A. Wagner, Richard L. Venezky, and Brian V. Street. Boulder, CO: Westview Press.

———. 1994. *The World on Paper: The Conceptual and Cognitive Implications of Writing and Reading.* Cambridge: Cambridge University Press.

———. 1991. "Literacy and Objectivity: The Rise of Modern Science." In *Literacy and Orality,* ed. David R. Olson and Nancy Torrance. Cambridge: Cambridge University Press.

Sella, Marshall. 2001. "The Crawl. The Year in Ideas: A to Z." *New York Times Magazine,* December 9, 66.

Winchester, Simon. 2001. "Where Is It Written? Right Here." Review of *Wide as the Waters* by Benson Bobrick and *In the Beginning* by Alister McGrath. *New York Times Book Review,* April 8, 8.

Chapter Five

◆ Reading: How We Learned to Read

> *The history of written communication in the West may be divided into two broad fields of inquiry. The first comprises the discipline of the history of reading, the second constitutes the history of literacy. The history of reading deals with the qualitative question of how people have evolved diverse cognitive techniques to extract meaning from written or printed text. The history of literacy is concerned with quantitative questions relating to the diffusion of these various reading skills to different strata of society.*
> —Paul Saenger, "The History of Reading"

What does Paul Saenger mean, in the epigraph to this chapter, by the "qualitative question" of learning to read? How, over the centuries, have we developed mental strategies for finding meaning in the written or printed page? In other words, what goes on in my mind as I read? And how has this process changed over the millennia? Furthermore, has the appearance of the written page changed since ancient times, and if so, how? And if it has changed, in what subtle and significant ways did it alter how I read? Very simply, but not surprisingly, all these changes in language and in writing format have come about for one reason: to make reading easier. And we modern readers enjoy the advances in reading made by legions of humble, dedicated authors and scribes over the centuries.

WHAT WE DO AS WE READ

We who are already fluent readers are unaware of these changes. For the most part, we know nothing of how language has changed, and how the printed page looks to our eyes lies below the level of conscious thought.

If we ask an accomplished reader, What do you do as you read? she might answer something like this: "What do I do as I read? I look at the page before me and figure out what kind of reading I'm up against. If it's a newspaper or magazine article, I expect to read in a certain way. If it's a page in a textbook, another way. Of course, if I read a poem, or even in a great while, if I read a play, I read them in still different ways. However, if I read a play of Shakespeare's, which is a play in poetry, then I have an altogether different way of reading."

This reaction reveals how the fluent reader adjusts to varied reading material, but it doesn't say precisely what cognitive processes are going on as we read. How have we come to the ability—an utterly amazing skill—to read silently, by ourselves, and with great speed? And to make sense of all kinds of reading material? Have we always read the way we read today? Did readers develop this ability as soon as alphabetic script was invented by the Greeks, sometime during the eighth century B.C.? No. Although as naive readers we might assume that we have forever read as we read today, that is simply not the case.

How has the radical change in reading occurred? Essentially, the appearance of the written page and later of the printed page—the "text format"—has been modified over the millennia. As the format of the page has evolved, so the very structure of the language used in writing has also been transformed. As a result, our mental abilities have also evolved to keep pace with these changes.

When alphabetic writing was first invented, people from many different cultures with varied languages used a variety of cognitive strategies to comprehend writing. No matter how many techniques we have employed over the centuries, however, there are two main elements of all written documents determining the cognitive processes we use to decode meaning from print: the structure of the language and the format of the written or printed page.

First is the very structure of a language—its grammar and syntax. What syntax does the language exhibit? Does it show meaning by inflections—by word endings—as, for example, in ancient Greek, Latin, Old English, and modern German? Or does the syntax show meaning by word order and function words (for example, articles and prepositions), as in modern English, whose most common sentence order is subject-verb-direct object or predicate nominative?

What do we mean by a language representing meaning by inflections? Take this simple Latin sentence, for instance:

Puer puellam amat.

If we ignore the Latin inflected endings and just transcribe the words, one at a time, into English words, keeping the word order, we have

Boy girl loves.

But if we now translate the sentence into English, that is, if we translate the inflected words in Latin, which uses word endings to convey meaning, into English, which uses word order to convey meaning, we have

The boy loves the girl.

In Latin, we do not need to have our English word order because Latin uses word endings to show meaning. The word *puer* means "boy," and since it is the subject of the sentence, it is in nominative case and so does not have any special added ending. The word *puellam,* "girl," is in the objective or accusative case, as is shown by the word ending *-am,* and so is the object of the verb *amat.* The verb *amat,* we know from its inflection *-at,* is the third person singular form of the verb *amare,* "to love":

amo, "I love"
amas, "you love"
amat, "he, she, or it loves"

Also note that as we conjugate the verb *amare—amo, amas, amat—*the word endings signify what in English is signified by the pronouns "I," "you," and "he, she, or it." Since English is not heavily inflected, we need the pronouns to show meaning.

Because both ancient Greek and Latin are highly inflected languages, the ancients first wrote out highly inflected languages, which many times place the verb last in sentences. It was common for medieval authors to place verbs last in sentences, in imitation of classical authors. Even with the simple sentence we have used as an example, we are obliged to read to the end of the sentence before we can tell what it means. Imagine how difficult a long, complicated sentence with the verb at the end would be. Such a sentence, which we cannot understand until we reach its ending, is called a "periodic" sentence, and it was a favorite grammatical construction for ancient writers. Common sense tells us, and research has revealed, that sentences in ordinary word order are much easier to read than are sentences with an inverted word order.

Vocabulary also determines how easy or hard a text is to read. What is the proportion of short, simple words to long, multisyllabic words in a sample of writing? Of common, well-known words to specialized words that refer not to familiar objects and creatures but to abstract concepts? Do we immediately recognize these words, or is it the first time we have met them? All such factors affect our ability to read.

Page format is the second major element determining difficulty or ease of reading. Again, we take for granted the modern printed page with all its graphic aids. What are some of these formatting features of modern print that make reading easy? Capitalization and punctuation, as well as paragraphing, running heads, bullets, outlining, marginal notes, and even page numbering—"foliation" or "pagination," as this practice is called—all help us read more easily.

And of course, for effortless reading, we must include standard-ized spelling, formally known as "conventional orthography." We didn't agree on common spellings for English words until the eighteenth cen-tury. Before that time, for the most part, all writers spelled phonetically. For example, in the sixteenth and seventeenth centuries, Shakespeare spelled his own name several different ways. We finally agreed to spell English words uniformly, as always, to make reading easier.

Surprisingly, probably the most important feature of the written and printed page for making reading easier is the simple but profoundly important practice of leaving spaces between words. It is hard to imag-ine that the ancients first read writing with no spaces, just continuous strings of lowercase printed letters. (Cursive had not been invented yet.) Even for an especially trained, able, and conscientious elite, reading was slow and arduous, and those few who could read were forced to read out loud in order to make sense of frequently puzzling pages. All the aids to reading—the most important being word separation—were yet to be invented.

Recent scholarship has made an attempt "to explain the physio-logical and psychological influence of word separation on the reading process and to trace . . . the path of the adoption of word separation— the crucial element in the change to silent reading in medieval script" (Saenger 1997, x).

How do different types of present-day writing systems affect chil-dren's ability to learn either to read silently or to read out loud? First, there may be as many different systems for transcribing spoken lan-guage—including nonalphabetic systems—as there are tongues. Even so, scholars have observed that there are only two basic ways for chil-dren to learn how to "read" these systems, either a "hard" system like the one for writing Chinese, or a comparatively "easy" system like the one for writing English.

With a "hard" writing system, one devoid of word separation, children must spend a great deal of time and effort sounding out letters and then syllables before they can understand the meanings of words. Thus, beginning readers spend a long time on oral reading and rote memorization before they can advance to reading for meaning. Reading a language with a "hard" writing system is so difficult that those who learn to read this way may be doomed to read out loud—slowly and laboriously—as long as they live.

On the other hand, present-day research shows that children who learn to read a language, like English, with a simpler writing system are taught in a different way and follow a different path. Remember that we write modern English in an alphabetic script, the words are separated by spaces, and we have a number of graphic devices to make reading easier. All these factors make English—contrary to criticisms that written English is notoriously irregular—an easier language to read than are many ancient and present-day nonalphabetic languages with scripts without word separation.

As a result of reading in this "simpler" system, once children have spent a relatively short period learning that letters and syllables do not *have* sounds but, rather, *stand for* sounds, they generally move quickly to silent reading. "These [hard] writing systems require a longer training period, one that features oral reading and rote memorization and that continues, in some instances, even in adulthood. Examples from several modern languages, as well as from ancient Greek and Latin, illustrate these differences" (Saenger 1997, 2).

Research into how children learn to read in Chinese, Burmese, Japanese, Korean, and Vai (a modern language spoken in Liberia) related to oral and silent reading produces remarkably consistent findings. In the written language of Vai, for instance, which requires teachers to spend a great deal of initial oral practice in phonetics before the children are taught how to make sense of words, "it is not surprising to find that oral recitation forms an important part of elementary reading instruction" (Saenger 1997, 4, 5).

As further evidence that script printed without spaces compels readers to read out loud, scholars have observed that fifth-graders given a text typed in capital letters with no word separation or punctuation automatically read the script out loud.

> This phenomenon [of oral reading] is a continuation of a habit that originates when the child initially pronounces words syllable by syllable in order to gain access to meaning. When visual focus is blocked, the brain's aural system for word recognition predominates. Young children tend initially to write in *scriptura continua* [an ancient method of writing rows of printed letters with no spaces between words] because they see its continuity as a faithful representation of an uninterrupted oral speech. (Saenger 1997, 5, 6)

If young, beginning readers *are* introduced to print in which words are separated by spaces (as all modern English print is) and if their initial reading instruction deals mainly with first detecting words by sounding out syllables—and internalizing the idea that in alphabetic script, letters stand for speech sounds—then the children tend to move easily and directly to understanding word meanings.

In order to read silently and eventually easily and rapidly, children, then, while becoming familiar with print in which words are separated by spaces, internalize the concept of sound-symbol correspondences in alphabetic writing. They grasp the crucial notion that written symbols *stand for* the oral sounds of a language, the letters of the script, of course, being in themselves without meaning. If beginning readers perceive this relationship between the symbols of a script and the sounds of a language, they generally move naturally and easily to the next stage of reading, in which they instantaneously recognize words as whole units of meaning and then advance to comprehending what words mean and learning how to pronounce them.

HOW WE FIRST READ: TEXTS WITH NO WORD SEPARATION

How did the ancients read texts in which the words—without capitals or periods or other marks of punctuation to show sentences and units within sentences—were all written together? Slowly and strenuously.

The change from reading texts with no word separation to reading modern, word-separated print format was a slow process; ancient script took many centuries to evolve into modern text. "In the West, the ability to read silently and rapidly is a result of the historical evolution of word separation that, beginning in the seventh century, changed the format of the written page, which had to be read orally and slowly in order to be comprehended" (Saenger 1997, 6).

How was this process of reading script without word separation qualitatively different from modern reading? What psychological processes did ancient readers go through? As they read out loud, ancient readers had to keep their eyes ahead of their voice, so to speak, as they struggled to make sense of unseparated script. This process, so familiar to ancient Greeks and Romans, was thus a kind of "elaborate search pattern." How they read, a process followed for centuries by Greek and Roman readers, was an incredibly complicated and sophisticated mental action in which the readers' eyes were constantly searching back and forth over strings of letters, unseparated and unpunctuated. As they scanned the letters, readers had to identify words by sounding out syllables and then trying to figure out how they formed words—a complicated mental and visual probe, if you will.

As we now know from contemporary research on the mental processes involved in reading, our eyes move across a page not in a steady, continuous rate but in a series of "fixations" and "jumps," called "saccades." Just think how taxing the mental effort must have been for ancient readers. They made sense of unseparated scripts without the luxury of having words separated and without the additional help of our modern graphic devices. We can only assume that the ancient reader expended at least twice the mental energy we do to process all kinds of print.

Not only did the ancient readers need to scan the unseparated writing *forward* to search for words, they also had to look *backward*—making what are called "ocular regressions"—in order to make certain that the words they found did indeed contribute to the overall meaning of a sentence. Only rarely do we read today by ocular regressions. Obviously, there is no need for contemporary readers to make sure they have correctly separated words. But sometimes modern readers who are skimming print move so fast across the page that they make a mistake. As they continue reading, they realize that a previously scanned word does not make sense in the sentence being read, and they must reread. For ancient readers, ocular regression must have been a common mental act. For the most part, that is not the case for us today.

What other barriers did the unseparated script erect for the ancients while they read? Since they read by sounding out a script syllable by syllable, they were able to process visually only a few chunks of letters at a time. Because of this radically reduced field of vision, with a great many more fixations and saccades, the ancients were forced to read very slowly. Instead of keeping one, two, or even three words in their minds, as we are able to do with modern separated text—especially on a topic we are already familiar with—they could remember only a few syllables or at best short words, which in turn, they needed continually to identify and verify. Imagine how very difficult—next to impossible—it would have been for ancient readers to process current expository texts in this fashion.

Still other factors made reading unseparated text an arduous task for ancient readers. Not only did they have to pick out words within continuous strings of letters, they also had to deal with grammar or punctuation that we would find awkward and frequently puzzling (and often, by today's criteria, "incorrect"). For instance, ancient writers might join two declarative sentences without a conjunction or any mark of punctuation—called "parataxis"—as in the clauses, "It was hot we remained in the shade."

Another syntactical problem was that the ancients—apparently for rhetorical purposes—frequently used periodic sentences, with the verbs at the end. Placing the verbs finally meant that readers had to wait until they finished the sentence before they could grasp its meaning and that they had to move back and forth through the strings of unseparated letters before the overall meaning of a sentence revealed itself.

Furthermore, as the ancients read this unseparated script, they had to do a kind of "prereading," called *praelectio*, an initial preparation before they read "for real." By first reading a text out loud, ancient readers kept in their minds those fragments that might be confusing until they had worked their way through complete sentences and were confident they understood them.

Some ancients reported they read not exactly silently but with a suppressed, muffled voice so they could enjoy privacy or concentrate on understanding the text. "Saint Augustine suggests that Ambrose read silently either to seek privacy by concealing the content of his book or to rest his voice." Nevertheless, "no classical author described rapid, silent reference consultation as it exists in the modern world. For the ancients, *lectio*, the synthetic combination of letters to form syllables and syllables to form words, of necessity preceded *narratio*, that is, the comprehension of a text" (Saenger 1997, 8, 9).

If reading continuous letters out loud made reading such a painfully slow act, why did it take so long for writers to make reading easier by leaving spaces between words? There are several reasons why the ancients hung onto *scriptura continua*.

First, we need to keep in mind that the continued use of *scriptura continua* was possible only with an alphabetic script, with letters for both vowels and consonants making up a fairly complete set of symbols for transcribing the sounds of a language. Before vowels were added to consonants in the Greek script, "all the ancient languages of the Mediterranean world—syllabic or alphabetic, Semitic, or Indo-European—were written with word separation by either space, or 'points' [called "interpuncts," these dots were used throughout the Middle Ages to show syllable separation], or both in conjunction. After the introduction of vowels, word separation was no longer necessary to eliminate an unacceptable level of ambiguity" (Saenger 1997, 9).

In short, once vowels were added to the Greek script, writers felt no need to separate words by spaces. The addition of vowels to a script with consonants only and the widespread use of *scriptura continua* went together. If ancient scripts had been written in consonants alone with all letters strung together without spaces, the scripts would have been nearly impossible to read.

A puzzling question remains. Some ancient writers added symbols for vowels to the consonants so that readers could make sense of unseparated script. In scripts for other languages with signs for consonants only, such as for Hebrew, scripts were written with word separation. Why didn't some ingenious scribe simply compose a script with symbols for both consonants and vowels and with word separation all at the same time?

The answer cannot be that scribes in one language were unaware of how language was transcribed in another because recovered fragments of ancient writing show that Greeks, Romans, and Jews were all aware of each other's writing. Why, then, were the two systems not combined? We can only guess at the reasons, but it seems that the ancients had a cultural view toward reading and writing that we now find incomprehensible. First, the ancients showed no desire to make reading easier because few "reference texts," such as theological and scientific books, had yet been created. Even though the ancients had access to the writings of Plato and Aristotle, for the most part they read a relatively few literary texts, which they had read over and over and knew by heart. These texts were well known; they were not novel texts with new ideas, and therefore they could be read slowly and savored. Thus, there was no need to copy such familiar texts in unseparated script.

Moreover, it may be the ancients felt no need for a separated text with both consonants and vowels because the idea that many people could become literate did not occur to them. There was no movement for universal literacy in the ancient world. Besides, professional readers, educated scribes who were often slaves, did virtually all the reading for their masters anyway. "It is in the context of a society with an abundant supply of cheap, intellectually skilled labor that attitudes must be comprehended and the ready and pervasive acceptance of the suppression of word separation throughout the Roman Empire understood" (Saenger 1997, 11, 12).

Although most ancient Roman and Greek books were written in an unseparated fashion and were copied without any signs of punctuation, the fact remains that it was the practice of separating words in scripts and eventually adding graphic aids such as punctuation that would allow readers to read silently and in private and that would be a major factor in the centuries-long change to how we now read.

> The importance of word separation by space is unquestionable, for it freed the intellectual faculties of the reader, permitting all texts to be read silently, that is, with the eyes alone. As a consequence, even readers of modest intellectual capacity could read more swiftly, and they could understand an increasing number of inherently more difficult texts. Word separation also allowed for an immediate oral reading of

texts, which eliminated the need for the arduous process of the ancient *praelectio.* Word separation, by altering the neuro-physiological process of reading, simplified the act of reading, enabling both the medieval and modern reader to receive silently and simultaneously the text and encoded information that facilitates both comprehension and oral performance. (Saenger 1997, 13)

THE BIRTH AND EVOLUTION OF MODERN READING

For some nine hundred years after the fall of Rome, written texts continued to be copied without word separation or with marks of punctuation in *scriptura continua.* The task of separating words within strings of letters fell to the readers, not to the scribes. What a chore reading must have been! The readers had to read out loud, moving forward and backward along a line of printed letters, sounding out syllables, picking out words made up of these syllables, and then testing the words, still out loud, as to their meaning, and finally checking to see whether or not the words fit into the overall sense of a sentence. Very few of us would now be literate if that was how we had to read!

And what were these basic changes in reading that occurred between ancient and early modern times? What happened to how we read from the seventh century to the fifteenth century?

We went from reading scripts of unseparated letters to scripts in which there were spaces between words. We went from reading unseparated scripts with no graphic aids to reading scripts with all the present-day aids to reading—punctuation marks, paragraphing, tables of contents, indexes, glossaries, and page numbering, to name a few—enjoyed by modern readers. As a result of these technical innovations, we went from reading out loud slowly and in a tiresome manner to reading silently, quickly, and most of the time, almost effortlessly. We went from a time when only scholastics and some of those in religious orders could read to one in which laypersons, beginning first with royalty, nobles, and wealthy urban leaders, could read. Finally, we went from reading only Latin to reading in the vernacular languages of Europe.

What historical processes caused these dramatic changes in how we read, and how did this transformation alter the cognitive processes needed to call forth meaning from writing or print?

To understand these momentous changes, we need to recognize just how desperate the situation of literacy was in Europe after the fall of Rome. In the sixth century Gregory of Tours made this dismal comment on the state of literacy in Europe: "In these times when the practice of letters declines, no, rather perishes in the cities of Gaul, there has been no scholar trained in ordered composition to present in prose or verse a picture of things which have befallen" (quoted in Cahill 1995, 193).

The first impetus for this change was the trouble Irish scribes in the seventh century, who were copying Latin manuscripts, evidently had in reading the Gospels in classical Latin *scriptura continua.* The scribes were Celts, to whom Latin, the native tongue of Roman scribes, was a foreign language. How did these Irish scribes revise this foreign writing—a supremely precious scripture—to make it easier to read for those who found Latin foreign and difficult?

The Irish scribes noticed that in the Syriac Gospels they were copying, there were spaces between words, and they imitated this format in their work. They, and the Anglo-Saxon scribes they trained, realized that if they separated words, readers would no longer need to read out loud to make sense of what they read. And thus we began the long journey of learning how to read the way we read today.

In short, "the postancient period of the history of reading and of script began in Ireland and England at the end of the seventh century when Celtic monks, for whom Latin was a foreign tongue . . . introduced word separation and syntactic punctuation (i.e., punctuation that isolated units of meaning) into Latin and Greek texts." (Saenger 1999, 12).

Not only did the scribes begin to use word separation, but they also developed a process of writing comments between the lines of Latin script. These interlinear notes now made it possible to understand complicated and ambiguous Latin sentences without reading out loud. The scribes found this new script so successful that they immediately used it for a new kind of prayer book, one intended for those who could read it silently and in privacy. This separated script, though, was little known outside the British Isles, and except for Brittany, on the coast of what is now France, and in some insulated Celtic and Anglo-Saxon monastic colonies, it remained isolated there for some three centuries.

READING AT THE BEGINNING OF THE EARLY MODERN ERA

Although the idea of separating continuous strings of letters into words and using punctuation to isolate units of meaning began in the seventh century in Ireland, it was restricted to Ireland and southern England for some three hundred years. Not until the tenth century do we find evidence of word-separated scripts in the writings of monks in France and

Switzerland. By the beginning of the thirteenth century, this new script was used in England, northern France, and in Germany, and it later came to be used in southern France, Italy, and Spain. After centuries of changes in the format of ancient Latin *scriptura continua,* we could finally read silently, privately, and easily. This script now allowed us to read complex treatises and books on theology, philosophy, and science.

> By the thirteenth century, all of western Europe, from Scotland and Denmark in the north to Spain and Italy in the south, had adopted a single and generally homogeneous form of written Latin that incorporated both the graphic conventions of canonical separation and the principles of word order and syntactic word grouping. This new Latin, which was so different from the Latin of antiquity, became the medium of intellectual discourse for scholars. It was a medium with minimal ambiguity, compared with the writing system that had preceded it. (Saenger 1997, 256)

The general adoption of the new word-separated script transformed all aspects of literacy. The script radically changed the way university students were taught to read, the physical nature of libraries, the rise of heretical thoughts, and the development of texts in languages other than Latin—vernacular languages such as Italian, French, German, and English. It contributed to the rise of humanism, first in Italy and then throughout the rest of Europe, and because of an increase in private, silent reading, it allowed for the rapid spread of individual, personal thought and expression.

> Throughout Europe, the reading that separated script made possible profoundly affected the nature of thought and culture across a range of phenomena, from political subversion . . . to the intensification of personal piety. With the general acceptance of separated script and the practices it made possible, Europe entered the modern world as we know it. (Saenger 1997, 256)

By the thirteenth century, all literate persons—which meant primarily scholastics and specially trained person in religious orders—read word-separated texts silently. Throughout the late Middle Ages, from the thirteenth through fifteenth centuries, scribes continually modified the ancient Latin *textualis* (a formal Latin script used almost exclusively for copying manuscript books, called *codices*), and this mode gradually became the means by which new philosophical arguments were broadcast.

These changes in scripts did not just allow for the expression of new ideas. They also changed the physical act of writing itself. Ancient authors had written on wax tablets. Now scholars composed on "quires"—sets of usually twenty-four sheets of parchment—and writers enjoyed a much less taxing mode of composition. They now could revise what they wrote, move sections around on separate sheets of parchment, and refer on one sheet to ideas on other sheets. Because parchment came in sheets, readers could move back and forth from one argument to another without going through a whole scroll or searching individual wax tablets to find a particular passage. During the thirteenth century, authors began to write notes—glosses and commentaries—in the margins of manuscripts. Writing on tablets was slow, hard work. In reaction to this practice, scribes and authors developed a looped script, physically easier to do than the old manner of printing, and so cursive was born.

The following quotation from Umberto Eco's novel *The Name of the Rose* provides a delightful description of the work of scribes during the fourteenth century. In this case, a scribe copies "the pages of a richly illuminated psalter":

> They [the pages] were folios of the finest vellum—that queen among parchments—and the last was still fixed to the desk. Just scraped with pumice stone and softened with chalk, it had been smoothed with the plane, and, from the tiny holes made on the sides with a fine stylus, all the lines that were to have guided the artist's hand had been traced. The first half had already been covered with writing, and the monk had begun to sketch the illustrations in the margins. The other pages, on the contrary, were already finished, and as we looked at them, neither I nor William could suppress a cry of wonder. (Eco 1994, 76)

Not only was the traditional Latin *textualis* unsuited for expressing abstract statements, but printing it was just plain hard work. In illuminations—miniature pictures in the books of the time—we see scribes printing books in what looks to be a physically demanding way. Early illuminations show scribes with quill in one hand and a knife in the other. Writers used the knife to sharpen their quills, but they also used the arm with the knife to balance the writing hand. The hand with the knife also held the parchment firmly in place while the scribes printed the traditional *textualis*. The new way of writing was essentially the way we write today. Medieval illuminations show writers—just like us except for their dress, robes and cowls—holding a parchment in place with one hand while writing a flowing cursive script with the other.

Because of word-separated writing, scribes and scholars could now copy or compose silently and in delicious privacy. They no longer needed to read out loud while printing with the help of other scribes. Solitary authors, now writing in a strikingly user-friendly script, could move back and forth from one quire to another, for the first time getting a sense of an entire manuscript. They could make cross-references throughout their writing, adding supplements, and finally revising an overall manuscript before submitting it for publication to scribes in a scriptorium.

The new cursive, word-separated script also led to significant changes in methods of instruction in the medieval university classroom. We need to note that the educational practices described here deal almost exclusively with teaching university students and those in religious orders how to read and write. Although some persons were taught by private tutors, all others became literate in university classrooms or in religious environments.

In the late medieval period, we first observe a university teaching method that has persisted for centuries: A professor reads from a textbook while students follow in identical texts of their own. Even though more and more academics and their students began to read silently in private, the public lecture was the primary method of teaching. What were the ramifications of such a practice? There was the usual problem of students who failed to bring their texts to class. To resolve this dilemma, universities required students, by statute, to bring their texts to class. In 1259, for instance, the Dominican house of the University of Paris insisted that students come to class with copies of the text the professor was explicating. The lecture method was also adopted for public worship, and "collective prayer could be enriched by individuals gazing on the text of a written prayer as it was collectively pronounced" (Saenger 1997, 259). Here again is another modern practice for both university classrooms and churches, first started in the Middle Ages.

What were poor students to do if they could not afford personal copies of texts? They did about what poor students do today. In what may have been the beginning of student aid, students too poor to buy their own texts were allowed to borrow them from libraries, such as that of the Cathedral of Notre Dame of Paris. Benefactors made contributions to help defray the costs of stocking libraries with multiple copies of texts for poor students. (Could this have been the creation of charitable bequests to educational institutions?) At this time, universities also came up with a solution to another problem still faced by university libraries: ensuring that students returned their borrowed books. "The statutes of the Sorbonne [in Paris] provided for lending books against security deposits" (Saenger 1997, 259).

In the late Middle Ages, many additional changes in the text format of thirteenth-century and fourteenth-century manuscripts went along with silent reading. We know that when unseparated texts were read orally in the early medieval period, persons read aloud great chunks of texts. This practice was probably a result of a time when persons read from scrolls. Unlike readers of books, who can look up chapter headings or refer to indexes that point to specific topics on specific pages, readers of scrolls were forced to scan a continuous script from beginning to end in order to find a particular place. Because of this habitual way of reading, texts were seldom divided into parts smaller than chapters. In the thirteenth to the fifteenth centuries, however, scribes began to divide texts into logical subdivisions.

Those who wrote these new works and copied old ones introduced other features of text format. Not only did authors and perceptive scribes divide books into chapters and break up chapters into more easily manageable parts, which were called *distinctiones*, but they also devised such further aids to reading as tables of chapter headings, lists of subjects arranged alphabetically, and the titles of texts or of chapters on every page of a sheet of parchment, now known by printers as "running heads" or "running titles."

From the thirteenth century on, scribes began to use a new kind of punctuation, the colored paragraph mark, which pointed out various intellectual units. "Illuminated capitals were employed in the fourteenth century to help clarify the new sequential argumentation, in the fashion of *ad primum, ad secundum,* and so on" (Saenger 1997, 260).

These imaginative scholars and scribes also added brief explanatory notes and sometimes translated foreign words or puzzling technical terms, either in the margins or between the lines of a text. These helpful additions, called "glosses," are still in use today, especially in specialized technical textbooks. A list of such words, arranged alphabetically, we now know as a "glossary."

Writers also used intricate diagrams to help readers unravel the mysteries of complex texts, but the readers who used them were obliged to follow them while reading the texts they made visual. Such schematic plans were necessary additions, for instance, to new humanist translations of Aristotle's works.

All these changes and additions to the format of the written page were devised to aid the late medieval reader as he read, silently and privately, complex translations of old books and the many complicated new books. "The complex structure of the written page of a fourteenth-century text presupposed a reader who read only with his eyes, going swiftly from objection to response, from table of contents to the text, from diagram to the text, and from the text to the gloss and its corrections" (Saenger 1997, 260). Without word separation and all the typographical devices we have noted, the development and dissemination of new knowledge that occurred from this time on would have proceeded at a much slower pace or might not have happened at all.

It is a common belief that students of the Middle Ages produced their own texts by copying down verbatim the lectures by professors in university classes. Contemporary scholars report no evidence to support this idea. Instead, all the illustrations of the period, the "iconographic" evidence, show individuals not writing while professors lectured but, rather, creating books by copying from other books. Students, in fact, would have found it impossible to copy a professor's lecture word for word. At that time, there was no precise system of shorthand that would allow even professional scribes to write sufficiently rapidly and accurately (Saenger 1997, 260).

How, then, were medieval texts produced before the invention of the printing press? By the thirteenth and fourteenth centuries, the *pecia* system was in place, in which professional scribes were employed to turn out "correct," very legible copies of all of the standard texts used throughout the university curriculum. It is recorded, for example, that the scribes at the University of Angers could finish an acceptable copy of a text within a month for a fairly reasonable price. University "stationers"—as medieval publishers and booksellers were called—rented standard copies of textbooks to students and guaranteed the quality of the exemplary texts. Once the printing press was instituted, of course, the problem of making identical texts available to university students was solved. And so the modern university bookstore was born!

Not only were these textbooks with their gradually developed reader-friendly page formats necessary for students to understand the intricacies of public lectures, but books with such formats became indispensable for private reading, now an accepted part of university life.

> Paintings and illuminations of the fourteenth and fifteenth centuries in vernacular books intended for the lay reader showed motionless scholars reading in libraries, both in groups and in isolation, with their lips sealed, an unmistakable iconographic statement of silence. Inexpensive Latin and vernacular compendia of large treatises became popular to serve the growing student need for private study. (Saenger 1997, 261)

Changes in reading, as we might expect, brought about significant physical changes in libraries (including the introduction of special furniture) and in the ways these libraries were used. What were libraries like before the invention of word-separated reading? In ancient libraries, within secluded convents and monasteries, almost all the time, everyone read out loud. Those persons who did study by themselves in cloisters and carrels, which were isolated by stone walls, were able to read softly to themselves in low voices or to dictate to secretaries without disturbing their neighbors. By the end of the thirteenth century, however, library architecture and even furniture had been dramatically altered to accommodate silent reading.

> At Oxford and Cambridge colleges and at the Sorbonne and other Paris colleges, libraries were installed in central halls and were furnished with desks, lecterns, and benches where readers sat next to one another. Important reference books were chained to lecterns so they could always be consulted in the library. The first such reference collection was established in Merton College, Oxford, in 1290. (Saenger 1997, 262–263)

Reference texts were chained to the desks because they were valuable, one-of-a-kind works. Reference texts included such books as alphabetical dictionaries and "concordances"—alphabetic indices of all words in a text or body of texts, showing occurrences of particular words. Other standard reference books were the works of Thomas Aquinas, biblical commentaries, and works frequently cited by scholars. The statutes published by libraries of the time stated that books were to be chained to desks so all could refer to them: They existed for the common good. The secured reference books of the late Middle Ages were forerunners of another feature of modern libraries: the precious reference collection. In present-day libraries, reference works do not circulate. Rather, reference materials—now including such items as microfilm and microfiche—are open and available to all. Was the practice of keeping references for common use the beginning of free public libraries?

But the new physical spaces for silent reading in libraries, places of near-absolute silence, meant that patrons could no longer read out loud. At Oxford University in England, for instance, the regulations of 1412 stated that the library was a place of quiet. The rules of the library of the University of Angers in 1431 prohibited all talking, even "conversation and murmuring." By the fifteenth century, the rules laid down by the Sorbonne library, which had been in effect for decades, "proclaimed the chained library of the college to be an august and sacred place, where silence should prevail" (Saenger 1997, 263). Until recently, all libraries, including public libraries and not just college and great university libraries, were places where serious students could study in comparative silence. It is only lately that open reading spaces, especially in public libraries, have become more social than academic. It is not uncommon for students to do homework with each other and for teachers to tutor students out loud in these reading rooms. Nor is it uncommon for the libraries to serve as after-school meeting places for students.

As the physical design of libraries was transformed by the silent reading, scribes devised new reference tools, such as catalogs with the names of authors arranged alphabetically. From the eleventh century on, scribes and "rubricators," under the supervision of specially designated scholars, "corrected" previously written manuscripts by adding *prosodiae*, accepted punctuation marks. The job of professional rubricators was to provide rules or short commentaries in a book. A "rubric" (from the Latin word *rubrica*, "red earth," "red ocher," from *ruber*, "red") later referred to the practice of coloring a title, a heading, or even an initial letter of a book section in red. Eventually, a rubric became the label for any authoritative rule written in red.

Just as modern students underline words, sentences, and passages or use markers to highlight passages, write notes in the margins of texts, and use all sorts of figures—lines, arrows, crosses, asterisks—to note important items, so readers in the late medieval period wrote phrases, idiosyncratic symbols, and assorted doodles in books. Early readers were apparently as bothered as we are by books with notations by former readers: Late medieval universities ruled that critical editing—"emendations"—should *not* be done by students and should be the same in all standard books. Scholarly texts follow the same practice today by publishing "authorized" editions of texts.

In an amazing fashion, private, silent reading made possible, in an age of intellectual conformity, the spread of independent thought, especially of opinions or doctrines at odds with accepted religious beliefs and political doctrines of the day. "The transition to silent reading and composition, by providing a new dimension of privacy, had even more profound ramifications for both the lay and scholastic culture of the late Middle Ages. Psychologically, silent reading emboldened the reader because it placed the source of his curiosity completely under personal control" (Saenger 1997, 264).

During the ninth century, when most reading was done out loud, it was hard to make heretical thoughts public. Since authors dictated their ideas and presented them in public lectures—*lectios*—religious and political orthodoxy could be effectively maintained. But just two centuries later, in the eleventh century, those who read in seclusion were often accused of heresy. Since readers could now read privately, new speculations, especially subversive ideas in "tracts"—papers or pamphlets making appeals by representatives of religious or political groups—were not subject to censorship by the group. "Private, visual reading and private composition thus encouraged individual critical thinking and contributed ultimately to the development of skepticism and intellectual heresy" (Saenger 1997, 264).

University professors, ever conscious of their right to free expression, knew that students could read writings of unacceptable ideas privately and outside the lecture hall because we have records from the thirteenth century of university statutes forbidding attendance by students at public readings of heretical books. In the fourteenth century, censorship of books, including book burning, was common. In 1323, for instance, the general chapter of the Dominican Order decreed that all books on alchemy—the ancient chemical philosophy that had as its aim the conversion of base metals into gold—were to be burned. Some prohibited books, however, were officially allowed to exist, primarily so that theologians could prove them false.

What was the effect of this new script, first developed and used exclusively by those in religious orders and in universities, on the reading habits of laypersons? For a long time, not much. It took centuries before laypersons moved from reading orally to reading silently and from reading Latin texts to reading books written in the vernacular languages of Europe.

But during the late Middle Ages, momentous changes in vernacular texts occurred. Whereas once only ecclesiastics and academics read, now laymen, such as kings, nobles, and aristocrats, read. Reading practice changed from oral reading in groups to silent, private reading. Reading matter expanded from a body of well-known theological and philosophical texts to include new scientific works. Writing changed from print to cursive script. The format of reading materials changed from pages with few reading aids to pages with such modern graphic aids as paragraphing, punctuation marks, standardized spelling, and even underlining (which in modern print is shown by italics). And as the changes in print were made more available, terms were devised to describe and talk about these new ways of presenting print. As always, we need to keep in mind that all these changes in the appearance of the written page came about for a single purpose: to help us read better. "The transformation from an early medieval oral, monastic culture to a visual scholastic one had at first only a limited effect on the reading habits of lay society, particularly in northern Europe, where oral reading and dictation of vernacular texts were commonly practiced at least until the thirteenth century" (Saenger 1997, 265).

Why did silent reading by laypersons lag behind silent reading by academics or religious persons? Until the mid-fourteenth century, French kings and nobles had no reason to learn to read. They had scribes who did all their reading for them. When a prince like Saint Louis did read orally, he commonly read aloud as a member of a small group.

What did the royalty and the nobility read? Although they duti-fully studied liturgical works, for the most part they read histories, verse, and long narrative poems rather than the newly created scholastic, philosophical, and scientific texts. We might suppose that was so because the laymen knew the poetic epics by heart. Reading the new prose texts was a different and more difficult matter. These laymen enjoyed historical accounts—chronicles, that is, events arranged chronologically—of their countries. They read romances and chansons de geste, epic poems recounting the adventures of heroic characters, and the verse of the troubadours, poets popular in northern France dur-ing the twelfth and thirteenth centuries. Most of the works written in verse were intended to be recited orally in court performances. The *Roman du Lancelot,* for instance, and the *Histoire ancienne jusqu'à César,* an account of ancient history up until the reign of Caesar, were composed to be read aloud for kings and noblemen. Even at this time, "much of medieval vernacular poetry and prose was composed, memo-rized, and performed orally and only later set down in writing" (Saenger 1997, 266).

Because the first vernacular texts were meant for listeners rather than for silent readers, the tradition of composing vernacular texts by dictation and the development of cursive writing fell behind the use of cursive for scholastic texts. Even during the thirteenth century, when scholastic scribes employed cursive script on unbound sheets and quires, vernacular texts were still being written in the traditional *textu-alis,* the time-honored, hand-printed script used for centuries for copy-ing medieval manuscript books.

Another problem was that scribes, familiar with writing Latin, had problems writing down vernacular languages. In France, as late as 1300, even knowledgeable scribes, who had been trained in word-sepa-rated Latin texts, were unsure where to leave spaces between syllables to show correctly written vernacular words. The scribes also had trouble positioning parts of speech, especially prepositions. They were con-fused by the many variations in the spellings of words and by the lack of punctuation in various texts. These factors kept the practice of reading vernacular books almost solely oral.

Eventually, after many years, the scribes who did copy down vernacular texts began to use the techniques they had acquired copying word-separated medieval Latin texts. Incorporating the new aids to reading, the scribes gradually brought about changes in vernacular texts; most important, they spelled words more consistently and changed the word order of sentences away from the ancient periodic sentence order. And with a practice that changed the very nature of modern languages, scribes dropped word inflections and introduced natural word order in sentences. For example, the scribes changed, in writing, the very structure of Old English, from a heavily inflected language to that of early modern English, an analytic language, in which meanings are conveyed by word order and function words.

Not only were words in the vernacular now spelled more uniformly, but they were also spelled less phonetically than they had been in Latin. What did this have to do with reading? When words were spelled uniformly rather than phonetically, once readers of vernacular script saw a new word and heard it pronounced, they could immediately recognize it when they saw it again, instead of sounding it out phonetically, and they were able to read it from then on without trouble. For instance, in Middle English, the English word "knight" was pronounced "kuh-nik-ta." Although the pronunciation of the word over the centuries has changed to "nite," the spelling has remained the same as it was in the Middle Ages. We are able to read the word because we have seen it, learned what sounds it now stands for, and without hesitation, understand it whenever we encounter it in print. "Word separation, particularly in Middle French and English, allowed vernacular spelling to be less phonetic than that of Latin, for once vernacular words had a distinct image, the original spelling was retained, even when gradual changes in pronunciation rendered certain letters silent" (Saenger 1997, 266, 267).

Only at the beginning of the fourteenth century did scribes, using Gothic cursive script along with an accepted word-separated text format, first begin to transcribe vernacular texts. At the same time, illiterate princes of France evidently realized that their realms had become so large and complex that they needed to keep records and communicate in writing with other princes in order to manage them. This meant they must now learn to read and write. It was no longer appropriate for royalty to rely on professional readers, as they had before, and kings started a custom that persists to this day of having secretaries write out draft letters and official documents in cursive and in the vernacular. The kings would then edit the documents before signing them. One such forward-looking chief operating officer, Charles V of France, made corrections to drafts of letters and then signed edited copies. We have evidence that a century later, certain official letters were written by the kings themselves, and frequently letters from kings bore the royal "autograph signature." Busy administrators today seldom compose their own first drafts of letters, documents, or speeches. They may dictate letters and other documents to secretaries, though, or even have highly knowledgeable and trusted assistants listen to their thoughts and then create draft copies for their bosses to edit.

It was not until the mid-fourteenth century that the French nobility finally began to accept the custom of silent reading and the use of cursive writing. During his reign, John II was responsible for having a great deal of Latin literature translated into vernacular French. This effort was successful because the scribes translating Latin into French now had before them examples of recent scholastic texts with a syntax that, unlike that of the difficult ancient Latin texts, was much closer to the word order of the contemporary vernacular.

Other French kings continued to support reading and writing in the vernacular. Charles V, after the death of John II, carried on his work by ordering more translations of vernacular books. Charles V has the distinction of being the first king to establish a royal library, fittingly enough in a tower of the Louvre, with furniture like that found in university libraries. Scribes painted miniatures of King Charles "seated in his library, motionless, not declaiming, reading with sealed lips in silent and tranquil isolation. Manuscripts also depicted the king attending lectures, visually following a copy of the text in the university fashion as he listened to the lecture" (Saenger 1997, 268).

Along with reading vernacular texts silently went a new precise vocabulary to describe these innovations. In the Middle Ages before silent reading, monks had used the term *silentio* to describe how they read their Latin texts orally: in a low, muffled voice, called *submissa* or *suppressa vox*. "In the fifteenth century, vernacular authors employed a new, explicit vocabulary of silent reading, describing mental devotion from a written text as reading with the heart, as opposed to the mouth" (Saenger 1997, 268). French aristocratic texts employed the phrase *lire au coeur*, "reading from the heart," to designate private, silent reading.

Now that royals and nobles had learned to read vernacular texts and found they liked reading, they hungered for more and more books to read. But what kinds of books? Because of private, silent reading, vernacular books changed from traditional treatises and literary texts to newly created books "almost exclusively in prose." "French authors composed for the nobility new reference books, including alphabetical dictionaries of saints and gazetteers" (Saenger 1997, 269). And as the types of books being read changed, the format of the new vernacular prose books was also altered. Scholars and other authors added to them all the features of page layout that had already become common in the scholastic books of the thirteenth, fourteenth, and fifteenth centuries: tables of contents, alphabetically arranged glossaries, subject indexes, and running heads. Authors now agreed more and more on standard spelling of words, and as a result, this period may have seen the beginning of teaching reading by word recognition. By this time, words were separated and were spelled in a fairly consistent way, so once readers learned a word, they did not have to sound it out over and over again. They now were familiar with the word and read it without hesitation. In these new vernacular texts, "orthography became increasingly standardized, enabling the reader to recognize words by their global image, as in Latin, rather than to decode them phonetically by an ad hoc synthetic combination of phonemes" (Saenger 1997, 269).

This was also a time of illustrating books, of painting pictures and miniatures as teaching devices to help lay readers understand prose texts. This practice was a logical extension of the scholastic technique of using diagrams to explain unfamiliar academic and theological texts. Authors also transferred another visual aid from scholastic to vernacular texts, called "banderoles," ribbon-shaped figures written in the margins of books and containing useful information; this was another device to help readers understand the prose they encountered. All these graphic aids—paragraphing, illustrations, miniatures, banderoles, illuminated letters (many times stories in themselves)—look comfortably like the modern reading aids we accept without question, such as magazine and book illustrations, photographs, and now computer-generated visual aids. Only in scholarly books and textbooks do we still find page after page of long paragraphs uninterrupted by pictures, diagrams, or illustrations.

Before the 1300s, when professional readers read to kings and nobles, books were composed in *textualis,* the traditional script exclusively used in copying Latin manuscript books. This was all right because university readers were familiar with this writing. As we might imagine, when laypersons began to read in the vernacular for the first time, they found *textualis* too hard for them. One particular barrier to comprehension was the practice in *textualis* of printing all letters in lowercase figures and of writing the letters "m," "n," "i," and "u" in the identical, vertical "minim" strokes.

The scribes, aiming to please the lay readers for this new reading market in the last twenty years of the fourteenth century, created a "new improved" script, written rather than printed, called *cursive formata*. In the first half of the fifteenth century, the authors and scribes came up with a new version of *cursive formata*. Because this advanced script was written in cursive but was still part *textualis*, it was called *lettre batarde*, "bastard script." Modern scholars, who cannot pinpoint the precise date and place of its invention, identify this type of writing by a more polite name, *hybrida*, "hybrid" script. So successful was *lettre batarde* or *hybrida* that authors and scribes began to use it for transcribing Latin as well as for copying vernacular texts. It is interesting to note that until this time, all the innovations in vernacular script were copied from scholastic, Latin writing. However, with the appearance of *hybrida*, we find, for the first time, vernacular writing influencing academic writing.

Laypersons, who might be able to pronounce words in Latin texts phonetically without understanding them, could now read vernacular texts silently with full comprehension. The changes made in the script and text format of vernacular texts made reading possible by a wider range of persons. The change from oral to silent reading was virtually completed. No longer did readers read texts out loud with the intention of using them as guides to oratorical performances. Now readers could read and understand ideas, arguments, and scientific observations in the books that were being produced and disseminated at an increasingly rapid rate.

> In certain vernacular *lettre batarde* books, punctuation was borrowed from Latin university books and was calculated to guide the eye of the private reader, rather than to regulate the voice of the professional reader. Aristocratic books of the fifteenth century regularly used paragraph signs, underlining, and capitalization to divide texts into intellectual, rather than rhetorical units (Saenger 1997, 270–271).

The changes from common, out-loud reading to private, silent reading of word-separated vernacular script took place in Italy during the first half of the fourteenth century, a full fifty years earlier than in northern Europe. It may not be an overstatement to say that without word-separated script, with all its accompanying graphic aids, the Renaissance—the rebirth of learning in Europe, which began in Italy—and the spread of humanism might not have taken place, or at least might have been delayed for many years. For instance, two books of Dante's *Divine Comedy*, the *Inferno* and the *Paradisio*, were composed in Italian and enjoyed a wide readership. Because more and more lay aristocrats and members of the great Italian families desired books written in the vernacular, scribes copied them in a version of the highly readable *cursive formata,* created in Italy specifically for transcribing lay literature.

Some Italian scribes revered the ancient texts written in unseparated *scriptura continua* and still used this ancient script for "display" books—those to be placed on exhibition—but these scribes were practical enough to realize that the new word-separated script was here to stay. The scribes also imitated those distinctive features of earlier scripts that would make vernacular, word-separated scripts still easier to read. For instance, they extended the vertical stroke of the letter "t" above the height of the other letters. They used capital letters for proper names. They marked divided words to be continued on the next line of a manuscript, using not our hyphen but a mark like the acute accent. And they used Arabic numerals—very non-Roman—to foliate the pages. These humanist Italian scribes also used what we would now recognize as commas, periods, and capital letters. But, we are told, "[the] humanist scribe's most original contribution was the parenthesis, a mark designed to give a graphic representation of the aside, a device of ancient oratorical eloquence. The parenthesis in fifteenth-century humanist texts permitted the private, silent reader to recreate vicariously what in antiquity had been an oral experience" (Saenger 1997, 272). Scribes also used the parenthesis in a very specialized way, for "parsing," that is, explaining difficult grammatical constructions, a practice once valuable for ancient orators.

The dramatic "aside," which moderns may find strange in Shakespearean theatrical soliloquies, was a natural continuation of the time-honored, ancient aside. We still use the upright curved lines of the parenthesis—the singular form referring to either or both of the marks—to show explanatory or qualifying phrases and clauses. The use of dashes to set off written asides has now become common, especially in informal writing, even though traditional writers believe the dash should be used sparingly, for they consider it not acceptable in formal, standard prose

The spread of the new modes of writing—the *lettre hybrid* and the improved humanistic *textualis*—throughout western Europe in the late fourteenth and fifteenth centuries brought about significant changes in the reading habits of the aristocracy and the urban elite. First, authors who once wrote dense and complex theological, scholastic, and scientific books in Latin now wrote books in the vernacular on those topics for educated lay readers. "Just as separated written Latin had facilitated the birth of scholasticism, separated vernacular writing allowed for the transference of the subtleties of fully developed scholastic thought to a new lay audience" (Saenger 1997, 273). Aristocratic laypersons, for example, read arguments on the abstruse debate between the philosophical doctrines of nominalism (the idea that concepts, such as truth and virtue, have no reference in reality but exist only as names) and realism (the counterargument that universals are more genuine than so-called real objects in the natural world). These lay readers in the privacy of silent reading could study philosophical debates—just as their scholastic contemporaries did—and make their own decisions as to which position they accepted as valid.

At the same time, since lay readers could now read silently and in private, they could share unpopular political thoughts. For instance, Charles of France, the brother of Louis XI, left lying around, for anyone who might just pick it up and read it, a copy of the Roman author Cicero's *De officiis,* with juicy passages advocating the assassination of tyrants underlined. In effect, during the second half of the fourteenth century, the vernacular book became the primary source for ideas urging resistance to oppressive rulers.

And finally, the new private, silent reading had a potent effect upon individuals' religious devotions. As they read vernacular religious books privately, readers were able to work out for themselves their personal relationships to a higher being. Thomas à Kempis, the renowned writer of *The Imitation of Christ (De imitatione Christi),* originally written in Latin for his fellow monks, allowed the popular book to be quickly translated into French. The work was soon widely read by members of the Burgundian court in southeastern France.

It is at this time that we first find expressions of the "sacred" nature of the written word, of the idea that readers should read in silence in order to reach the most intense level of spiritual experience. The author Jean Mansel, for instance, in the prologue to his book *Vie de Christ (Life of Christ),* "declared that the spoken word is fleeting, while the written word endures, and he called upon knights and princes disposed to devotion for the profit of their souls 'to see' *(voire)* the content of his book" (Saenger, 1997, 275).

Writers of vernacular texts constantly instructed readers to separate themselves from groups in order to read and offer up their individual, silent prayers. Authors of vernacular religious books, of course, used all the graphic aids evolved over the centuries for scholastic Latin texts (punctuation now also included a modification of the medieval *diastole,* a large, comma-shaped mark placed under a line to indicate word separation).

The wave of religious fervor, which spread throughout Europe in the fifteenth century, was made possible largely by religious vernacular books. At the same time, however, silent reading of vernacular religious texts may have contributed to readers' feelings of spiritual inadequacy, and this in turn probably contributed to religious reform. Changes in word-separated text had so radically altered reading that lay readers could now hold nonconforming opinions in private and share them with others in writing, which acted as a catalyst to the spread of the Protestant Reformation. The printing press obviously facilitated the spread of radical ideas, but the mode of writing, developed painstakingly by multitudes of unsung scribes and authors over a period of some eight hundred years, was a major factor in the dissemination of new ideas about political and religious freedom, individual study, religious contemplation, and personal expression, which, in turn, all contributed to the modern period of Western civilization:

> The printing press would play an important role in the ultimate triumph of Protestantism, but the formulation of reformist religious and political ideas and the receptivity of Europe's elite to making private judgments on matters of conscience owed much to a long evolution that began in the late seventh century and culminated in the fifteenth century in the manner in which men and women read and wrote. This enhanced privacy represented the consummation of the development of separated writing and constituted a crucial aspect of the modern world. (Saenger 1997, 276)

And that is how we learned to read.

SUMMARY

The changes in the way texts were written from the late seventh century in Ireland though the fifteenth century in Europe changed the way we read. But the changes in writing also altered the way our minds work, the way we process and acquire knowledge. And some authors maintain that such changes in written language actually affected the physical makeup of our brains.

Of particular importance in page composition were changes in word separation and the addition of punctuation marks. In addition, the language and style of written language changed from that of formal Latin, conveying meaning by inflections and using long, complicated periodic sentences, to that of the analytic vernacular languages, using the word order normal to them; in the process, writing changed from unseparated print to word-separated cursive. We changed from a chaotic, individual way of spelling to a generally agreed upon system of spelling. We changed from writing mostly about well-known literary works to writing new books on theology, philosophy, and science. And we changed from writing in Latin to writing in the vernacular languages spoken in Europe.

According to recent scholarship on how we learn to read, the late Middle Ages was a remarkable time for change in three main areas. The first change was in language. Ancient Greeks and Romans were able to read unseparated, hand-printed, Latin *scriptura continua*—a script fraught with ambiguities—because it represented the language of persons who spoke it. The Latin script of the twelfth century, even though it was now more legible and easier to read, was a second language to its readers. The change from Latin to word-separated script in the vernacular was responsible for an enormous increase in the number of people who could read. In fact, more people could read at the end of the Middle Ages than could read in ancient Rome. "In 1500, although it is difficult to measure with quantitative precision, a larger percentage of the general population in England and France were competent to read vernacular texts than had ever been the case in ancient Greece or Rome" (Saenger 1997, 14).

The second great change in reading was in how books were produced. In antiquity and in the early Middle Ages, books were not only transcribed by hand but were put together manually, a lengthy and time-consuming process. Such books were extremely precious, but there were not many around to read. With the onset of word-separated script in Ireland in the seventh century, however, scribes no longer had to copy books from the dictation of a colleague. Scribes now transcribed books privately, following a script visually. Word separation thus changed the reading psychology—the actual mental processes—of the scribes. "When copying a word separated book, a medieval Latin scribe, like a modern typist, could with minimal effort, duplicate a literary text by replicating a linear series of word images and signs of punctuation" (Saenger 1999, 14). In short, instead of listening to another scribe read the pages of a book and attempting to reproduce in writing the spoken words phonetically, the scribe now could simply copy down "word images"—word-separated word for word-separated word—along with the accompanying signs of punctuation. This was still a slow and difficult task, but it was a great deal easier than any previous method.

This practice of copying books visually rather than by dictation was later standardized through a *pecia* system of producing "perfect" books. After the invention of movable type and the printing press in the mid-1400s, the publication of books increased at a furious pace. As a result, "in 1500 books of a legible quality . . . were widely available at moderate prices to a readership extending from London to Warsaw" (Saenger 1999, 14).

The third major change in reading in the late Middle Ages was the opening of new schools in which reading and writing were taught to an ever-increasing number of people. What the teachers taught may sound familiar to us: Instruction included "word separation, punctuation, and standardized orthography" (Saenger 1999, 14). The theory of the "whole word" method of teaching reading, which was first used in medieval Celtic teaching, was even a matter of debate.

The spread of schools to teach reading and writing did not alter the psychology of reading; rather, it was a factor in spreading literacy. As schools were established, the society of late medieval Europe was transformed, for widespread schooling ensured that people other than those in religious orders, scholastics, royalty, or aristocrats could read.

> Rich and poor and men and women deciphered meaning by approximately the same processes. The social context of reading thus became crucial in the early modern period when fluent reading, which had largely been the privilege of a restricted elite in the Middle Ages, was translated into the vernacular and disseminated via printed books to the majority of the inhabitants of western Europe. (Saenger 1999, 15)

REFERENCES

Cahill, Thomas. 1995. *How the Irish Saved Civilization: The Untold Story of Ireland's Heroic Role from the Fall of Rome to the Rise of Medieval Europe.* New York: Doubleday.

Eco, Umberto. 1994. *The Name of the Rose.* San Diego, CA: Harcourt Brace.

Saenger, Paul. 1999. "The History of Reading." In *Literacy: An International Handbook,* ed. Daniel A. Wagner, Richard L. Venezky, and Brian V. Street. Boulder, CO: Westview Press.

———. 1997. *Space between Words: The Origins of Silent Reading.* Stanford: Stanford University Press.

Chapter Six

●← Reading Literature: Literature as a Way of Knowing

Let me begin by setting out my argument as baldly as possible and then go on to examine its basis and its consequences. It is this. There are two irreducible modes of cognitive functioning—or more simply two modes of thought—each meriting the status of a "rational kind." Each provides a way of ordering experience, of constructing reality, and the two (though amenable to complementary use) are irreducible to one another. Each also provides ways of organizing representation in memory and of filtering the perceptual world. Efforts to reduce one mode to the other or to ignore one at the expense of the other inevitably fail to capture the rich ways in which people "know" and describe events around them.

—Jerome Bruner, "Narrative and Paradigmatic Modes of Thought"

What does the cognitive psychologist Jerome Bruner mean by "two irreducible modes of cognitive functioning"? We need to read his words carefully because, incidentally, he is writing a particular kind of text, one very different from literary composition. This kind of writing is a prime example of paradigmatic language, of abstract ideas presented within a logical structure.

He argues that we have two different ways of using our minds. He also uses the technical term "cognitive functioning" to describe the ways our brains operate. Each of these two ways, he maintains, is a distinctly separate method of "ordering experience," of trying to make sense of the terribly complex and confusing world in which we live. Each method helps us to put into some sort of order what we remember, to call up our memories and make sense of them. These mental aids (human "inventions," for that is what they are) act as frames—or filters, to use Bruner's term—that assist us in perceiving and understanding our environment. It is crucial to note here that Bruner does not use the word "thinking." Rather, he employs the word "perceiving," which carries the meaning of apprehending reality through both our minds and our feelings, for we have evidence that our brains have the capacity to "think" as well as to "feel" (see Blake 1978, 83–94).

According to Bruner, the ways our brains work are essentially different from each other. Taken together, though, the two modes make up a whole way of apprehending reality, in other words, they complement each other. So if we use one mode only to the exclusion of the other—if we primarily think by rational means and neglect how we feel and how we learn through intuition—then we do so at our own peril and run the risk of denying ourselves a potentially rich and full life.

LITERATURE AS A WAY OF KNOWING

What are the two ways of dealing with our world? How do we describe them? Bruner calls them the "narrative" and the "paradigmatic" modes of thought, what we generally know as stories and exposition. Others call the two modes "literary knowing" and rational, logical, or "scientific knowing."

Why should we be concerned with the idea of two ways of perceiving reality in a consideration of reading? Because it follows that since narration and exposition are two entirely dissimilar ways of knowing, we need to learn how to read the various texts that represent the two modes. To put it simply, we tell and write stories not to provide factual, scientific information but to create, through words, emotional experiences. (We do learn from stories, of course, but not in the way we learn from informational writing.) And conversely, we read exposition expressly not allowing our feelings to intrude, reading, rather, to process information as clearly, dispassionately, and in as logical a structure as possible.

Let us turn to examples of the two kinds of writing that illustrate the two modes. Both selections deal with the same topic, the exotic and beloved giant panda, but the selections represent two very different kinds of reading.

> *Panda* is the name of two species of Asian mammals that differ greatly in appearance. The *giant panda* is a large, black-and-white animal. The *red panda,* also called the *lesser panda,* is reddish-brown and much smaller. Both species live in bamboo forests on upper mountain slopes

of western and southwestern China. Giant pandas are rare and are protected by law in China.

Pandas eat bamboo. The giant panda eats bamboo stems and leaves. The red pandas eat bamboo leaves. Pandas grasp the bamboo between their fingers and an "extra thumb." This thumb, which is a bone covered by a fleshy pad, grows from the wrist of each forepaw. Pandas also have true thumbs, which they use as fingers. Unlike most plant-eating animals, pandas have inefficient digestive systems that cannot easily change plant food into energy. As a result, pandas must eat large quantities of bamboo to get enough energy. For example, giant pandas eat as much as 85 pounds (39 kilograms) of bamboo shoots per day.

The *giant panda* has a white, chubby body with black legs and a broad band of black across the shoulders. It has a large, round head; small black ears; and white face with black patches around each eye. This panda commonly grows to about 5 to 6 feet (1.5 to 1.8 meters) long and has a short tail. Adults weigh about 200 to 300 pounds (90 to 140 kilograms).

Scientific classification. The scientific name for the giant panda is *Ailuropoda melanoleuca.* (Snyder 1999, 129)

The ridge lunged upward like a dragon's spine bristling with fir and birch, and clouds were low and flying out from the mountains. Snow from a late-winter storm balanced on boughs and logs. When a riffle of wind stirred the branches, the snow drifted down in crystal veils that added a ghostlike radiance to the forest. Bamboo grew in the understory, the crowded ranks of stems claiming the hillside so completely that the light beneath the bamboo's canopy was a translucent undersea green. The sunless scent of moss and moldering wood choked the gloom. The bamboo was rigid with frost, and a dense silence hung over the ridge; there was no movement and seemingly no life.

In the stillness, leaves suddenly rustled and a stem cracked like breaking glass. Shrouded in bamboo was a giant panda, a female, slumped softly in the snow, her back propped against a shrub. Leaning to one side, she reached out and hooked a bamboo stem with the ivory claws of a forepaw, bent in the stem, and with a fluid movement bit it off near the base. Stem firmly grasped, she sniffed it to verify that it was indeed palatable, and then ate it end-first like a stalk of celery. While her powerful molars sectioned and crushed the stem, she glanced around for another, her movements placid and skillful, a perfect ecological integration between panda and bamboo. She ate within a circle of three feet, moved a few steps and ate some more, consuming only coarse stems and discarding the leafy tops; she then sat hunched, forepaws in her lap, drowsy and content. Within a circle of three thousand feet was her universe, all that she needed; bamboo, a mate, a snug tree-den in which to bear young.

Minutes later, she ambled in her rolling sailor's gait to a nearby spur where, among gnarled rhododendrons, she halted. No bamboo grew here. A shaft of sun escaped through a fissure of cloud and penetrated the twilight. Among bamboo the panda's form and color had seemed blurred and difficult to define; now in sun the panda shone with sparkling clarity. Near her was a massive fir. She knew that tree: it was a landmark, it defined the edge of her favored haunts, it served as a scentpost. The tree's many dimensions helped give her an identity. The snow around the tree was unmarked by tracks, but when she sniffed the bark, she learned that a male had marked the site with his anal glands a few days before. Though she fixed the scent in her mind, she did not cover his odors with hers.

She angled down to the nearest bamboo patch and there once again foraged, the recycling of bamboo being the essence of her existence. She lived leisurely. Alone in these heights, the panda conveyed a sense of absolute solitude, an isolation that was almost mythic. A flock of tit-babblers skittered like airborne mice through the bamboo above her head, yet her small dark eyes showed no awareness. Having eaten, she rolled over to sleep, her body at rest in the snow against a log, her dense coat making her impervious to the elements.

From below, near where forest gave way to field, came the sound of an ax. The bamboo around her like armor against intruders, she listened and then moved away, shunning any possible confrontation. She traveled on a private path along the slope, insinuating herself from thicket to thicket, moving like a cloud shadow, navigating with precision through the sea of stems, with only her tracks a record of her silent passing. (Schaller 1993, 1, 2)

The first selection, from *The World Book Encyclopedia*, is a fine example of exposition, that is, writing aimed at presenting ordered information that is a consequence of systematic observation and disciplined thought, the result of what we call the "scientific method." The writing is arranged in a clearly logical structure and is presented in a plainly straightforward manner. There are, for instance, no examples of figurative language such as similes and metaphors or other examples of figurative language. It presents not an emotional experience open to varied interpretations but unambiguous information by way of a specialized vocabulary. The text presents the following information about the giant panda: physical appearance, habitat, species classification, diet, and scientific labeling of the panda. The author makes general statements about pandas based on data collected through observations of many individual pandas.

Observe carefully the kinds of direct sentences used, and notice in particular that the author writes not of an individual panda but of the general behavior of all pandas, employing the words "*the* panda" and "pandas." (An exception comes in the last paragraph, but even there, "this panda" means "this species of panda," not an individual panda.) The text, then, is a model of inductive thinking, a form of logical reasoning in which we draw conclusions about members of a group after observing a number of the members of that class. Although we simply accept this kind of writing, usually assuming it has always been with us, it is a fairly recent invention, perhaps some five hundred years old (see chapter 4).

Now let us turn to the second piece of writing. In order to tell in detail the kind of writing it represents, we describe at length how one of the authors of this book first read the piece and subsequently went over it several times:

As I start reading it, I am immediately tipped off that what I have here is not a purely informational piece. Even if I had begun with the intention of concentrating on facts, I shortly discard this intent and find myself entering into the world of the panda. As I read along, I am drawn into her eerily quiet, protective world. If I had to select the most important phrase or sentence in the passage, the one that stands out in my mind, I would choose the statement that "the panda conveyed a sense of absolute solitude, an isolation that was almost mythic." Only at the end of the piece do I feel a sharp terror that shatters her splendid, innocent isolation when I learn that she hears the "sound of an ax," from faceless but ominous intruders far below her, "near where forest gave way to field." After my first emotional encounter with the work, I say to myself, "Wow! What a beautiful piece!" Only after I have first lived through the experience evoked by the writing do I reread it to find out how the writer did it. After experience comes analysis.

This kind of writing, unlike the objective explanation of the first piece, uses words designed to evoke images, concrete details, and strong feelings in order to create an emotional spell, almost a hypnotic trance, *if I allow myself to enter the experience.* How does the writer create this emotional effect? After I have moved though the piece the first time—without consciously picking out specific details, merely allowing myself to become emotionally involved—I make an uninhibited, intuitive response to the writing. The total effect may be that I have a sense that I am there on that snow-covered mountaintop in splendid isolation with this strange and exotic creature. The writing casts such a spell that I even may feel myself become the panda. Narrative writing like this is worlds apart from exposition of informational writing. The purpose is different, the effect is different, and one must read it differently.

Now I reread the text to see how the great naturalist George Schaller does it. First, he uses words to conjure up precise, visual images: The ridge "lunged" up; a "riffle" of wind stirred the branches; the bamboo's "canopy" was a "translucent undersea green." He also uses figurative language, such as similes and metaphors, which compel us to see in fresh ways by comparing what we normally think of as unlike objects and creatures in unusual ways: The ridge was "like a dragon's spine"; the panda ate a bamboo shoot "like a stalk of celery"; she ambled in "her rolling sailor's gait"; a flock of tit-babblers skittered "like airborne mice"; the bamboo around her was "like armor" against intruders; she traveled "like a cloud shadow." The overall effect of the words is to evoke an intensely powerful, lived-through experience.

Furthermore, in contrast to the logical structure of the encyclopedia entry, the organization of Schaller's piece is "spatial": The writing moves from "far to near," acting like the zoom lens of a camera, moving from a wide-angle view of the snowy mountain forest to a series of close-ups of an individual panda. Since he is a dedicated and compassionate naturalist, Schaller even tells us what one "theme" of his writing is, that her "movements placid and skillful" represent "a perfect ecological integration between panda and bamboo." Another literary writer might have omitted such an explanation and left it to the reader to infer such a conclusion.

The author here uses the techniques of description, compelling us to enter into the world and life of a single panda and helping us create a personal, emotional understanding of what in essence a single panda is like. As a result, we read this writing in an entirely different way from the way we read scientific, rational, informational, paradigmatic writing.

But is it accurate to say that there are two "irreducible" ways of knowing and that we must read each kind in a different way? And just how are these two kinds of knowing different? The debate about this question is as old as language, and we need to go back centuries to arrive at the root of the argument.

To understand how literature and rational thought are markedly dissimilar, we turn to an account of the historical roots of literary knowing and rational thought in Western culture. (For a more extensive discussion of the subject, see chapter 4, in which we review the main linguistic and philosophic bout of Western history, in which Homer and Plato duke it out.)

According to the classical scholar Eric Havelock, all cultures—if they are to survive and thrive—must have a "cultural book," or in a complex culture like ours, a series of "books," either oral or written repositories of useful and valuable information that all members of the culture need to know, an encyclopedia of ethics, politics, history, technology, religious instruction, theology, and religious and moral training (Havelock 1976). Because the ancient Greeks were nonliterate this information was passed on orally to successive generations, primarily through the recitation of such folk epics as the *Iliad* and the *Odyssey.*

Because the long narrative poems were presented before a non-literate audience, they made extensive use of mnemonic devices. They dealt with well-known myths, legends, and stories of great heroes in monumental events. They were composed in regular rhythms and rhymes, creating a continual repetition of sounds. They were presented as full-scale productions, accompanied by a lyre and by dancers performing formalized dance movements.

But the intent of the performances was not solely to give pleasure. The epics, and later the ancient plays, were designed to instruct as well as to delight. The epics served a didactic purpose. They were created to teach—through oral, regular, rhythmic stories told to people who could neither read nor write—what was worthwhile in a culture to retain. Primarily, the epics taught through the action of highly placed individuals—such as Achilles, Hector, Odysseus, and Antigone—how to behave. These heroes' actions revealed matters of public law *(nomos)* and family rules of behavior *(ethos).*

If literature was such an important way of knowing to the ancient, nonliterate Greeks, what happened to it? What way of knowing—what cultural mind-set—stands in opposition to literature as the primary way of knowing? The other way of knowing is the mode of thinking done not by the artist but by what we have called the intellectual, an individual who is capable of abstract reasoning. To understand this way of knowing in Western culture, we turn to the Greek philosopher Plato, who if he did not invent abstract language, its way of thinking, and its new way with words, at least codified a model of abstract, rational knowing rather than literary knowing.

For Plato, as we know from reading *The Republic,* literature as a way of knowing is dangerous. Poetry is too emotional, too ambiguous, and too undependable, incapable of dealing with rational, abstract thought. No wonder he banished the poet and poetry—especially the poetry of Homer—from his ideal city-state. Poetic language, in Plato's view, is at third hand from reality, which resides in the realm of the ideal. We find a notorious example of Plato's basis for dismissing poetry and the poem in his explanation of the various levels of reality for the idea Bed. The poet describes a "bed," which is a symbolic copy of an actual bed created by a carpenter, which is but a representation of the abstraction of "bedness," an ideal, never-changing, concept Bed. The poet, and his mode of thought, cannot be trusted, for he shows shadows, ever-changing events, and the actions of inconsistent heroes, the effect of which is to send the enthralled audience of a poetic performance into a virtual trance from which the spectators cannot perceive the reality of existence.

How does Plato's way of knowing—unchanging, abstract thought—differ from literary knowing? The intellectual—one who is obsessed by rational thought—*thinks;* the poet *feels.* The intellectual reasons; the poet intuits. The intellectual generalizes, dealing with abstractions arrived at from observing creatures and events; the poet creates ways of behaving by observing humans in stressful situations.

Is the contention that there are two modes of knowing valid today? Is Bruner correct in stating that these modes of knowing are not only still a part of our culture but are inherently "irreducible"? There is considerable agreement among scholars not only that these two modes are still alive but that the rational, "scientific," paradigmatic mode is ascendant in our culture.

For instance, Elliot Eisner, an art educator, broadens the idea of "literary knowing" beyond literature to include other arts and calls all these activities "aesthetic" modes of knowing (Eisner 1985, 23–36):

> The phrase "aesthetic modes of knowing," presents something of a con-
> tradiction in our culture. We do not typically associate the aesthetic
> with knowing. The arts, with which aesthetic is most closely associated,
> is a matter of the heart. Science is thought to provide the most direct
> route to knowledge. Hence, "aesthetic modes of knowing" is a phrase
> that contradicts the conception of knowledge that is most widely
> accepted. (Eisner 1985, 23–24)

Not only do we encounter aesthetic modes of knowing through the arts, including literature, but according to Eisner, many scientists frequently use aesthetic modes of knowing in their pursuit of scientific knowledge; Eisner cites the scientist Alfred North Whitehead in this regard: "Scientists, Whitehead believed, are drawn to their work not by epistemological motives but by aesthetic ones. The joy of inquiry is the driving motive for their work. Scientists, like artists, formulate new and puzzling questions in order to enjoy the experience of creating answers to them" (Eisner 1985, 27).

We acquire knowledge through the aesthetic mode of knowing, believes Eisner, in two ways: First, we come to understand the world through the structures or forms that we create through the aesthetic modes of knowing. Homer "created" the form of the oral folk epics the *Iliad* and the *Odyssey* to present the elements of Greek culture, especially the Greek warrior culture, to its people. Likewise, the Irish writer James Joyce "created" the form of the "stream of consciousness" in such novels as *A Portrait of the Artist as a Young Man* and *Ulysses* to reveal the Irish culture to his people. A second kind of knowing received from the aesthetic mode is the pleasure one enjoys by surrendering to an emotional experience triggered by particular piece of art.

The most provocative argument for the value of the aesthetic mode of knowing is the claim that through this mode we *create* knowledge. The general opinion toward the scientific mode is that in that mode, by contrast, we *find* or *discover* knowledge. The scientist *finds* the knowledge that the earth is round and that it revolves around the sun. Sophocles in *Oedipus Rex* and Shakespeare in *Hamlet,* on the other hand, *create* the knowledge that parricide, the killing of one's father, is a universal taboo.

If we confuse the aesthetic with the scientific mode, maintains Eisner, the aesthetic is diminished by our cherished belief that we search for knowledge rather than create it. Knowledge is considered by most in our culture as something one discovers, not something one makes. Knowledge, according to this viewpoint, is out there waiting to be found, and the most useful tool for finding *it* is the scientific method. "If there were greater appreciation for the extent to which knowledge is constructed—something made—there might be a greater likelihood that its aesthetic dimensions would be appreciated" (Eisner 1985, 32).

Eisner believes that artists—broadly conceived to include musical composers, painters, and architects as well as writers and sometimes even scientists—are capable of using the aesthetic mode. If this is so, and we believe it is, we would prefer to think of the aesthetic mode of knowing as best viewed as being situated on a continuum, with the purest form of aesthetic knowing at one end and the least aesthetic, the most scientific mode, at the opposite end.

For the cognitive psychologist Bruner, the two modes of knowing—what he calls the "narrative" and the "paradigmatic" or "logico-scientific"—cannot be placed on a continuum; rather, they are "irreducible." Our concern here is to ask, If there are indeed two essentially different modes of knowing, what are the characteristics of each, and more crucially, how do we "read" each?

This is Bruner's argument: Each of these modes of knowing provides a way of making sense out of experience and of then constructing our individual realities. Attempting to reduce one mode to the other or to ignore one at the expense of the other fails to capture the rich ways by which we describe and know what happens around us. Each way has operating principles of its own and its own criteria for well-formedness. The methods, however, differ radically in their procedure for establishing "truth." There is no direct way by which a statement derived from the scientific mode can contradict or support a statement derived from the aesthetic mode, or vice versa. For example, the statement made by the wife in Robert Frost's narrative poem "The Death of the Hired Man," that "home is a place I thought you somehow shouldn't have to deserve," cannot be proved by empirical evidence.

What, then, are the two modes like? According to Bruner, the paradigmatic, the most fully developed in our culture, fulfills the idea of a formal system of description and explanation. It is based upon the rational functions of categorization and conceptualization. Because the paradigmatic mode has been developed over the millennia in Western culture, we know a great deal about it and have developed powerful man-made systems—mental "prosthetic" devices, he calls them, analogous to artificial limbs—for carrying on paradigmatic thought, such as the human inventions of logic, mathematics, and the algorithms used by those in the so-called hard sciences (e.g., physics, chemistry, and astronomy) to conduct their research. Paradigmatic knowing leads to "good" theory, tight analysis, logical proof, and empirical discovery guided by reasoned hypotheses. And, of course, this kind of knowing requires a special kind of reading.

Bruner describes the narrative mode, on the other hand, as the one that leads to rousing stories, elegant poems, gripping drama, believable historical accounts, and even perceptive case histories for physicians and psychiatrists (see Robert Coles's 1989 book *The Call of Stories: Teaching and the Moral Imagination*). Seldom do we find in hard science writing narrative or poetic license (naturalists like George Schaller, as we have seen, do use the narrative mode in their reports for popular audiences), and when we apply "scientific" techniques of criticism to narrative, "we replace the narrative by a paradigmatic structure" (Bruner 1985, 99). Any detached, purely analytic, rational analysis of a story, poem, novel, or play then exhibits paradigmatic thought rather than a narrative perception of a literary text. Not only do we read a literary text in a different way from the way we read a strictly scientific text, we need two different kinds of language to talk about the two modes of knowing. The literary critic Caroline F. E. Spurgeon once did an exhaustive count of dominant images in Shakespearean plays "to throw new light on the poet and his work" (Spurgeon 1952, ix). In the play *Hamlet,* she found a great many "images of sickness, disease or blemish of the body, . . . and we discover that the idea of an ulcer or tumour, as descriptive of the unwholesome condition of Denmark morally, is, on the whole, the dominant one" (Spurgeon 1952, 316).

Bruner, a psychologist himself, finds it unfortunate that the psychology of thought has concentrated on the paradigmatic mode to the virtual exclusion of the narrative mode. At the same time, psychology's parent, philosophy, has been concerned only with studying how paradigmatic knowing works, "how mind comes to know the world, to represent it, to reach right conclusions about it, to avoid errors, to achieve generality and abstraction" (Bruner 1985, 102). The reasons for this state of affairs, believes Bruner, is that scholars in psychology and philosophy desire their disciplines to be more like the "hard" natural sciences, more rigorous and scientific, than the social sciences. As evidence, Bruner offers this example:

> Piaget, for all his genius, saw the growth of mind as paralleling the growth of science—or vice versa. There is no reasoned way in his system of characterizing the difference between the prattling of the Department gossip and a Homer, a Joyce, or a Hardy. For some reason, the nature and growth of thought that are necessary for the elaboration of great stories, great histories, great myths—have not seemed very attractive or challenging to most of us [cognitive psychologists]. So we have left the job to the literary scholars and linguists, to the folklorists and anthropologists. And they have studied not the process, but the product, the tales rather than the tellers. (Bruner 1985, 103)

In short, Bruner believes that the "outcomes produced by the two modes of thought could neither contradict nor corroborate the other" and that this "is a very radical claim" (Bruner 1985, 112, 113).

But it is not really so radical as that. Not only do most of us unconsciously accept that there are two mutually exclusive modes of knowing or that many times we confuse the two modes; we may try to retrieve "facts" from a poem or attempt to prove a piece of empirical evidence by a feeling or opinion. The reality of a story cannot be proved true or false by empirical evidence. At the same time, we verify paradigmatic thought not by opinion or by feeling but by logic, rational thought, so-called objective observation, and by the accumulation of empirical data. "Each [narrative and paradigmatic thought] is a version of the world, and to ask which depicts the real world is to ask a question that even modern metaphysicians believe to be undecidable" (Bruner 1985, 113).

To recapitulate, the philosopher, the psychologist, and the art educator we have referred to speak of different modes of knowing: Plato speaks of the poetic and the intellectual; Bruner, the narrative and the paradigmatic; and Eisner, the aesthetic and the scientific. Another respected cognitive psychologist, Howard Gardner, addressing the problem of "human knowing" in another way, identifies seven discrete ways of knowing in his *Frames of Mind: The Theory of Multiple Intelligences* (1985): linguistic, musical, logico-mathematical, spatial, bodily-kinesthetic, and the personal intelligences, which he divides into the interpersonal and intrapersonal intelligences (Gardner 1985). In a later book, Gardner considers "several new candidate intelligences, including 'naturalist,' 'spiritual,' 'existential,' and 'moral' intelligences" (Gardner 1999, 4).

In *Frames of Mind,* Gardner divides the personal intelligences into two types: the "interpersonal," knowing about others within a community, and the "intrapersonal," knowing about one's self in relation to others, the most helpful for illuminating the idea of modes of knowing.

How do people best learn the personal intelligences (which we maintain are directly related to literary knowing)? As Gardner explains, we learn them through core myths, rituals, and commonly shared stories. As we participate through experiencing familiar tales, we learn and eventually internalize crucial intrapersonal and extrapersonal skills. As does Bruner, Gardner points out that the presently dominant way of knowing—that is, what is generally perceived to be "intelligence" in our schools and in society at large—is the logical-mathematical intelligence; this view exists primarily because of the writings of the developmental psychologist, Jean Piaget. Gardner acknowledges that Piaget's view of knowing—together with his theory of intellectual development—is a powerful one, but he believes it is the narrow viewpoint of the laboratory scientist, a "brilliant portrait of that form of intellectual growth which is valued most highly in Western scientific and philosophical traditions" (Gardner 1985, 20). Gardner also has problems with Piaget's theoretical model of knowing. First, Piaget's theory is only one kind of mental development, and it is one that is less important to people in non-Western cultures and, as we have learned, for nonliterate people. Indeed, Piaget's view of how people know may "be applicable to only a minority of individuals, even in the West" (Gardner 1985, 20). In

addition, Piaget's model ignores the steps in developing mental competence in occupations or professions other than those of laboratory scientists and similar workers; the mental development of artists, writers,
dramatists, musicians, lawyers, athletes, and political statesmen are not
addressed. And the tasks developed by Piaget are all drawn from the laboratory benches and blackboards of the biologist. In short, virtually the
only model of intellectual development taught directly in our schools,
which thus becomes a part of our cultural knowledge, is Piaget's theory
of the development of scientific knowing.

If Gardner is correct in his view that Piaget's theory of cognition
deals exclusively with scientific knowing, what does he say about other
intelligences? And of what relevance is his theory of "multiple intelligences" to our concern with "literary knowing"? And ultimately, just
how do we read these two different kinds of texts?

Let us examine Gardner's descriptions of the personal intelligences to see whether or not they relate to our discussion of a narrative
mode of thought. Here are Gardner's descriptions of the personal intelligences. The core capacity of an intrapersonal intelligence is understanding of our own feelings, access to the full range of our emotional
person. If we have a sophisticated intrapersonal intelligence, we discriminate among our feelings, call them by name, and understand how
they work in all aspects of our lives. At the simplest level, we use our
intrapersonal intelligence to tell the difference between elementary
pleasure and pain. At the highest level, though, intrapersonal knowing
allows us to note and translate into language our own highly complicated and subtle feelings. Examples of persons with supremely developed intrapersonal intelligences are novelists, dramatists, poets, psychiatrists, and therapists.

What is interpersonal intelligence like? The core capacity of
interpersonal intelligence, which turns us from within ourselves outward to others, is the ability to note and make distinctions between
feelings in individuals, in particular, in their moods, temperaments,
motivations, and intentions. When we are children, interpersonal intelligence allows us to discriminate among people around us and to
become aware of their various moods. At the advanced stage, our
mature grasp of interpersonal intelligence permits us to read intentions
and desires in the many people we come in contact with—even when
their intentions are not explicitly stated and may even be hidden to
themselves—and enables us to act upon this information. What kind of
people are known for their superior grasp of interpersonal intelligence,
for understanding the behavior of many people and having the talent of
influencing those people to behave in certain ways? They come from all

walks of life, but they are especially political and religious leaders, such as Mahatma Gandhi, Abraham Lincoln, Eleanor Roosevelt, and Martin Luther King Jr., as well as ordinary people who are skilled in the helping professions, such as teachers, ministers, priests, therapists, counselors, and wise elders.

This fully developed sense of self—as represented in the personal intelligences—is the highest achievement of human beings and is the "crowning capacity which supersedes and presides over more mundane and partial forms of intelligence" (Gardner 1985, 242). The essence of these intelligences is the skill to use symbols, and without a sophisticated grasp of language and literary knowing, broadly conceived, we are able to cope with only the most elementary and unorganized discrimination among feelings. Armed, however, with a refined command of the personal intelligences, we have the potential to make sense of the full range of human experience from all the people we encounter. In summary, Gardner writes, "The less a person understands his own feelings, the more he will fall prey to them. The less a person understands the feelings, the responses, and the behavior of others, the more likely he will interact inappropriately with them and therefore fail to secure his proper place within the larger community"(Gardner 1985, 254).

The personal intelligences are crucial to our very existence, but how do we learn them? Well, we do not learn them through scientific, logico-mathematical knowing, which deals primarily with the human inventions of logic, mathematics, systematic and objective observation, and abstract theory. We acquire a sophisticated personal intelligence by mastering symbol systems, myths, legends—the common core literature of a culture. Generally speaking, we reach this goal by mastering literary knowing. (The linguist Martin Joos calls this precious literature of a culture, the texts we will not let die, "frozen language." Such texts as Lincoln's Gettysburg Address and Second Inaugural Address, which are so revered they are inscribed on marble, are examples of "frozen language" [Joos 1967].)

But simply reading worthwhile literature by ourselves is not enough to teach us the personal intelligences. We need to recognize that experiencing literature is—as it was for the ancient Greeks—a social activity. We need to read and see literature—including movies, TV shows, and plays—but it is essential that we allow ourselves to experience these works together, to respond orally and in writing to what we have experienced, and to discuss our responses with others. Only through this process can we learn about ourselves, about how we feel and think and learn about others. These are the social and cultural knowledge and social skills that worthwhile literature can impart. In essence, "through formal tutoring, or through literature, rituals, and other symbolic forms, the culture helps the growing individual to make discriminations about his feelings, or about the other persons in his milieu" (Gardner 1985, 251).

The personal intelligences overarch all other intelligences, believes Gardner. "Perhaps," he hypothesizes, "it makes more sense to think of knowledge of self and others at a higher level [than that of the other intelligences], a more integrated form of intelligence at the behest of the culture and of historical factors, one more truly emergent, one that ultimately comes to control and to regulate more 'primary orders' of intelligence" (Gardner 1985, 274).

We can, in fact, provide other, anecdotal, evidence, not from philosophy or psychology, for the existence of two modes of perceiving. Janet Malcolm, in a magazine article, tells us about Russian short-story writer and playwright Anton Chekhov's expository piece on his three-month visit to the prison colony of Sakhalin, Russia. Malcolm describes the problems Chekhov faced when he wrote not a story or play about the prison but, rather, a scientific account, "The Island of Sakhalin," first published in 1895. She tells us that Chekhov wrote his work "not from memory" but from "file cards and scholarly books and reports" and that he thought of it as a report, as a work of social and natural science rather than as a literary text. Chekhov even briefly considered submitting it to Moscow University's medical school as a dissertation attesting to his qualification to teach there (Malcolm 2001b).

What happened when this supremely accomplished master of literary knowing tried his hand at writing scientific prose? Malcolm describes the result like this:

> His customary artist's fearlessness gives way to a kind of humility, almost servility, before the ideal of objectivity and the protocols of scientific methodology. Like a convict chained to a wheelbarrow (one of the punishments at Sakhalin), he drags along the burden of his demographic, zoological, and botanical facts. He cannot omit anything; his narrative line is constantly derailed by his data. In an autobiographical note he wrote for a reunion of his medical class, Chekhov registered his awareness that the "principles of creative art do not always admit of full accord with scientific data; death by poison cannot be represented on stage as it actually happens." In the Sakhalin book, the conflict between science and art is always resolved in science's favor. Chekhov tells it like it is, and allows his narrative to go where his mountain of information pushes it, which is all over the place, and ultimately nowhere. Chekhov's horror at the harshness and squalor of life in the

colony, his contempt for the stupidity and callousness of the adminis-
tration, and his pity for the convicts and settlers sometimes do break
through the posture of scientific detachment. But, in rendering the suf-
ferings on this island of the damned, Chekhov could not achieve in
three hundred pages what he achieved in a four-page passage at the
end of the story "The Murder," first published in 1895, about Sakhalin
convicts in fetters waiting to load coal onto a steamer on a stormy
night. (Malcolm 2001b, 62)

In short, when Chekhov attempted to write scientific prose, he
was intimidated by the requirements of this mode of thought, although
he did, for the most part, meet the requirements of objectivity, detachment, and disinterested observation and analysis.

In yet another striking example of the tensions between scientific
and narrative knowing, we learn how the novice child psychiatrist
Robert Coles attempted to reconcile two views toward treating patients,
one a clinical, scientific method, the other a narrative approach, by simply attending to the stories his patients told. One of Coles's psychiatric
supervisors, Dr. B., told him to read more in the scientific treatises about
a particular mental illness, to diagnose what his patient's problem was,
and to prescribe what action was indicated to help the patient become
better—a classic case of a clinical, scientific approach to a medical situation. Here is an account of Dr. Coles's meeting with Dr. B.:

In our first meeting Dr. B. urged me to read more in the psychiatric literature so that I might understand "the nature of phobias." He could
see that the suggestion puzzled me. "She is phobic, and you've got to
work around her defenses." It was clear, however, that I hadn't a clue as
to how I might follow his advice. "Best to see her in your office. Have
the nurse bring her." A pause, and then an explanation: "Phobics are
power-conscious. You'll do well to make it clear that you're the doctor,
and that you intend to see her in your office at a time of your choosing." (Coles 1989, 3–4)

Dr. B. told Dr. Coles to "formulate" the case about the phobic
woman, using such terms as "treat," "patient," "diagnose," and "work
around the patient's defenses" and telling him, "Phobics are hard to
treat." Dr. B., known as a brilliant theorist, asks him, "What are the psy-
chodynamics here?"

The other psychiatric supervisor, Dr. L., who listened attentively
to Dr. Coles during their meetings, appeared to be hard of hearing and

seemed to have little to say. At the beginning of one of their meetings, Dr. L. told Dr. Coles he was going to tell him a story and proceeded to recount a tale of a patient who was almost paralyzed by worries and fears. The story was so riveting that Dr. Coles forgot he was listening to a patient's clinical history. Then Dr. L. told him the patient had been struck by a car on the way to a lecture at an art museum. Dr. L. stopped. He sat silently for a while and then asked, "Do you see her in your mind?"

"Yes," replied Dr. Coles.

"Good," Dr. L. said. "I have just told you a story."

"What happened?" blurted out Dr. Coles, responding to the storyteller, not to the doctor, the psychiatrist, the supervisor.

> Then he told me "what happened." Afterward there was a different kind of silence in the room, for I was thinking about what I'd heard, and he was remembering what he had experienced. Finally he gave me a brief lecture that I would hear in my head many times over the next three decades: "The people who come to us bring their stories. They hope they tell them well enough so that we understand the truth of their lives. They hope we know how to interpret their stories correctly. We have to remember that what we learn is *their story*." (Coles 1989, 7)

In the following chart, we present, in an admittedly oversimplified way, what we perceive to be the striking differences between what we have discussed as two ways of knowing, and thus of two ways of reading. We are well aware that such outlines render extremely intricate situations less complex, but the description we hope will at least provide food for thought and a basis for discussion. We are not as sure as Bruner is that the two modes are irreducible. Rather, we believe we can better understand the characteristics of the two modes by thinking of them as occurring along a continuum. Besides, if we view the characteristics of the two ways of knowing as being opposites, we come to think of them as antithetical in nature, as one mode as versus the other, when we know from reading many kinds of texts that in fact many writers use both kinds of language within the same texts. The historian Shelby Foote, for instance, uses the techniques of fiction in his acclaimed and immensely popular three-volume history, *The Civil War,* and he aptly enough identifies the way of knowing it represents in the book's subtitle: *A Narrative.* On the other hand, the philosopher Plato, explaining the ultimate of abstract ideas, that of the abstract nature of reality, uses the poetic device of metaphor in his famous description in "The Cave."

Logico-Mathematical (Scientific) and Literary Knowing

Logico-Mathematical (Scientific) Knowing	*Literary Knowing*
Deals with abstractions and generalizations, especially in pure mathematics. It is considered by most people in our culture to be the highest form of knowing. Unfortunately, only a few "philosopher kings," to use Plato's term, are capable of abstract thinking.	Deals with reality through the concrete and specific, such as objects, events, creatures, and human beings.
Seeks to discover absolute truths, ideal never-changing realities such as Good, Right, gravity, and the Pythagorean theorem.	Teaches us to tolerate ambiguities and to accept irony and paradox in our lives.
Perceives reality by disinterested, objective observation and logical, rational methods such as equations, propositions, rules, and laws.	Approaches reality through stories, poems, songs, and plays about people.
Generally ignores what cannot be explained by a logical system of reasoning and believes that if something cannot be observed and measured, it does not exist.	Concedes that there are forces in life not perceived by rational means alone. Hamlet's observation seems apt here: "There's more than is dreamt of in your philosophy, Horatio."
Insists on objective detachment on the grounds that emotions distort observations and judgments.	Requires involvement and participation within a human and ever-widening community.
Usually amoral and does not admit the ethical concerns of good and evil.	Constantly deals with the notions of good and evil, right and wrong. Herman Melville's *Billy Budd,* Nathaniel Hawthorne's *Scarlet Letter,* Mark Twain's *Huckleberry Finn,* Toni Morrison's *Beloved,* Sophocles' *Antigone,* and Shakespeare's *Macbeth* spring to mind as outstanding examples of works with this focus.

continues

Logico-Mathematical (Scientific) and Literary Knowing (cont.)

Logico-Mathematical (Scientific) Knowing	*Literary Knowing*
Ignores a divine being as an explanation of reality.	Insists on the preciousness of the individual—as the spiritual sings it, "His eye is on the sparrow."
	Frequently is concerned with universal matters, such as the existence of a divine being, tending to believe, with Hamlet, that "there's a divinity that shapes our ends, rough-hew them how we will."

SUMMARY

It seems clear to us that there are two ways of knowing—two modes of cognition, to use the technical term—and thus two ways of writing and reading. One is known by many names: The ancient Greek philosopher Plato labeled it abstract thinking. We have variously called it logico-mathematical, rational, and scientific. The other kind of knowing is generally called literary knowing, which includes poetry, drama, and narrative, and it is far older and was at one time far more influential than the scientific. The archetypal examples of literary knowing in Western culture are Homer's great narrative epics the *Iliad* and the *Odyssey*.

Recent scholars and writers call these ways of knowing by different names. Cognitive psychologist Jerome Bruner calls them the paradigmatic and the narrative; art educator Elliot Eisner identifies the literary as part of the aesthetic. Psychologist Howard Gardner creates his own category for the literary: the personal intelligences, made up of the interpersonal and the intrapersonal intelligences. Author Janet Malcolm, in her account of the Russian short-story writer and playwright Anton Chekhov's attempt to write a scientific report, makes the distinction between "a work of social and natural science" and "a literary text." Child psychiatrist Robert Coles describes two ways of talking about mental patients as the difference between a clinical, scientific method and a narrative approach, which amounts to nothing more than the psychiatrist's listening to patients as they tell their stories.

Are these two ways of knowing—the scientific and the literary—mutually exclusive, irreducible one to other? We do not believe so. Would it not make more sense to think of actual examples of the two ways as being placed on a continuum or along a mental spectrum, with the purest forms of scientific and literary knowing placed at the two ends and with various examples of each lining up somewhere between the two extremes?

First of all, we know that except for the most unadulterated examples—say imagist poetry at one end and higher-level, pure mathematical equations at the other—most worthwhile texts exhibit both expository and poetic language.

Furthermore, we argue that if we continue to think of the two ways of knowing as being mutually exclusive—as being one *versus* the other—then do we not set the modes up as antagonistic? Is it not more accurate to think of them as simply two arbitrary ways of knowing that we all should be aware of and that we all should learn to read and write? If we experience one to the exclusion of the other, are we not really depriving ourselves of a command of the widest range of potential language ability and thus of a full mental and emotional life?

REFERENCES

Blake, Robert W. 1978. "Composing for the Left Hand." In *Facilitating Language Development*, ed. Patrick J. Finn and Walter T. Petty. Amherst: State University of New York at Buffalo.

Bruner, Jerome. 1985. "Narrative and Paradigmatic Modes of Thought." In *Learning and Teaching the Ways of Knowing*, ed. Elliot Eisner. Chicago: University of Chicago Press.

Coles, Robert. 1989. *The Call of Stories: Teaching and the Moral Imagination.* Boston: Houghton Mifflin Company.

Eisner, Elliot. 1985. "Aesthetic Modes of Knowing." In *Learning and Teaching the Ways of Knowing*, ed. Elliot Eisner. Chicago: University of Chicago Press.

Gardner, Howard. 1999. *Intelligence Reframed: Multiple Intelligences for the Twenty-First Century.* New York: Basic Books.

———. 1985. *Frames of Mind: The Theory of Multiple Intelligences.* New York: Basic Books.

Havelock, Eric A. 1976. *Origins of Western Literacy.* Toronto, Ontario: Institute for Studies in Education.

———. 1963. *Preface to Plato.* Cambridge, MA: Harvard University Press.

Joos, Martin. 1967. *The Five Clocks.* New York: Harcourt, Brace, and World.

Malcolm, Janet. 2001a. *Reading Chekhov: A Critical Journey.* New York: Random House.

————. 2001b. "Three Journeys: Anton Chekhov on the Road." *New Yorker,* October 29, 62–69.

Schaller, George C. 1993. *The Last Panda.* Chicago: University of Chicago Press.

————. 1985. *The Giant Pandas of Wolong.* Chicago: University of Chicago Press.

Snyder, Gregory. 1999. "Panda." In *The World Book Encyclopedia,* vol. 15: P. Chicago: World Book.

Spurgeon, Caroline F. E. 1952. *Shakespeare's Imagery and What It Tells Us.* London: Cambridge University Press.

Chapter Seven

●◆ Reading Literature: New Criticism— Theory to Practice

Some literary students and critics are likely to be worried by the idea that a literary text does not have a single "correct" meaning, but probably not many. They are more likely to be engaged by the idea that the meanings of a text do not lie within them like wisdom teeth within a gum, waiting patiently to be extracted, but that the reader has some active role in this process. Nor would many people today be disturbed by the notion that the reader does not come to a text as a kind of cultural virgin, immaculately free of previous social and literary entanglements, a supremely disinterested spirit or blank sheet on which the text will transfer its own presuppositions. Most of us recognize that no reading is innocent or without presuppositions. . . . there is no such thing as purely "literary" response: all such responses, not least those to literary form, to the aspects of a work which are sometimes jealously reserved to the "aesthetic," are deeply imbricated with the kind of social and historical individuals we are.
—Terry Eagleton, Literary Theory: An Introduction

The critic Terry Eagleton, with his deceptively breezy and irreverent tone, has described a change in the way we now read literature, a way radically at odds with the way we have read literature for at least the last century.

What are these changes? First, we see a transformation in the way we talk about reading: We now speak of "reading" and "responding" to literature rather than of "interpreting" or "criticizing" literature. Second, as Eagleton so clearly states, we no longer believe there is any single, "correct" meaning in a literary text; rather, we believe that meaning does not reside solely within the text, that we play a dynamic role in reading literature and have an active, not passive, transaction with a text. As a result, rather than "finding" the "correct" meaning of a literary text, we "construct" our own personal meanings. Third—and this idea is powerfully evident—our personal reading of a literary text is entirely dependent upon what we, as unbelievably complex individuals, bring to texts. In other words, how we read an open—or worthwhile—text is a result of a bewildering array of accumulated influences, including age, gender, intelligence, race, education, childhood experiences, family background, genetic makeup, society in which we live, and so forth and so forth. The so-called factors affecting our reading are, of course, labels to describe all the influences that have gone into making us the unique persons we are. Our presuppositions, often below the level of consciousness, overlap—"imbricate" as Eagleton so elegantly puts it—to form who we are. Fourth, we have changed in our reading of literature from criticizing literary texts as texts to reading and responding to texts, a potent transformation that broadens our understanding of a text beyond the "text itself" to wider and broader readings, including social, political, psychological, and moral considerations. We remember, for example, a class in which college students read D. H. Lawrence's "The Rocking Horse Winner." They moved inexorably from a literal reading of the story, of a boy who tries to please his cold-hearted, money-obsessed mother, to an outward interpretation of the story dealing with a society in which many members are concerned mainly with material possessions. Such a reading, they pointed out, is not irrelevant to our present culture. And fifth, it seems to us that as a result of new ways of thinking about how we read literature, a momentous alteration is occurring, that we are moving from a time when only privileged, specially trained university students and scholars are able to interpret literature to a more democratic era when everyone will be encouraged to read and create his or her own personal response to literature. We have, in other words, democratized the reading of literature. We are no longer bound to the "received" interpretations of literary texts; instead, we are becoming courageous readers: independent, confident, and perceptive.

In this chapter and in chapter 8 we will discuss what we believe have been the two most influential theories of literature during the twentieth century, New Criticism and Reader Response, and the school practices derived from each.

A word here about "theory": Although those of a rational, scientific bent hold theory sacred, as the hallmark of the scientific method, those who have been schooled in the humanities, especially in the study of language and literature, distrust theory as "merely" abstract ruminations or solitary speculation. Possibly we all need to be reminded that the word "theory" derives from the Greek verb meaning "to observe" and a noun meaning "a viewing," which, interestingly enough, is also directly related to a modern word of ancient lineage, "theater." For an example of how nonscientists may view the idea of theory, we turn to an account of child psychiatrist Robert Coles's description of his first experiences with different notions of theory in his psychiatric training. One of the novice psychiatrist's supervisors, Dr. L., told him that the idea of theory, rather than referring only to an abstract, scientific statement, originally referred to "observing" or "contemplating" something, that the word "theory" in Greek meant literally "I behold," as what we view in the theater, originally in the ancient Greek theaters where such plays as *Oedipus Rex* and *Antigone* were performed. Dr. L. told Dr. Coles, "We hold something visual in our minds; presumably, the theory is an enlargement of observation" (Coles 1989, 20).

Over the centuries, however, as we have developed scientific knowing, theory has come to be seen as something very different from an "enlargement of observation." Today many people think of theory only by its scientific meaning. Such a definition includes a set of assumptions and accepted methods for analyzing and predicting behavior in the natural world. With a valid theory, we have a general set of principles that we believe can be applied in a wide variety of circumstances.

We need to remember that there are two modes of knowing, that there are two ideas of theory, one the scientific and the other literary. A problem arises when we attempt to use scientific principles to construct a theory of literature. Many teachers of literature distrust or dismiss (and many times for good reason) the literary theorists who, for the most part, populate the universities. And we grant that the "lit-crit" technical language of the university theorists may be an impenetrable jungle of jargon. Some schoolteachers go so far as to claim that they have no theory undergirding their daily teaching of literature, that they rely on "common sense" in their instruction. Of course, the apparent lack of theory is itself a structured way of teaching, a "theory," if you will.

Why should we bother our heads with thinking about theories of literature? We agree with Terry Eagleton that a common response by students at the mention of theory is that theory has no relation to the "real" world and that theory gets between readers and what they read. Eagleton's reply to this stance "is that without some kind of theory, however unreflective and implicit, we would not know what a 'literary work' was in the first place, or how we were to read it. Hostility to theory usually means an opposition to other people's theories and an oblivion of one's own" (Eagleton 1996, x).

READING LITERATURE: BACKGROUND

In order to understand where we are now with reading literature and where we have come from, we turn to the groundbreaking research by the British critic I. A. Richards as presented in his book *Practical Criticism*—as opposed to "theoretical" criticism we might surmise—published in 1929. It is important to note that the subtitle of the book is *A Study of Literary Judgment*. Some scholars have identified this work as a forerunner of Reader Response theory. James Squire, for instance, states that *Practical Criticism* is "generally regarded as the first study of reader response" (Squire 1994, 637). However, we would regard it as a precursor to Reader Response *only* because Richards examined the written responses of a group of selected Cambridge University students and others as they "criticized" thirteen mostly unfamiliar poems, not because Richards or the respondents were aware of Reader Response theory.

This report is also important because not only does it give us a rich description of the prevailing attitude of the time toward literary criticism, but it also reveals matters of literary study that we have dealt with for the rest of the twentieth century.

What was Richards trying to find out? What was his research design? What in fact did he discover? What did his findings mean to him? And most importantly, what do his findings mean to us?

First of all, what was Richards trying to find out? Through the study of how university students and others interpreted poems, Richards aimed "to introduce a new kind of documentation to those who are interested in the contemporary state of culture whether as critics, as philosophers, as teachers, as psychologists, or merely as curious persons" (Richards 1929, 3). Such an aim, it seems to us, casts a pretty wide net to capture the influence of poetry, a mesh trapping the entire culture. His second aim was to present a new technique for persons to "discover for themselves what they think and feel about poetry (and cognate matters)" (Richards 1929, 3). And third, he aimed to provide educational methods "more efficient than those we use now in developing discrimination and the power to understand what we hear and read"(Richards 1929, 3).

What was his research design? He gave copies of thirteen poems, without the names of the poets, to a small group of privileged readers. Notice who they were: The majority were undergraduates at Cambridge University "reading" (that is, studying) English in hopes of earning an Honours Degree. Many were also top students "reading" in other subjects as well, and a few were nonacademic men and women. They were, we conclude, a pretty select group.

Richards left the poets' names off the copies of the poems so his readers would not be influenced by the fame of noted poets. He also played a rather underhanded trick by including poems generally agreed to be "mediocre" as well as poems by such masters as Christina Rossetti, John Donne, Edna St. Vincent Millay, Gerard Manley Hopkins, D. H. Lawrence, Alfred Noyes, George Meredith, and Henry Wadsworth Longfellow. As we read the poems today, we are struck by how regular they are in rhythm and rhyme scheme and by how "literary" their vocabulary is. It is as if no professor at Cambridge had ever heard of the American poet Walt Whitman.

Richards asked the members of the group to "comment" in writing, at their leisure outside of class, on their readings of the poems, noting how many readings they finished in one sitting. Multiple readings completed during a single sitting counted as one "reading." Some readers worked over ten to a dozen readings. A small number made fewer than four "attacks" on any of the poems. Richards was convinced that the readers gave more thorough readings than were ordinarily accomplished in any university course.

By this method of collecting responses, Richards hoped to make the study of poetry an

> eminently suitable *bait* for anyone who wishes to trap the current opinions and responses in this middle field [between the descriptive sciences at one end of a continuum and, at the other end, the concrete affairs that can be handled by rule of thumb and generally accepted forms of discussion] for the purpose of examining and comparing them and with a view to advancing our knowledge of what may be called the natural history of human opinions and feelings. In part then this book is the record of a piece of field-work in comparative ideology. (Richards 1929, 6)

It appears the aim of his research was far broader than merely to assess students' critical responses to a group of poems.

How did Richards analyze these samples of literacy criticism? First, he divided the responses into two classes. Into one category he lumped all "statements," those readings in which readers interpreted what they had read and were concerned with what meanings they found in the poems. All other responses he categorized as "mental operations," comments that revealed his readers' thought processes. By making these distinctions, Richards states he is primarily interested in the "history of criticism," which he considered "a history of dogmatism and argumentation rather than the history of research." His second aim was to "improve" the "technique of literary criticism" (Richards 1929, 8).

How did Richards intend to make the study of poetry a result of "research" rather than merely of "dogmatism and argumentation"? Again in his own words, the guiding principles of literary criticism are discovered through the "indispensable instrument" of "psychology," and thus "the whole apparatus of critical rules and principles is a means to the attainment of finer, more precise, more discriminating communication. There is, it is true, a valuation side to criticism" (Richards 1929, 11). In short, by using the techniques of psychology, he hopes to discover the "rules" and "principles" of literary criticism.

But what happened when he studied these responses? Generally, Richards was dismayed by the "astonishing variety of human responses" to the poems, a variety that prevented him from achieving a "systematic scheme" for analyzing the responses. He therefore created the now notorious "arbitrary list of the principal difficulties that may be encountered by one reader or another in the presence of almost any poem" (Richards 1929, 13). Here are the chief difficulties of criticism, arranged in hierarchical order from the "simplest . . . up to the most insidious, intangible, and bewildering of critical problems" that Richards found in the responses:

1. First, the readers found it difficult to state the *"plain sense"* of the poems in, we assume, ordinary, clear English.
2. They had difficulty in perceiving the rhythm of words in sequence, that is, with what Richards calls the "sensuous apprehension" of the poems, with noting the effects rhythm and rhyme had on their criticisms of the poem.
3. They had difficulty in picking out and evaluating "visual images" and in judging the "value of a poem by the images it excites in them." Laments Richards, "There is a troublesome source of critical deviation" (Richards 1929, 15).
4. They allowed "irrelevant intrusions" of feelings, memories, and associations. What Richards labels "mnemonic irrelevances" intrude upon their readings. "These are misleading effects of the reader's being reminded of some personal scene or adventure, erratic association, the interference of emotional reverberations from a past which may have nothing to do with the poem" (Richards 1929, 15).

5. The readers had difficulty with the "critical traps" of "Stock Responses." "These have their opportunity whenever a poem seems to, or does, involve views and emotions already fully prepared in the reader's mind, so that what happens appears to be more of the reader's doing than the poet's" (Richards 1929, 15). While reading a poem, then, a "button is pushed," and the reader relates the first things that come to mind.

6. They showed too much emotion, revealing too much "sentimentality." We can only assume they were not objective or detached enough.

7. But the readers also frequently lacked any emotion, displaying what Richards labeled "Hardness of Heart." How precisely the readers were able to walk a fine line between too much emotion and disinterestedness, we do not learn.

8. They had difficulty in criticizing the poems when they applied their personal views and beliefs to their readings of poems. "If so," asks Richards, "what bearing has the truth-value of the views upon the work of poetry?" For readers to bring their own values to their readings is thus a particularly heinous mistake: "Difficulties at this point are a fertile source of confusion and erratic judgment" (Richards 1929, 16).

9. They had difficulty in evaluating the poems on the basis of their technical aspects. If they judged poems on the basis of technical aspects alone, they put means before ends. Richards called such difficulties "technical presuppositions."

10. And finally, the readers allowed their prior knowledge of the nature and value of poetry to affect their readings. These preconceived notions "intervene endlessly, as the history of criticism shows only too well, between the reader and the poem" (Richards 1920, 17).

For Richards, the difficulties were interconnected and overlapping, but he believed he had identified most of the "principal obstacles and causes of failure in the reading and judgment of poetry" (Richards 1929, 17).

Richards's research into literary criticism is deservedly noted as the first and one of the most important studies of literary criticism in the modern era. What are we to make of it in the light of current literary theory and practice, especially the contributions by what we believe to be the two major theories of the twentieth century, New Criticism and Reader Response? What light does Richards's study and his conclusions shed on the state of literary criticism of his day, and what influences have his thoughts had upon criticism throughout the twentieth century?

First, his subjects form an especially privileged elite: They are young, white, upper-class or upper-middle-class, privately educated university students with formal training in English language and literature at Cambridge, one of the great universities of the world. Although Richards is surprised by their readings, we should not be, because we are now aware that people respond to literature according to their social and educational backgrounds. As Eagleton puts it, Richards's readers' responses "were deeply entwined with their broader prejudices and beliefs. This is not a matter of *blame:* there is no critical response which is not so entwined, and thus there is no such thing as a 'pure' literary critical judgment or interpretation" (Eagleton 1996, 13). More responsible for Richards's judgment of the readers' responses is Richards himself, the young male Cambridge don who was unable to recognize the beliefs of the readers, which he himself shared.

Furthermore, Richards also failed to recognize what we now accept as an axiom: that students interpret literature according to the methods used to teach them. In other words, how the readers in his study criticized the poems in the study was, for good or bad, a direct result of how they had been taught to criticize poetry.

Richards was also dismayed by the "astonishing variety of human responses" made by the readers in his study. It seems to us that his consternation implies that there were acceptable responses and that he, Richards, knew what they were. The idea of essential, inherently "correct" responses is one of the assumptions underlying New Criticism, and the idea that readers create their own personal responses to literary works—varied as the responses may be—is one of the assumptions of Reader Response theory.

It is important for us to note that Richards's approach to his research is based upon "psychological principles," that is, he wished his study to be rigorous, systematic, and (we may infer) scientific, an important element of New Criticism.

To us, the "difficulties" the readers had in criticizing poems add up to a series of methods for overcoming these difficulties as they interpreted the sample poems.

In summary, what implications does Richards's groundbreaking study, published in the first third of the twentieth century, have for us at the beginning of the twentieth-first century? What issues concerning literary criticism does he explicitly identify and what issues are suggested by his work?

First, we are forced to consider a basic epistemological question: What is the nature of meaning in literature? Do we "find" meaning in a literary text? In other words, is it there in the work, for us to find if only we use accepted critical techniques and search hard enough and long enough to discover the "correct" meaning?

Or is the meaning in a literary text a result of our "negotiating" or "transacting" with the text? Do we "create" meaning as we read and respond to the text as a result of our idiosyncratic, absolutely unique personalities? If a written text is in fact an inert bunch of meaningless symbols—think of a native speaker of English trying to make sense of the original Russian-language version of Fyodor Dostoevsky's *Crime and Punishment*—until a reader is able to understand the text and create a unique response to the piece, then this philosophical position may make some sense.

Next Richards raises the question of what, exactly, literary criticism is. How do we go beyond reading to how we criticize literature? Do we—or should we—use scientific techniques, arrived at from a discipline like psychology? Or do we read and respond to literature not as a self-contained, objective structure but as a special way of knowing, a text in which feelings, memories, associations, images, figurative language, and rhythm—as well as technical procedures—inform and contribute to our own personal responses?

If we review the "difficulties" Richards found in the criticisms made by the readers in his study, we can infer what Richards considered acceptable methods for criticizing poems. It also seems evident to us that it is these methods, the ones Richards would accept, that have, for the most part, been the methods of literary criticism for at least the first two-thirds of the twentieth century.

What would be Richards's acceptable method of literary criticism? First, critics state in plain, unadorned language the plain-sense meaning of a literary text. Then they pay attention to the technical aspects of the poem—such as rhythm and visual images—and relate them to the meaning of the poem. As they do this, they should not be distracted by such "mnemonic irrelevancies" as strong feelings, memories, and associations brought on by words, images, and situations in the poem. Critics should go beyond "Stock Responses"—which express the first things that come to mind while reading—to find the poem's deep, below-the-surface meaning. Critics may show some emotion, but not too much. And they should not bring their opinions or prior knowledge of criticism to the critical evaluation.

Finally, the results of Richards's study reveal an element of literary criticism that has persisted for most of the last century and that still persists today: Only a privileged class of students, rigorously trained, should read the standard works of the literary canon and should be taught the accepted principles of literary criticism. Since the study of literature had become academic, theoretical, and guided by rigorous scientific principles, then only students in literature courses read the standard literary texts and were trained in literary criticism. One of the authors of this book, because he was an English major, as an undergraduate read the standard texts in English, American, and European literature, but his classmates majoring in other disciplines, such as the hard sciences, economics, or history, had little or no training in reading literature. And when the author taught high school English, only the college preparatory students studied such standard literary texts as *Hamlet, Macbeth, The Scarlet Letter,* or *Huckleberry Finn.* The non-college-preparatory students read special "abridged" texts or "adolescent literature," especially aimed at them.

The other author of this book, a French major as a college undergraduate with a diploma from the Sorbonne in Paris, read such French literary texts as Victor Hugo's *Les Misérables,* Gustave Flaubert's *Madame Bovary,* and Honoré de Balzac's *Le Père Goriot,* using strenuous methods of "close reading" (a technique known in French as *explication de texte*). Her classmates in other disciplines had few or no courses in literature. One friend, a student in dentistry, asked her quite seriously, "Why does anyone need to read Shakespeare?" Another student in prelaw, again seriously, asked her, "Why does anyone need to take a class to read a novel?"

What are we to make of such distinctions concerning formal literature study? First, we believe the discrimination occurred primarily because academics co-opted literature as they made its study rigorous, scientific, and abstract. As we know, only a few people in any population are capable of abstract thinking, but all of us can respond to literature. And as we also know, the great folk myths, plays, and epics and the English mystery and miracle plays were popular with people from all classes of society, most of whom were nonliterate.

Shakespeare's plays stand as the perfect example of folk literature being taken over by the academics. We know that all kinds of people flocked to Shakespeare's histories, comedies, and tragedies—from nonliterate groundlings (people who stood on the ground in the theater) to well-educated nobles. Now, however, when we study a Shakespeare play in school, we study such matters as the time in which the play was written and the sources Shakespeare used as the bases for his plays, and we read the play word by word, line by line, scene by scene, and act by act, looking up the meaning of every archaic word in Shakespeare's vocabulary. But Shakespeare never meant his plays to be studied in classrooms by a small group of select readers. He meant them to be enjoyed by all persons, including those without special training in literary theory and analysis.

So what are we to make of all this? Finally, and very importantly, we may be moving from a time when only a privileged few—like those in I. A. Richards's study—are allowed to study literature to a time when we take literary study out of the grasp of the academics and give it back to all the people. In effect, Richards's study of *Practical Criticism* lays the foundation for a new way of "reading" literary texts. He may call the process "criticizing" or "interpreting" literature, but essentially he is addressing the age-old question of how we read this special way of knowing we call literature.

NEW CRITICISM: THEORY

From the nineteen-forties on, the Age of Criticism [a tag given by Randall Jarrell, a poet and critic of the time] had been especially fruitful, and had multiplied so many literary exegetes and ruminators that, with all their differences, they had come to constitute an establishment. They might call themselves Southern Agrarians, like Allen Tate and John Crowe Ransom, or neo-Thomists, like Eliseo Vivas, or formalists, like Cleanth Brooks—but, whatever the rubric and whatever the tendency, the mantle of New Criticism fell over all of them. Nowadays, the jingling mantra of their illustrious names is a faded archaism, together with their monastic tenets. The chief dogma of New Criticism, irresistible and indisputable, was *explication de texte*, or close reading, which meant the exclusion of all external interpretive biases: no politics, no past, no social forms, no ethics. Instead, the isolated purity of metaphor, image, "tension," irony—elements that were said to be objectively inherent in the work, which was looked on as a self-enclosed artifact. In the most up-to-date graduate schools of the time (I was fresh from one of these), all this was felt not as a literary movement but as a theology linked to eternity. It was with such a credo—New Criticism as sacrosanct truth—that I arrived at Trilling's [Lionel Trilling, whom Ozick calls the "greatest literary critic of the day"] office door. (Ozick 2000, 116)

In this quotation, the brilliant writer of fiction Cynthia Ozick gives us a richly written summary of what the philosophical position we call New Criticism means to her. Her quote addresses, in a spectacular fashion, the basic questions raised by New Criticism: What is literature? How do we read literature?

Although this quotation is an example of exposition rather than a piece of literature, we must read it carefully, paying strict attention to Ozick's precise use of words and the exact meanings we attach to them. Let us do a close reading of this passage.

First, although the New Critics had many differences, they came to "constitute an establishment." As the Cambridge don J. A. Cuddon wrote in his *Penguin Dictionary of Literary Terms and Literary Theory*, New Criticism was a "term which refers to a kind of 'movement' in literary criticism which developed in the 1920s (for the most part among Americans)" (Cuddon 1999, 544).

The main focus of New Criticism, remembered Ozick, was the idea of *explication de texte*, known popularly in U.S. criticism as close reading. This term is basic to the New Criticism, as well as to the reading of all dense, complex prose, so we explain it here. Close reading is a detailed analysis of a particular text. In a poem, this means a word-by-word, line-by-line, stanza-by-stanza inspection. In fiction, short fiction particularly, this means word-by-word, sentence-by-sentence, paragraph-by-paragraph analysis. After several readings, we relate all the discrete parts to each other and find a general pattern relating the parts to each other and to the overall piece as a whole. One author remembers reading Chaucer's *Canterbury Tales* in class at a major university in the early 1950s. The method was for the students to recite in turn, proceeding line by line through a tale, each giving translations of individual words. In another graduate class in American literature, the students—with questions and comments from the professor—explained each successive, numbered paragraph of Ralph Waldo Emerson's essays. In the purest and most pristine practice of close reading, we read literary works, especially short poems, by analyzing texts solely as texts, with no consideration of such "outside" elements as history, culture, ethics, or morality. Instead, we focus our attention, like lasers, on words and textual elements such as metaphor, image, irony, tension, and ambiguity.

After we have read Ozick's piece closely and noticed a pattern of words forming an overall theme, we are struck by the way the words all add up to an overall notion of New Criticism as a religious calling. We notice these words and the meanings we attach to them: "Exegetes" make critical analyses of texts, especially of the Scriptures. A "rubric" is a red title or direction in a liturgical book. A "mantra" is a sacred phrase used in prayer; it possesses magical power. A "monastic tenet" is a religious doctrine held by a monk, one who lives in contemplative seclusion. A "dogma" is a principle or belief considered to be an absolute truth. The literary text is a "self-enclosed artifact," an artifact being something man-made that is of historical interest. New Criticism, to Ozick, was not so much a literary movement as it was "a theology linked to eternity." The author's credo—the term is derived from *credo,* "I believe," the first word of the Apostle's Creed—was that New Criticism was "sacrosanct," a sacred and inviolable truth.

Generally, we might say that the Age of Criticism, especially as exemplified by New Criticism and as illustrated by I. A. Richards's 1929 study, *Practical Criticism,* flourished in the United States from the 1920s through the 1950s. However, it was not until 1941 that the movement earned its official title, with the publication of a book by the poet-critic John Crowe Ransom entitled, appropriately, *The New Criticism.* We now remember the book because it provided the name for one of the preeminent movements in literary criticism of the twentieth century, but the work is also instructive because it outlines typical methods of New Critical analysis and provides examples of New Criticism.

In the preface to *The New Criticism,* for instance, Ransom illustrates the New Critical methods of critic R. P. Blackmur. Here is Blackmur's New Critical analysis of an Emily Dickinson poem. We provide an extended sample of Blackmur's reading because it is a striking example of what came to be the New Criticism.

> Renunciation
> Is a piercing virtue,
> The letting go
> A presence for an expectation—
> Not now.

> The words are all simple words [writes Blackmur], parts of our stock vocabulary. Only one, *renunciation,* belongs to a special department of experience or contains in itself the focus of a particular attitude, a department and an attitude we condition ourselves to keep mostly in abeyance. We know what renunciation is; we know it turns up as heroism or hypocrisy or sentimentality; and we do as little as possible about it. Only one word, *piercing,* is directly physical; something that if it happens cannot be ignored but always shocks us into reaction. It is the shock of this word that transforms the phrase from a mere grammatical tautology into a metaphorical tautology which establishes as well as

asserts identity. Some function of the word *pierce* precipitates a living intrinsic relation between renunciation and virtue; it is what makes the phrase incandesce. (Quoted in Ransom 1941, viii, ix)

What strikes us most sharply in this quotation is the unnerving use of the word "incandesce." Most of us are familiar with the adjective "incandescent" as in "incandescent light," but we were surprised, even shocked, to find someone who applies the verb "incandesce" to the phrase "Is a piercing virtue," literally claiming that the phrase becomes white with heat, actually glows from its effect upon us, making our heart stop with surprise and shock. Here the critic finds the effect of words, not ideas, at the core of the phrase's existence. Perhaps it is here that we find an explanation of a phrase Ransom uses, "ontological critic." Ontology is the branch of philosophy that deals with the essence of existence, of "being," what we hear in Hamlet's soliloquy, "To be, or not to be." So the ontological critic may be one who finds the "being" of a poem in its special patterning of words. The primary method of New Criticism was to focus on words, what they mean by plain sense, what they mean in all their reverberations, and how they mean in particular orderings.

What else does Ransom say about New Criticism? He describes critical writing as that which has been "turned over a great many times" and which has provided "the light of the visual illumination." The writing itself is "close, and a little difficult." (The New Critic "has mastered" some or all the critical systems Ransom treats in the book.) Later, he argues that "criticism is an extraordinarily difficult thing to get right, and this [the sample analysis quoted] is a new criticism." The New Criticism, Ransom feels, should not be damaged by at least two "specific errors of theory, which are widespread. . . . One is the idea of using the psychological affective vocabulary" and the other is "plain moralism, which in the new criticism would indicate that it has not emancipated itself from the old criticism. I should like to see critics unburdened of these drags" (Ransom 1941, xi).

Ransom's most illuminating argument for a New Criticism is what he regards as

the most fundamental pattern of criticism: criticism of the structural properties of poetry. The sciences deal almost entirely with structures which are scientific structures; but poetic structures differ radically from these, and it is that difference which defines them. The ontological materials are different, and are such as to fall outside the possible range of science. (Ransom 1941, xi–xii)

Although the structure of a literary text is "radically" different from scientific structures, it is a structure nevertheless, one that has an observable existence, one that can be approached only by a strenuous, close reading.

Other critics of the time substantiated these positions. As we have observed, Richards found an expression of emotion one of the "difficulties" faced in correctly criticizing a literary text, and we discover that Ransom also believed that one of the "specific errors of theory" was to reveal emotion in criticism, to use a "psychological affective vocabulary." In one of the most widely quoted statements made by New Critics, W. K. Wimsatt Jr. and Monroe C. Beardsley (now known to all of us older critics affectionately as simply Wimsatt and Beardsley) in their book *The Verbal Icon*—which imprinted another phrase in the mind of would-be New Critics—proclaim the "Affective Fallacy" as a "feared obstacle to objective criticism" which leads "away from criticism and from poetry" (Wimsatt and Beardsley 1954, 21).

For Wimsatt and Beardsley, the Affective Fallacy is an egregious sin in literary criticism because it is "a confusion between the poem and its *results* (what it *is* and what it *does*), a special case of epistemological skepticism. . . . It begins by trying to derive the standard of criticism from the psychological effects of the poem and ends in impressionism and relativism. The outcome . . . is that *the poem itself* [italics ours] as an object of specifically critical judgment tends to disappear" (Wimsatt and Beardsley 1954, 21). Note that the phrase "the poem itself" implies that because of the intrusion of emotion in reading poetry the poem "disappears," another revered phrase in the New Critical mantra.

One more enduring pronouncement by Wimsatt and Beardsley relates to the second major obstacle to objective criticism, the "Intentional Fallacy." The authors argue "that the design or intention of the author is neither available nor desirable as a standard for judging the success of a work of literary art, and it seems to us that this is a principle which goes deep into the differences in the history of critical attitudes" (Wimsatt and Beardsley 1954, 3–4). The authors go on to explain why the Intentional Fallacy is indeed a misleading notion in reading poetry:

> The poem is not the critic's own and not the author's (it is detached
> from the author at birth and goes about the world beyond his power to
> intend about it or control it). The poem belongs to the public. It is
> embodied in language, the peculiar possession of the public knowl-
> edge. What is said about the poem is subject to the same scrutiny as

any statement in linguistics or in the general science of psychology. (Wimsatt and Beardsley 1954, 5)

And pointedly, the authors maintain in another of the lasting statements of New Criticism that

> "a poem should not mean but be." A poem can *be* only through its *meaning*—since its medium is words—yet it *is*, simply *is*, in the sense that we have no excuse for inquiring what part is intended or meant. . . . Poetry succeeds because all or most of what is said or implied is relevant; what is irrelevant is excluded. . . . In this respect poetry differs from practical messages which are successful if and only if we correctly infer the intention. They are more abstract than poetry. (Wimsatt and Beardsley 1954, 4, 5)

We can understand these authors' distaste for any reference in the reading of a poem to a writer's intended meaning when we understand that for them, the Intentional Fallacy is a romantic one. It is the idea in literary criticism, an idea that persisted for centuries, that a literary text was the result of the poet's genius and inspiration. If this view is valid, then to read a poem "correctly" we merely have to discover what the author intended the poem to mean.

And finally, in our hasty review of statements made by New Critics, we note the tendency by at least a few writers to advocate that we need to read poetry in a scientific way, that in fact, we need to use scientific methods to arrive at nonscientific, literary knowledge. Remember that in 1929, I. A. Richards touted his methods of literary criticism as being based upon the science of psychology. Almost a decade later, Ransom argued that although literature is of course generically different from scientific knowing, we should use rigorous, unemotional, "scientific-like" methods to read literature: "Criticism must become more scientific, or precise and systematic, and this means that it must be developed by the collective and sustained effort of learned persons—which means that its proper seat is in the universities" (Ransom 1941, 329).

Not only should we read literature by scientific methods, but (we must infer) because writing New Criticism is so difficult, its critical apparatus can be learned only through a long and arduous apprenticeship to critical masters; in all matters of reading literature, we must defer to the infallible, specially anointed university professors. We may ask, So what? What does it matter that only special university professors can tell us how to read a literary work? Or that only the professors—or their acolytes, including secondary school English teachers, who have been trained by professors in university English departments—can tell us what a literary piece means? The answer to such questions gets at the core of how one reads literature. If it is true that only specially trained professors and teachers can tell us the meaning of a literary text, then the best students can do when they read poems or stories is to find their inherently, objective "meanings," as announced by the professors and teachers.

What were the New Critics reacting to in their theoretical statements? It appears they were in opposition to the "old critics," whom they accused of being subjective, romantic, and impressionistic. For instance, two New Critics, Cleanth Brooks and Robert Penn Warren, in their enormously influential college textbook *Understanding Poetry,* identify "confused approaches to the study of poetry," "substitutes" for the poem itself (Brooks and Warren 1950, xi). It is their view that if a poem is worth teaching at all, then it is worth teaching as poetry; nevertheless, many teachers fell prey to the temptation to make substitutes for the poem the focus of study. There are many confusing replacements, but these are the most common: "1. Paraphrase of logical and narrative content; 2. Study of biographical and historical materials; 3. Inspirational and didactic interpretation" (Brooks and Warren 1950, xi).

To illustrate some of these confusing substitutes, the authors cite examples from popular textbooks of the time. They quote the solitary critical comment, for instance, on "Ode to a Nightingale" as follows: "The song of the nightingale brings sadness and exhilaration to the poet and makes him long to be lifted up and away from the limitations of life. The seventh stanza is particularly beautiful" (Brooks and Warren 1950, xi). In the same text, they find this question for the student: "What evidence of love of beauty do you find in Keats' poems?" (Brooks and Warren 1950, xii).

Here is another example of the old criticism that Brooks and Warren—as well as other New Critics—are reacting to. The author of the questionable text makes this critical comment about William Blake's poetry: "To the simplicity and exquisite melodiousness of these earliest songs, Blake added mysticism and the subtlest kind of symbolism" (Brooks and Warren 1950, xii). This approach to reading poetry, Brooks and Warren believe, "raises more problems than it solves" (xii). Such general pronouncements offer no understanding of Blake's poems. What is needed for mature reading of Blake's poems is a careful reading with specific examples from the poems to substantiate a position toward them. How can a poet add mysticism and "symbolism" to poetry, we must ask the textbook author. Does the poem itself illustrate the mystical attitude through the use of words to stand for intangible ideas?

In summary, here are some of the principles that most New Critical theorists agreed upon.

Principles of New Critical Theory

1. *Meaning lies within a literary text.* The New Critics assert that meaning resides within the text. We read literature as a quest for its inherently objective meaning. A literary work stands alone, inviolable, as an autonomous object, a "verbal icon," with an intrinsic meaning. A literary text is independent from the writer who created it and a reader who responds to it. The text belongs neither to the author nor to the reader.

2. *The reader finds the meaning of a text.* It follows thus that we read literature, not to *create* our own personal meaning but to *find* the meaning of a text.

3. *We read literature as literature, not as biography, history, or psychology.* When we read a literary text, we respond to it as literature. We are not reacting to a biography of the author or to a historical account of the time in which it was created. Biographical or historical concerns have no place in "objective criticism."

4. *The discrete elements of a literary text make up an organic whole.* We analyze the separate elements of a literary text not to destroy the text but in order to put them back together again to make an analysis of an essential whole. The most important aspect of a literary text is its "organic unity." Content and form are inseparable, constituting a complete work of art. We should not, however, study any aspects of a literary text, such as character, plot, symbolism, images, or figurative language, in isolation.

5. *We should not confuse the meaning of a text with either the author's intention or with our own emotional reaction to the text.* The two most telling mistakes we make in reading literary texts are these: We are guilty of the Intentional Fallacy when we try to figure out what the author meant by his work, and we are guilty of the Affective Fallacy when we mistake the feelings the text arouses in us for its meaning.

6. *We should read literary texts in a scientific manner.* As we read literary texts, we should struggle to become more professional, more scientific, rather than reading like the old critics, who were impressionistic, nonrigorous, unsystematic, and nonsci-

entific. Only by our scientific methods can we transform the study of literature into a legitimate academic discipline.

NEW CRITICISM: PRACTICE

We are acutely aware of how difficult it is to turn theory into practice. Persons who are able to construct abstract theoretical structures are usually unable to translate structures into methods other persons can use. And conversely, pedestrian teachers who are unable to convert theoretical assumptions into practical methods many times simply repeat theoretical statements in the classroom. As Richard Beach writes, "Simply 'applying' a theory often entails no more than a reification of the traditional knowledge-transmission model, in which the teacher draws on theory to impart knowledge. The theory does not itself provide the creation of classroom situations in which students may create their own knowledge through active sharing of ideas" (Beach 1993, 3–4).

Though translating legitimate theory into pragmatic classroom methods is a nearly insurmountable task, trying to determine how and when an intellectual movement began, how it was spread, and when it ended is even more difficult. Here we would like to discuss how the general principles of New Criticism affected actual classroom practices. We make these statements based upon our reading and study, our observations of numerous classes in literature, and our own experiences over decades of teaching literature.

Most authorities believe that New Critical methods dominated literary criticism roughly from the 1930s through the 1960s. It is our view, however, that the influence of New Critical theories on instruction in universities, colleges, and secondary schools has never really died out.

Richard Beach describes the situation like this: New Criticism continues to "influence undergraduate and high school literature instruction. Despite the dramatic shifts in interest in literary theory in the past thirty years, secondary and postsecondary literature teachers in general continue to employ methods reflecting New Critical orientation" (Beach 1993, 2).

In a recent study of secondary literature instruction, Arthur Applebee found that the New Critical methods English teachers used to teach literature in 1989 had changed little since he had made a survey of how secondary school teachers taught literature in the 1960s. He wrote, "Teachers continue to focus on 'close reading' of literary texts, on the assumption that such texts are automatically integrated into organic wholes" (quoted in Beach 1993, 2).

Why is this so? Beach examined high school literature textbooks and found that exercises were set up for students to "focus on how the specific aspects of texts—setting, character, plot, language, and theme—fit together to form a coherent whole. Such approaches are often assumed by their practitioners to be merely 'commonsense' . . . methods of literary study, and to be untouched by 'theory'" (Beach 1993, 2, 3).

It appears that the theoretical principles of New Criticism are so deeply embedded in teaching practice that professors and secondary school teachers simply accept the methods as the natural way to teach literature. We are often tempted to dismiss these methods as overly mechanistic and as removing the spontaneous emotional excitement from the reading of worthwhile texts, but many of the New Critical techniques of literary analysis—leading to an understanding of how a literary text "works" and of why we "like" a particular work—are valuable. Teachers keep these New Critical methods because, to a large extent, they make sense and they work.

What precisely are the New Critical methods that secondary and postsecondary literature teachers in general continue to employ? Here, in Beach's words, are the assumptions he observed high school teachers held about teaching literature:

> These ideas served as a set of unacknowledged assumptions guiding literature instruction since the 1940s. Teachers assumed that texts were central; that they were best regarded as well-wrought urns, artistic objects that were endlessly rich and self-consistent; that students should appreciate their complexity; and that therefore the teacher's job was to teach the skills of close, concise, attentive analysis. Encouraging expression of and attending to differences in students' own response was considered less important. (Beach 1993, 15–16)

To us, these beliefs sound like unquestioning acceptance, whether or not consciously realized, of faith in New Critical tenets as a foundation for teaching literature. But we may wonder how such convictions led to classroom practices. Here, for instance, are some examples of teacher-made classroom activities and exams duplicated for a class of ninth-grade literature students from a suburban high school. These excerpts from homework assignments and a quiz are typical of how teachers taught under the unconscious worldview attributed to New Critical theory.

On a handout labeled "Reading Comprehension" for a ninth-grade unit on the "Short Story," for example, the teacher offers exercises like these:

"The Most Dangerous Game" by Richard Connell.

   A. Literal Comprehension

   1. As the story opens, Rainsford is on his way to hunt: a. tigers b. jaguars c. moose d. bear. . . .

   B. Inferential Comprehension

   5. All of the following could be logically concluded at the end of the story EXCEPT: a. Rainsford has gained valuable knowledge about the psychology of a hunted animal. b. Rainsford will take Zaroff's place on the island. c. Rainsford will never hunt again. d. Zaroff commits suicide.

And here are some short-answer questions from a quiz on Shirley Jackson's short story "The Lottery." Note that students are required to provide short-answer responses, not sentences, to the questions; the answers must fit within the brief blank spaces provided. There is no opportunity for students to make any sort of extended written interpretation.

   English 9 "The Lottery" Quiz

     1. In what month is the lottery always held?

     2. What does Mr. Summer use to hold the slips of paper? . . .

     9. Why is the ending of the story such a surprise to the reader?

And finally, here are some true/false items from a quiz on Edgar Allan Poe's "The Cask of Amontillado."

   TRUE OR FALSE

     8. Montresor feels no guilt for his crime.

     9. An example of irony is when Fortunado cries out, "For the love of God."

     10. Poe's expert descriptive abilities emerge when he describes the catacombs and the carnival.

Our first reaction to such study guides and quizzes is that although the questions may appear to the teacher who created them to require "close reading" techniques of items appropriate for literary analysis, in actuality they relate only to a low-level and superficial understanding of the short stories in question.

How well do such short-answer exercises and quizzes work? Do they help students understand literary texts? In our experience, not very well. Consider, for example, one soundly devised and carefully conducted study dealing with how three various writing activities (restricted writing, personal analytic writing, and formal analytic writing) affected, among other things, eleventh-grade American literature students' understanding of three short stories by J. D. Salinger, "The Laughing Man," "Just before the War with the Eskimos," and "Pretty Mouth and Green My Eyes" (Marshall 1987). At least from the evidence of this study, short-answer activities and quizzes are far less successful in helping students to understand worthwhile but potentially ambiguous stories than are extended essay assignments. Marshall found that

> the form of school writing that proved most limited in its effects on these students' understanding of literature was short answer questions. Though widely used in classrooms and textbooks such assignments were associated with lower posttest scores when compared to extended writing, and in some cases, when compared to no writing at all. . . . these tasks [short-answer questions] did not allow the students to elaborate upon their analyses by embedding them within the context of the story. (Marshall 1987, 59)

Short-answer questions simply prevented upper-level high school students from explaining in any detailed way why they wrote the short answers they did. But even more restricting, short-answer questions prevented the students from crafting coherent, fully articulated interpretations of the story. Marshall continues,

> Moreover, the examination of the writing protocols suggests that when the students completed short answer questions, they shifted rapidly from one area of focus to another, from one operation to another, as they responded to different questions. The short answer questions, by discouraging the students' construction of a coherent and elaborate representation of the story, may have interfered with their developed sense of the story's meaning. (Marshall 1987, 59)

And finally, Alan Purves, one of the most knowledgeable and respected authorities on teaching literature, reported that "secondary school students whom I have studied over the past years report that they perceive school literature study as comprising the reading of literary texts in order to take tests on them." Furthermore, he noted, the literature tests that serve as the focus of instruction are trivial, and like the examples given above, they test low-level knowledge in the guise of "understanding": "The tests the students report taking and that I have studied are frequently atrocious, calling for low-level recall of details and the derivation of a summary or set theme—what is called 'comprehension.'" In an indecorous answer to a question of how they viewed their literature tests, some students called them "plot vomit" (Purves 1993, 352, 353).

To recapitulate, from our observations and from reports of several studies on teaching literature in secondary schools, teachers generally applied the principles of New Criticism they had been taught in a way that trivialized the principles.

This is not to say that what the New Critics set out to accomplish was not admirable and that what they believed did not, in fact, radically change how literature was taught in colleges and schools. The New Critics desired fervently, almost messianically, to change literary criticism from an impressionistic, subjective, and inexact practice of reading literature into a precise, predictive science with newly developed tools and methods, a complete critical apparatus. These New Critics were committed to the idea that systematic thought and rigorous analysis were the keys to the most complex problems in literary interpretation. If only we looked at a literary text long enough—read it, reread it, studied it, analyzed it, and made generalizations about it—we should find the objective, inherent meaning of a poem, story, novel, or play. What the New Critics most wished to do was to make literary criticism a legitimate academic discipline, and to this aim, they instructed their students in this new undertaking.

For us, the textbook that had the most influence on generations of college and university professors and ultimately on the secondary school teachers they prepared was *Understanding Poetry* by Cleanth Brooks and Robert Penn Warren (hereafter called simply Brooks and Warren), first published in 1938 and revised for a 1950 edition.

So how do we actually teach poetry—and by extension all literature—by the New Critical methods? For Brooks and Warren, the answer is simple, but to our way of thinking, simple but not easy. Here is their unassuming but profound statement, which appeared in the 1938 textbook and in the revised 1950 complete edition on how to teach literature according to New Critical principles:

> The editors of the present book hold that a satisfactory method of teaching poetry should embody the following principles.
>
> 1. Emphasis should be kept on the poem as a poem.
> 2. The treatment should be concrete and inductive.
> 3. A poem should always be treated as an organic system of relationships, and the poetic quality should never be understood as inhering in one or more factors taken in isolation. (Brooks and Warren 1938, xv)

So that is it. But how do we translate these bald statements into practical teaching methods? To us, this means our primary aim is to study individual poems by close, systematic examination. It means that in order for students to acquire gradually the critical methods, we teach poetic analysis by studying poems in order from the simplest to the most complex and most profound. And it means that ultimately by studying poems on an "ascending scale" and by being provided with more and more sophisticated analytical methods—with an entire critical apparatus—we become expert New Critics.

It is not a trivial matter to study poems that represent texts of ascending complexity and profundity. Rather than arranging poems to be studied in thematic groups like "families," "nature," and "love," we read poems to serve as models for teaching analytical principles. Here, in their table of contents, is the progression Brooks and Warren stipulate for teaching students to become competent critics. Note that they have students move from most accessible to most complex poems:

Contents
    Section I—Narrative Poems
    Section II—Descriptive Poems
    Section III—Metrics
    Section IV—Tone and Attitude
    Section V—Imagery
    Section VI—Statement and Idea
    Section VII—Poems for Study: New and Old
    Section VIII—Ambiguity, Added Dimension, and Submerged
Metaphor
    Section IX—How Poems Come About: Intention and Meaning
    Section X—The Poem Viewed in Wider Perspective. (Brooks and Warren 1950, xxviii–xxxii)

Although the critical methods used are chiefly analysis and interpretation, the primary aim is not to train technical critics, Brooks and Warren caution us, but rather to prepare competent readers of poetry. But for readers to appreciate poetry, they must go beyond the initial stage of simple passive enjoyment.

Brooks and Warren's original 1938 textbook for teaching students how to criticize poetry according to New Critical methods was used by legions of instructors. As the authors themselves note in the postscript to the 1950 second edition (added to the "Letter to the Teacher" of the first edition), the text was written to bring "something of the critical attitude, even at a very simple level, into the classroom," and it was apparent to them that "today the critical attitude has entered into hundreds of classrooms" (Brooks and Warren 1950, xxi).

The postscript was written in response to criticisms by instructors across the nation who had used the book. However, as the authors answered their critics, they emphasized in the clearest and plainest language possible that they had not budged one iota from their original stance: "We must confess that our fundamental approach to poetry remains the same. We still believe that poetry is worth serious study as poetry" (Brooks and Warren 1950, xx, xxi).

In what ways did they revise their thinking about criticizing poetry?

First, although some scholars had interpreted their remarks about studying the "poem itself" as meaning that the poem should be looked at without considering the historical background of the poem or biographical information about the poet relevant to a rich, full understanding of the poem, the authors now acknowledged that even though there should still be a "sharp focus" on the poem itself, they now viewed the poem in relationship to its historical situation and to the body of the poet's work. But such information, they cautioned, must at all times be related to the total poetic meaning.

A second criticism of Brooks and Warren's text was a common complaint made by students and teachers alike: "Aren't you just reading your own ideas into the poem?" they ask plaintively. "The poet couldn't have meant all that you've found in the poem." In answer to this criticism, the authors contended that both students and teachers (who should know better) may be confusing the idea that we need to find out what the author intended the meaning of the poem to be—the "authorial intent"—with what actually happens during the creative writing process. Many writers attest to the fact that as they create in writing, themes, ideas, and meanings simply emerge, frequently unconsciously. In other words, a finished literary text is often not at all what its author originally "intended," and it is up to readers to find not the author's intention but a meaning of their own. For instance, the Italian novelist Umberto Eco, the author of *The Name of the Rose,* explains the creative process like this: "And I would define the poetic effect as the capacity that a text displays for continuing to generate different readings, without ever being completely consumed." Eco even goes so far as to argue that "nothing is of greater consolation to the author of a novel than the discovery of readings he had not conceived but which are then prompted by his readers" (Eco 1994, 506). The intent of the author should be of no concern to the reader.

A third criticism is this cry of pain: "But if we pick the poem apart the way you want us to, we kill it!" Readers moan that if they analyze a poem closely and systematically, they destroy a beautiful thing. It is murder by dissection. We call this the "untouchable flower" syndrome. How do Brooks and Warren answer this complaint? They acknowledge that the criticism is a valid one, that it is natural to want to enjoy a literary text, but they believe we cannot appreciate a poem "until we have worked a little at [it]. Immediacy and innocence must sometimes be earned" (Brooks and Warren 1950, xxiii). Frequently, we need to understand how all the poem's elements work together before we can appreciate it on more than a superficial level.

And here the authors make a prescient observation: We must be moved intuitively by a poem before we can tell why we enjoy it and are moved by it. (One writer calls it being "possessed" by a poem.) "This is not to deny," they argue, "that the intuitive grasp may precede exegesis" (Brooks and Warren 1950, xxiii). Why is this observation so crucial to a new way of reading poetry? Remember that the authors stated in 1938 that their method must be "inductive," a term commonly associated with the scientific method, in which we gather a great deal of concrete evidence before we come up with a general statement describing a pattern emerging from a body of data—in this case with poetry. To us, the inductive method applied to reading poetry meant we had to move through a poem word by word, line by line, and stanza by stanza before we could discern the inherent, objective meaning of the poem. The authors have now revised their original notion and hold that we initially and intuitively—at a first reading and without any rational analysis—"grasp" the meaning of a poem before we analyze it, not the other way around. Such a distinction, especially in later Reader Response theory, is a radically new idea. Instead of finding meaning in poetry by a scientific process—which New Criticism implies—we may indeed create our own personal meaning for a poem through an initial, intuitive grasp of its meaning. Such an idea, however, was way ahead of its time—especially in the era of New Criticism—and it would take decades before many understood and grasped it.

Even though we may apprehend a poem intuitively, the authors continued, we still need to "grow up to the level of a poem" (Brooks and Warren 1950, xxiii) before we can experience this initial surprise of understanding, and criticism—New Criticism, we may assume—makes this experience possible.

But, they continued, we can never be completely sure that we have grown up to rich works like the *Iliad, Hamlet,* or William Butler Yeats's "Slouching toward Bethlehem." And this belief is another step in the transformation from the New Critical belief that individuals find a single, objective, inherent meaning in a literary text to a new belief that individuals may and indeed do grow up to rich poems by creating their own highly personal readings of literary texts. If we believe there is an official meaning for a literary text, then we—and our teachers—are in grievous error, we "falsify the whole matter" (Brooks and Warren 1950, xxiii). But does this idea make interpreting poetry—or any other worthwhile literary text—a simpler and easier process? Not at all; if anything, it is probably made more difficult by requiring more careful analysis and enlightened perception after the initial, intuitive "possession." But we let Brooks and Warren speak for themselves:

> The good reader of poetry knows that there are no "official readings."
> He knows that there is only a continuing and ever-renewing transaction
> between him and the poem, a perpetual dialectic. For this reason the
> process of criticism is a never-ending process. It cannot exhaust the
> good poem or the good poet. This means more criticism, not less. But it
> ought to mean a criticism constantly returning to the object and con-
> stantly refining itself by fresh appeals to intuition and perception.
> (Brooks and Warren 1950, xxiii)

Here we have two wise men—one a critic, the other a critic, poet, and novelist, both university professors—who, on the basis of their continued experience in teaching privileged young men how to "criticize" literature, revised their original, rather restrictive views regarding a New Criticism and modified their original theories as a result of continued practice in university classrooms.

The fourth criticism of the first edition goes something like this: "Your approach is too objective, too detailed, and even too stuffy. It doesn't deal with really important things in life like beauty and right and wrong." We all know only too well that New Criticism in the hands of unimaginative teachers can be all these things. The authors' reply that good poetry always, directly or indirectly, makes a comment on human conduct and human values and that since poetry evidently fulfills some basic human need, which cannot be fulfilled in any other way, the study of poetry is self-validating. But—and here they return to their overarching notion of "the poem itself"—until we read the poem as a poem, we cannot apprehend the values inherent in the poem.

Furthermore, the moral essence of a poem's meaning is embodied within its technical structure. In fact, the "meaning" of a poem is profoundly a part of the shape of the poem. In other words, the meaning of a good poem is represented in physical form within the structure of the poem—its rhythm, rhymes, and stanzas. Elinor Wylie's poem "Sea Lullaby" comes to mind: It is a simple poem written in a regular rhyme scheme and in a lullaby-like rhythm. Its structure contrasts with the plain-sense meaning of the poem, which deals with a personified Sea who has drowned an innocent little boy and now lingers beside him all night as if singing a lullaby to the lifeless body.

The idea that the form of a poem, of a well-made story, novel, or play—as well as of good paintings, musical pieces, and buildings—is a certain "morality" proves to be a troubling concept for beginning students of literature to comprehend. But here the authors make the most profound epistemological pronouncement: that we cannot separate the form of a worthwhile literary text from its "attitude" or "idea." Brooks and Warren write,

> The meaning of the poem is finally, in the kind of being the poem has and not in any particular statement (taken abstractly) that it may make. This is not to say that statements or ideas are not important in poetry. They are tremendously important; but they are important as elements entering into the total structure which is the poem and into the total experience of the poem. (Brooks and Warren 1950, xxv)

It seems to us that in their "Letter to the Teacher" (1938) and in the 1950 postscript, these two discerning men ask the most basic questions about how we read literature, a type of reading much different from our reading of expository prose:

- What is a good poem? Good literature?
- What is a good poet?
- Who is a good critic?
- How do we grow up to reading good literature?
- What is the proper relationship between a good poem and a good reader?
- Why do we have literary criticism?
- What part do reason and rational analysis play in criticism?
- What part does intuition play in criticism?

SUMMARY

The theory of New Criticism was articulated as a reaction to the subjective, impressionistic, nonrigorous interpretations of literature, now known as "Old Criticism." Probably the single most influential textbook applying New Critical theories in schools, colleges, and universities was Cleanth Brooks and Robert Penn Warren's *Understanding Poetry*, first published in 1938. This book's influence, spread by English teachers who had been taught in their college and university classrooms by New Critical methods, was so pervasive that schoolteachers came to take the approach for granted, frequently accepting it as the only way to "criticize" literature, the method so obvious that it came to be thought of as the commonsensical approach. If they accepted one aspect of New Criticism over all others, school teachers emphasized the principle of close reading, although such a practice could be translated into study guides of low-level questions and tests of true-false, short-answer, and multiple-choice questions. Recent research has shown that extended written responses to literary texts help students understand and interpret literary texts better than do short-answer questions, but how can we expect secondary school English teachers to require all of their sometimes as many as 130 to 140 students to respond in written essays at least once a week to literary texts?

From the 1930s to the 1960s, teachers and professors of literature generally followed New Critical methods. In fact, for the most part, New Critical principles still survive in schools and colleges. It is only in the major university centers that formal discussions rage over such new theories of literature as structuralism, semiotics, deconstructionism, Freudianism, Marxism, feminism, postmodernism, and neocolonialism. Such debates, however, appear to have little influence on secondary school and most college classrooms.

In any event, here we list what we believe are the most commonly agreed upon practices—based upon principles of New Critical theory—that are still widely used in classrooms.

How We Read Literature Using Principles of New Criticism

1. *Emphasis on the text as a text.* We focus primarily on the poem as a poem, the story as a story, the novel as a novel, or the play as a play, not on historical and background information.
2. *Close reading of the text.* We use close reading techniques. With poetry, we read from beginning to end, word by word, line by line, and stanza by stanza, noting literary meanings (denotation) and emotional reverberations (connotation), rhyme schemes, meter, and other technical aspects such as tension, ambiguity, irony, and paradox. As we note the discrete elements of a poem, we keep our eyes peeled for repetitions, parallelism, patterns, and other factors such as foreshadowing.

Fundamentally, we ask ourselves, "What is going on here? How is the poet doing it?"

3. *Using systematic, rational, objective—scientific—strategies.* As we read closely, we are detached, nonemotional, and objective in our search for meaning. We do not allow our feelings to intrude on our close reading.

4. *Finding the meaning in the text.* Through close reading, we search for and (if we are successful) find the objective, inherent meaning in the text. We read and reread the text several times, "working at" our close reading. And if we look long enough and intensely enough—following accepted methods and using the right critical apparatus—we discover the intrinsic significance of the text.

5. *Treating the elements of a text as an organic whole.* Once we have taken the text apart—"dissected" it, as some critics maintain—we put it back together. We now treat the components— words, diction, images, rhythm, rhyme scheme, stanzaic form—as parts of an organic whole. Meaning then unfolds as much from the technical elements of the poem as from any implied or abstract statements. "The poem should not mean / but be" (MacLeish 1952, "Ars Poetica").

REFERENCES

Beach, Richard. 1993. *A Teacher's Introduction to Reader-Response Theories.* Urbana, IL: National Council of Teachers of English.

Brooks, Cleanth, and Robert Penn Warren. 1950. *Understanding Poetry. An Anthology for Students.* 2nd, rev. ed. New York: Henry Holt and Company.

Coles, Robert. 1989. *The Call of Stories. Teaching and the Moral Imagination.* Boston: Houghton Mifflin Company.

Cuddon, J. A. 1999. *The Penguin Dictionary of Literary Terms and Literary Theory.* Revised by C. E. Preston. New York: Penguin Books, Penguin Putnam.

Eagleton, Terry. 1996. *Literary Theory: An Introduction.* 2nd ed. Minneapolis: University of Minnesota Press.

Eco, Umberto. 1994. "The Author's Postscript." In *The Name of the Rose.* San Diego, CA: Harcourt Brace.

MacLeish, Archibald. 1952. *Collected Poems, 1917–1952.* Boston: Houghton Mifflin Company.

Marshall, James. 1987. "The Effects of Students' Understanding of Literary Texts." *Research in the Teaching of English* 21, no. 1 (February): 30–63.

Ozick, Cynthia. 2000. "The Buried Life." *The New Yorker,* October 2, 116–127.

Purves, Alan C. 1993. "Toward a Reevaluation of Reader Response and School Literature." *Language Arts* 70 (September): 348–361.

Ransom, John Crowe. 1941. *The New Criticism.* Norfolk, CT: New Directions.

Richards, I. A. 1929. *Practical Criticism: A Study of Literary Judgment.* New York: Harcourt Brace.

Rosenblatt, Louise M. 1978. *The Reader, the Text, the Poem: The Transactional Theory of the Literary Work.* Carbondale: Southern Illinois University Press.

Squire, James. 1994. "Research in Reader Response: Naturally Interdisciplinary." In *Theoretical Models and Processes in Reading,* ed. Robert S. Ruddell, Martha Rapp Ruddell, and Harry Singer, 4th ed. Newark, DE: International Reading Association.

Wimsatt, W. K. Jr., and Monroe C. Beardsley. 1954. *The Verbal Icon: Studies in the Meaning of Poetry.* Lexington: University of Kentucky Press.

Wylie, Elinor. 1921. "Sea Lullaby." In *Collected Poems of Elinor Wylie.* New York: Alfred A. Knopf.

Chapter Eight

⊶ Reading Literature: Reader Response— Theory to Practice

Fundamentally, a text, whatever it be (poem, short story, essay, scientific exposition), has no real existence until it is read. Its meaning is in potentia, so to speak. A reader completes its meaning by reading it. The reading is complementary; it actualizes potential meaning. Thus, the reader does not have, as has been traditionally thought and accepted, a passive role; on the contrary, the reader is an active agent in the creation of meaning. By applying codes and strategies the reader decodes the text.

—*J. A. Cuddon,* The Penguin Dictionary of Literary Terms and Literary Theory

Here we have a "definition" of the theory of reading literary texts called Reader Response, and in this quotation several salient ideas are presented about a very complex matter, including one problem that has beguiled philosophers for centuries: the nature of meaning. Where do we find meaning? Where is meaning in a literary text? Is it in the text itself? Or is it in a reader's mind as he or she reads the text? If, indeed, the meaning of a text lies within the mind of the reader, then what is this reader like? What does the reader bring to the text? What moves does he or she make in reading the work? And to complicate the matter further, are there different kinds of texts that must be read differently by the same reader?

Although it is beyond the scope of this book for us to explore the issue, we need to note that the Oxford-educated author of this quotation includes in his definition of Reader Response all kinds of writing—not just literary writing but also nonliterary essays and scientific exposition—in which the reader plays an active role in *creating* meaning. We have learned that the proponents of objective science—who believe adamantly that one *finds* objective meaning in scientific texts—consider such a thought appalling.

No matter which position is "right"—whether we find or create meaning—we are still left with the ancient questions of what meaning is and where we find it in a literary text. These problems remind us of the hoary question raised in our college course "Introductory Philosophy 101": "If a tree falls in the forest and no one hears it, does it make a sound?" If a poem or story is not read, does it have any meaning? (By the way, which position do you take with regard to the falling tree—or the meaning of a story?)

These are the questions—along with several others—we shall be dealing with in this chapter. We shall present a short and necessarily oversimplified summary of the various positions taken by notable Reader Response theorists and describe some ways gifted teachers have translated the theories into practical classroom methods.

We need to recall just how difficult it is to read abstract statements—a kind of reading very different from reading most literature—and to pull together sometimes conflicting ideas into an intelligible pattern. Another formidable task is summarizing how the elements of such theories translate into practice, in this case, how teachers make use of Reader Response theory in literature classrooms.

For us, the ideas from Reader Response theory that are used in classrooms are few but powerful. First is the thought that feelings are not only allowed but are a crucial part of reading literature. For decades, we have been taught that reading literature, at least in schools, is a serious, no-nonsense, even "glum" business. Personal emotions are simply not part of formal criticism.

The second is the idea, now accepted by some, not only that feelings are a good thing in reading literature but that emotions actually precede analysis of a literary text and should be an integral part of interpretation. In our hearts, we have always known that worthwhile literary texts have the power to arouse within us a sensory revelation, but we had been taught to tamp down this excitement. All of us have memories of being awe-struck after reading a story, poem, or novel or of having experienced an especially affecting movie, play, or even TV show. We remember the strong feelings we had after reading John Steinbeck's *The Grapes of Wrath,* our tears at the final curtain of Arthur Miller's *Death of a Salesman,* and our wonder and disbelief after the final page of Toni Morrison's *Beloved.* Only after we had recovered from our initial impressions could we analyze how the texts aroused these strong emotional responses.

Third, and this was possibly the most illuminating recognition of all, Reader Response theory moved the focus of reading literature from the text to the reader. It seems to us that if this is the right center of interest—and we think it is—then the reader is freed from the thrall of the all-knowing, high-priest professor or teacher of literature and becomes his or her own interpreter, what we call a "courageous reader." The reader no longer has to look to the teacher to find out whether or not he or she has the "correct" meaning of a poem or story. If you do not believe that most students have little confidence in their ability to arrive at the meaning of a literary text independently, simply ask students in any literature class what a particular poem or story means, and watch as they look uncomfortably around at the other kids and wait for you to tell them what the meaning is.

READER RESPONSE: THEORY

How did the Reader Response movement come about, and how did it develop? What were its main ideas, those that most Reader Response theorists would agree upon?

Primarily, the Reader Response theorists switched the emphasis of their study from the text—which the New Critics had insisted was the point of literary criticism—to the reader. They disputed the text-oriented theories of New Critics, which, they believed, failed to account for the reader's role in criticizing literary texts. Although Reader Response criticism was not and still is not a unified position, the "term has come to be associated with the work of critics who use the words *reader*, the *reading process*, and *response* to mark out an area" (Tompkins 1980, ix). Although such a definition is much too wide in scope, it will have to serve our purposes.

For Jane Tompkins, the Reader Response movement was in "direct opposition" to Wimsatt and Beardsley's New Critical objection to the Affective Fallacy (Tompkins 1980, ix). As we remember from the discussion in chapter 7, Wimsatt and Beardsley identified the Affective Fallacy as interpreting a poem on the basis of how we "feel" about it; in doing so, we confuse emotion with objective criticism. If we base our interpretation of a poem on our feelings, then our criticism ends "in impressionism and relativism" (Wimsatt and Beardsley 1954, 21). Horrors! Showing any emotion as we read a literary text!

Of course, there is more to New Criticism than a distaste for feelings, but the position certainly reflects a major tenet. The New Critics were understandably determined to rid criticism of mere unsubstantiated "aesthetic impressions" and to make it into a respectable systematic and scientific discipline.

So where do we start with our search for the roots of the Reader Response movement? James Squire identifies the beginning of the movement with I. A. Richards's *Practical Criticism* (1929), stating that "Richards' work is generally regarded as the first study of reader response" (Squire 1994, 637). That may very well be, but for us, Richards's study represents Reader Response only because Richards, rather than spinning a theory in his university office, actually analyzed the written responses of readers—male Cambridge University students and other adults—to poems. As we know from our previous discussion (in chapter 7), as Richards analyzed his students' written "criticism," he was struck by their "misreadings" of poems (some canonical poets were slighted, whereas mediocre ones were frequently praised), and he listed ten "difficulties" the students had with their criticisms (see chapter 7). Furthermore, he aimed at using scientific principles from the discipline of psychology to create a systematic, rational plan for criticizing literature. Such a position sounds rather far removed from a Reader Response; it sounds, in fact, more like a forerunner of New Criticism.

We prefer to turn to the work of Louise M. Rosenblatt as the forerunner of Reader Response theory. Her first book, *Literature as Exploration*, originally published in 1938 and reissued in 1968, was the result of her interactions with philosophers, psychologists, and anthropologists of the day and was based upon her fertile experiences teaching literary criticism to university students, dealing with how students actually respond to literary texts. What seems significant to us is that here she first articulates the idea of reading literature as a dynamic "transaction" between reader and literary text. Her aim, stated in the preface to the first edition, is to show that reading literature affects the well-being not only of students but of the society as a whole. For her, the "study of literature can have a very real, and even central, relationship to points of growth in the social and cultural life of a democracy" (Rosenblatt 1938, ix).

First of all, she chose the word "exploration" for her title rather than "discovery," for she recognized that the "word *exploration* is designed to suggest primarily that the experience of literature, far from being for the reader a passive process of absorption, is a form of intense personal activity" (Rosenblatt 1938, x). Later in the book, she first articulates the famous phrase, her deservedly celebrated epithet, "literature as transaction."

In chapter 2 of this work, entitled "The Literary Experience," she states that "the teacher's task is to foster fruitful interactions—or, more precisely, transactions—between individual readers and individual literary works" (Rosenblatt 1938, 26–27). She continues with her understanding of what happens as we read literary texts: "But no one can read a poem for us. The reader of the poem must have the experience himself" (Rosenblatt 1938, 33). And here we have one of her basic theoretical positions: "Sound literary insight and esthetic judgment will never be taught by imposing from above notions of what works should ideally mean. . . . The reader, too, [like the author] is creative. . . . the literary experience must be phrased as a *transaction* between the reader and the text" (Rosenblatt 1938, 33–35). With such statements, this wise teacher and writer foresees a future of reading literature in which we do not "criticize" or "evaluate" literary texts but, rather, read literary works by entering into "transactions" with them.

Besides stating her claim that reading literary texts should be seen as a transaction, in this 1938 text she also asks virtually all the big questions we have been wrestling with since then.

- As teachers, how do we foster literary "transactions"?
- How do we teach students to develop sensitivity to the way the elements of a literary text relate to an "organic whole"?
- What adolescent needs and interests should we be aware of?
- How does reading literature help us understand ourselves?
- How does reading literature help us understand our society within a broad context of feelings and ideas?
- Does close reading lead to an impersonal attitude toward literature?
- How can we teach students to read literature of higher and higher quality?
- Should reading literature help students learn to question traditional values and ethics?

Now we turn to a consideration of Rosenblatt's 1978 work, *The Reader, the Text, the Poem,* which is tellingly subtitled *The Transactional Theory of the Literary Work.* Why do we examine in some detail what Rosenblatt says in this book? First, although the book is highly theoretical and learned, since its publication it has become one of the most influential books in the field, particularly with its insistence on three simple ideas: first, that reading literature is a "transaction" between reader and text; second, that there are two ways of reading texts, one an "aesthetic" reading, in which the aim is to live through an emotional experience, and the other an "efferent" reading, in which the aim is to "take away" factual information; and third, that in order to study the process of reading literature, we should ask students to relate what they did as they worked their way through a literary text. For one such study, she asked her university students to read a poem, Robert Frost's quatrain, "It Bids Pretty Fair" (the students were given the poem without the author's name so that they wouldn't be influenced by his reputation). Unlike in Richards's study, rather than having the readers respond in writing outside of class after as many readings as they felt they needed, she had them write their immediate reactions to the poem as soon as they started reading. She told them not to "introspect" but just to jot down their immediate ideas and feelings. Rather than theorizing about how one "should" ideally read a poem, Rosenblatt built her theory upon what students did as they read poems.

As a result of her experience in teaching graduate university students and of her wide reading and association with the top thinkers of the day, Rosenblatt asked and answered three major questions about reading literary texts:

1. *Why is it important to focus on the reader as he or she reads a literary text?*

   Historically, as Rosenblatt reminds us, we paid attention to the author or to the text by itself, but recently the spotlight has been turned on the reader. But even as we shift our attention to the reader, we must not allow ourselves to move to the most remote limits of criticism, such as the extreme subjectivism of Freudianism, or the idea that the reader's mind is a tabula rasa—a clean slate, devoid of all experiences—on which the reading of the text leaves its imprint, or the notion that the literary text is something like an empty vessel, awaiting the content of the poem, to be added by the reader. Rosenblatt rejects all extremes of literary theory and insists that any discussion needs to begin with actual readers "encountering" a text and an analysis of what moves they make as they read a text.

2. *How does reading a literary text differ from reading a nonliterary text? Are there in fact two major kinds of knowing and thus two different ways of reading? And it follows, if literary knowing is different from nonliterary knowing, what are the characteristics of literary reading?*

   How does Rosenblatt approach the age-old philosophical and linguistic question of knowing? First, she considers the stance readers assume as they meet a text. "What kind of reading do I have here?" experienced readers ask themselves. Readers must first look closely at the words they encounter. In nonaesthetic reading, the words are chiefly related to their explicit meanings; the language is impersonal, with the words chiefly conveying unambiguous, literal meanings; and there is an almost total lack of personal references. If Rosenblatt were to place nonaesthetic reading on a continuum, then it would properly be at the midpoint between mainly aesthetic and mainly nonaesthetic.

Rosenblatt recognizes, however, that many texts contain examples of both aesthetic and nonaesthetic writing. The necessary introductory exposition in plays may be nonaesthetic, and much fiction includes both types of language. The lumbering novel *Moby Dick,* for instance, contains not only aesthetic storytelling but also long stretches of nonaesthetic information about whaling, but we realize the informative writing is absolutely necessary for the reader's understanding of the pell-mell aesthetic narrative later in the work. As we have already mentioned, Rosenblatt labels these kinds of knowing the aesthetic and the efferent.

To complicate further this matter of two kinds of reading, Rosenblatt points out that there are not only two kinds of texts but also different stances toward different texts, stances determined by age, gender, race, education, experience, and social, cultural, and religious backgrounds and at the same time by the matter of the same reader reading differently under different circumstances. For instance, in his recent review of Ronald C. White's *Lincoln's Greatest Speech,* about Lincoln's Second Inaugural Address, Max Byrd notes White's descriptions of the different ways various persons have perceived the speech. As might be expected, the poet Carl Sandburg described Lincoln's Second Inaugural as "the great American poem," but Byrd, a minister, remarks, "Yet, as must have been evident almost at once to the president's audience, it was not a poem but a sermon." Furthermore, when, at a White House reception, Lincoln asked former slave Frederick Douglass, who had been sitting in the audience, "How did you like it?" Douglass answered, "Mr. Lincoln, that was a sacred effort" (quoted in Byrd 2002, 12, 13). So three very different persons saw the identical text differently.

If there are indeed two kinds of texts, Rosenblatt asks herself, what are they like? The efferent is essentially rational, nonemotional, and unambiguous; the aesthetic is intuitive, emotional, and ambiguous. The efferent is unambiguous, precise, and declarative, and its words are denotative; the aesthetic is purposely ambiguous, imprecise, and suggestive, and its words generally have a connotative value. Whereas the reader of an

efferent text seeks explicit information, the reader of an aesthetic text seeks to live through an emotional experience while
transacting with the text.

3. *If there are two distinctly different kinds or reading—the efferent
and the aesthetic—how do we read a literary text? What
processes do we go through as we read a primarily aesthetic text?*
Here is Rosenblatt's description of how we read a poem, story,
novel, or play:

⇝ As we first meet a text, we determine by linguistic cues the
kind of we stance we should adopt.

⇝ We develop a tentative framework for understanding the
text.

⇝ As we read, we raise expectations about what will happen,
and these expectations affect our further reading.

⇝ Either we find our expectations are met, or as we read along,
we change our expectations.

⇝ If this process goes well, and we are satisfied with our "reading" of the text, we create a final interpretation of the text
(Rosenblatt 1978, 54).

In a recent study of how ninth-grade students read a poem they
have never seen before, Robert Blake and Anna Lunn found that students did indeed follow a process like the one Rosenblatt describes
(Blake and Lunn 1986, 68–73). The students were asked to talk into a
tape recorder as they worked through an accessible but fairly complex
poem, "Every Good Boy Does Fine" by David Wagoner. They were asked
to read the poem line by line and then to write out a final interpretation.
They were asked not to censor their thoughts and were told they could
reread the poem several times if necessary. They were also told that the
activity was not a test of any kind and that the researchers wanted to discover what the poem meant, not to a teacher or other grown-up, but to
them.

The students performed these activities as they read, pondered,
and interpreted the poem:

1. They read and reread the poem, sometimes several times.

2. They associated words and phrases with their own personal
experiences.

3. They interpreted frequently and confidently, their interpretations falling into these categories: hypothesizing, admitting
their lack of initial understanding, and finally arriving at satis-

fying interpretations of words, lines, stanzas, and the poem as a whole.

4. They restated and paraphrased lines in their own words.
5. They frequently quoted words and phrases verbatim from the poem.
6. They responded emotionally.
7. They "looped back" to words, lines, and stanzas read previously, a recursive process.
8. They connected elements of the poem, both perceiving patterns and creating their own structures.
9. They generalized by creating their own overall meaning for the poem and stating their ideas of general themes.
10. They revised their initial interpretations and evaluations of how "good" the poem was.
11. And finally, they evaluated the worth of the poem—by simply saying it was "good"—and showed pleasure with their accomplishment of interpreting a worthwhile but sophisticated poem.

The processes the students followed in their reading of an unfamiliar poem were *perceiving, interpreting,* and *enjoying.*

The researchers were amazed at how "incredibly complex the process is with even . . . a short, fairly accessible poem," as shown by the readers' accounts of their mental states (Blake and Lunn 1986, 72). And equally exciting for the researchers was the fact that one teenager especially, "—with little prior instruction in the apparatus of literary criticism, with no knowledge of special terms for figurative language or the technical aspects of poetry—is able to 'work through' and 'understand' a poem in a way that is eminently satisfying to her" (Blake and Lunn 1986, 72).

But back to Rosenblatt's consideration of the process of reading literature. In summary, Rosenblatt states that the systematic analysis of technical elements of a literary text as advanced by the New Critics should not be primary. Rather, a reader's primary approach to a text is a heightened awareness of the literary text as an "event," an emotionally charged experience. The dynamics of a literary reading involve activities that are interwoven, interacting, recursive, and often simultaneous, many times below the level of consciousness.

For Rosenblatt, these are the two major activities we perform as we read a literary text: becoming part of the text and then trying to make sense of our initial, intuitive experience. We first enter a text emotionally, creating a dialogue between ourselves and the writing. We notice especially the words we meet, for they serve as cues to our understanding of the work. As a result of our perception of the cues, we adopt what we believe is the appropriate stance toward the text, creating a preliminary idea about how we make sense of the total work. After this primary response, we strive to comprehend what we have experienced. We accept or reject our initial feelings and thoughts and give ourselves reasons for responding as we did. Inevitably, we come to a point in our reading when we feel "satisfied" with our interpretation and pleased with the tasks we have accomplished and with our ability to create a satisfying explanation of how our reading worked for us. As Rosenblatt sums it up, "Interpretation involves primarily an effort to describe the nature of the lived-through evocation of the work" (Rosenblatt 1978, 70).

What do other theorists say about Reader Response? As we might suppose, with so many different writers focusing on the role of the reader in interpreting literature, Reader Response theory is anything but a "unified position."

How do these writers envision the reader in Reader Response criticism? What follows are some of the speculations by a number of theorists who challenged the New Criticism position. To simplify the identification of the type of reader brought into being by each writer, we have attached a descriptive label to each writer's particular point of view.

The Submissive Reader

We call Georges Poulet's readers "submissive" because, although they yield their consciousness to that of the text, in effect, as they do so they share—merge, as Poulet puts it—their thoughts and feelings with another being residing in the text. For Poulet, when readers enter into a literary work, the "external" object of the book becomes an "interior" mental object. Reading literature, then, is the "interiorization" of an external object that becomes a mental object (Poulet 1970, 57–72).

For the authors, Poulet's account of reading literary texts is a profound analysis of the reader response theoretical position. As the critic Jane Tompkins interprets Poulet's point of view: "To read is precisely not to be aware of the structural and stylistic properties of the work but to be immersed in the author's mode of experiencing the world" (Tompkins 1980, xiv). Rather than concentrating on the form of a text—along with its elements of style—we focus intuitively, on the author's unique way of perceiving the world.

As he advances his argument, Poulet distinguishes between "exterior" objects, such as, for example, vases, statues, and books before they are read, and interior objects, such as literary texts once we commence reading them. As we read a literary text, the exterior book disappears, and the images, thoughts, and feelings latent in the text come into existence. Where do they now exist? Within the reader, states Poulet:

> There is only one place left for this new existence: My innermost self. . . . As soon as I replace my direct perception of reality by the words of a book, I deliver myself, bound hand and foot, to the omnipotence of fiction. I say farewell to what is, in order to feign belief in what is not. I surround myself with fictitious beings; I become the prey of language. There is no escaping this takeover. Language surrounds me with its unreality. (Poulet 1970, 58)

Reading this quotation, we notice the phrases he uses to describe his experience with reading literature: "deliver myself," "bound hand and foot," "the prey of language" "no escaping this takeover," and "language surrounds me." The first step in reading literature for Poulet is, in a striking fashion, to surrender his own personality to the spell cast by the consciousness of the text.

Poulet continues limning the experience he undergoes as he reads a literary text. As he reads, a remarkable transformation is wrought within him. The thoughts he reads are the thoughts of another, yet he the reader is the subject of the thoughts. He is changed by those thoughts, and he gives himself away to them. He feels that he is on loan to another, who thinks, feels, suffers, and acts within him. This possession takes place on two levels: on the level of objective thought (images, sensations, and ideas) but, at the same time, on a deeper level of his own subjective self. As the text takes over, a strange thing happens and he begins to sense in a new way who he is. "When I am absorbed in reading," states Poulet, "a second self takes over, a self which thinks and feels for me" (Poulet 1972, 61).

So if Poulet's account is an accurate description of how one reads a literary work, then what is the role of the reader? The reader's function is to go beyond mere comprehension of the parts of a particular text to a perception of the whole work itself—as it "stands alone." What is this essence of a freestanding literary work? It is what there is in isolation after an examination of the work. It is something created by the individual genius of the artist. When we have read and experienced worthwhile works of literature, after we have analyzed character and events in epics; setting, plot, and character in fiction; and images, figurative language, and structure in poetry, what do we take away from our total experience of each work? To me, what is the work "all about"? Isn't this the epiphany that Poulet is trying to explain? What, for example, is the fundamental meaning of Homer's *Odyssey,* of Hemingway's *For Whom the Bell Tolls,* of Frost's "Mending Walls"? Poulet here explains this process by acknowledging "that all subjective activity present in a literary work is not entirely explained by its relationship with forms and objects within the work" (Poulet 1972, 71).

A worthwhile literary work, we remind ourselves, exists on two levels. On the surface level, the work is represented by its objective form, such as plot, setting, character, images, and figurative language. There is, "at another level, forsaking all forms, a subject which reveals itself to itself (and to me) in its transcendence relative to all which is reflected in it" (Poulet 1972, 72). At this level of pure intuition (knowledge achieved without rational steps), we should not expect to define the piece rationally, nor should we use some outline or other structure to represent its meaning, and we must be prepared to accept that the essence of the text "is exposed in its ineffability and in its fundamental indeterminancy" (Poulet 1972, 72). Ultimately "criticism, in order to accompany the mind in this effort of detachment from itself, needs to annihilate, or at least momentarily forget, the objective elements of the work, and to elevate itself to the apprehension of a subjectivity without objectivity" (Poulet 1972, 72).

In other words, as we read a worthwhile literary work, we move from an exterior object to the interior, independent being of the work. We understand the statement that the work "reveals itself to itself" to refer to the fact that, as many authors report, a work assumes a life of its own as it progresses. The reader—as he or she enters into the experience of the completed work—finds himself or herself melding with the aloof thing that is the text. At this point, the work is ineffable, that is, virtually beyond expression, and indeterminate, that is, ambiguous and not able to be described rationally and precisely.

The Active Reader

Wolfgang Iser promotes the opposite kind of reader from Poulet's. Whereas Poulet's reader is submissive, Iser's is active. No matter, for both readers read only to arrive at the same point, that at which the reader and the text meet. Unlike Poulet's reader, who submits but still participates in reading, Iser's reader actively shares with the text in creating meaning. In effect, the reader becomes a cocreator of the work by supplying those parts that are not written—spaces—but that are implied only.

The foundation of Iser's theory is the fact that we cannot examine how we read without reflecting upon our response. Explains Iser, "As a literary text can only produce a response when it is read, it is virtually impossible to describe this response without also analyzing the 'reading process.'" In the case of the active reader, Iser argues: "Effects and responses are properties neither of the text nor of the reader; the text represents a potential effect that is realized in the reading process" (Iser 1978, ix). It is important to note at this point that Iser's analysis of the act of reading deals primarily with narratives, for narratives offer the widest range of examples relevant to his analysis of how we read.

For Iser, this is how we read a narrative text: "A description of the reading process must bring to light the elementary options which the text activates within the reader. The fact that the latter must carry out [a set of] instructions shows implicitly that the meaning of a text is something that he [the reader] has to assemble" (Iser 1978, ix).

Such an activity is a "dialectic" relationship among the text, the reader, and their interaction. But why is the relationship labeled an "aesthetic response," as it is called in the book's subtitle, "A Theory of Aesthetic Response"? Iser explains the term this way: "It [the reader's response] is called aesthetic response because, although it is brought about by the text, it brings into play the imaginative and perceptive faculties of the reader, in order to make him adjust and even differentiate his own focus" (Iser 1978, x). Good readers of good texts, we understand this to mean, are themselves by necessity creative—as authors of works have been—as they reconstruct and reassemble whole responses from incomplete texts.

Iser cautions us that his ideas may not be widely applicable and acknowledges that his theory has undergone no empirical tests. He is quick to assure us that he is not so much concerned with establishing the validity of his evolving theory as he is with creating a framework of assumptions about reading narrative that will serve as a guide to future studies. In effect, his aim is to formulate the right questions so that others can test his assertions.

Here we have Jane Tompkins's summary of Iser's notion of the active reader in Reader Response theory:

> The "concretization" of a text of any particular instance requires that the reader's imagination come into play. Each reader fills in the unwritten portions of the text, its "gaps" or areas of "indeterminancy," in his own way. But this is not to say that the text thus arrived at is a mere fabrication of the reader. The range of interpretations that arises as a

result of the reader's creative activity is seen rather as proof of the text's "inexhaustibility." (Tompkins 1980, xv)

The Semiotic Reader

In literary criticism, "semiotics is concerned with complete signifying systems of a text and the codes and conventions we need to understand in order to be able to read it" (Cuddon 1999, 805).

Umberto Eco, author of the critically successful and immensely popular novel *The Name of the Rose,* who calls himself a "semiotician," believes that in order to comprehend a literary text we must acknowledge the systems of cultural codes and subcodes—often below the level of consciousness—making up the world created in a text by an author. For example, we would not have a sophisticated understanding of Nathaniel Hawthorne's story "Young Goodman Brown" without knowledge of American Puritanism; of Toni Morrison's novel *Beloved* without a background knowledge of American slavery; or of *The Diary of Anne Frank* without an awareness of the European Holocaust.

Although Eco's works, especially his 1979 book *The Role of the Reader: Explorations in the Semiotics of Texts,* are dense and not for the fainthearted, his idea of the necessity for semiotic readings of literary texts and of a proposed distinction between what he calls "open" and "closed" literary texts are valuable for our understanding of how we read literature. As we approach an open text, we pay close attention to the text itself—literally reading closely—and actively collaborate with the text to create an individually satisfying meaning. An example of the ultimate open text in English is Shakespeare's *Hamlet,* which continues to generate new meanings throughout the world and over the centuries. On the other hand, as we read a closed text, such as a popular legal thriller or romance novel, we need not work at our reading; rather, we surrender to the headlong momentum of a "good read." In other words, we do not cooperate in creating meaning with a closed text. The text has predetermined the meaning we eventually arrive at.

The Subjective Reader

For David Bleich, particularly in his highly theoretical but persuasive 1978 work *Subjective Criticism,* all so-called facts, knowledge, opinions, and interpretations, as well as all literary criticism, are subjective. They can be nothing else, since every text—scientific as well as literary—is made up of humanly constructed symbols, which are in turn perceived by human minds.

In order to help us understand that the concept of subjectivity is only a human device—the word "subjective" having a negative connotation for many in our culture—Bleich argues that the notion of objectivity is also just another human invention. Where is meaning then? Is it "out there" to be found? Or is it potentially within each of us waiting to be created? According to Bleich, in both literary texts and in scientific observations meaning resides in the mind of the reader and at the same time in the eyes of what he calls the "scientific observer." The objective notion of finding meaning by systematic and rigorous observation is itself only another model, another human fabrication. Although some believe that methodical, objective observation and rational thought reveal "true," unvarying meaning, Bleich agues that as observers perceive—no matter how objectively and dispassionately they believe they are observing—what they watch attentively is influenced by their personal makeup. Bleich writes, "The process of observation interferes with what is being observed in such a way that the object of the observation appears changed by the act of the observation" (Bleich 1978, 17). In short, we see what we want to see. We cannot help it. And of course it follows that as we read literature, what we interpret is what we are destined to interpret. And we cannot help that either. All interpretations are a result of subjective mental processing.

Eventually Bleich articulates an idea we have previously considered, that knowledge is not discovered—as most persons who call themselves scientists believe—but created by humans. "Under the subjective paradigm, new truth is created by a new use of language and a new structure of thought. . . . Knowledge is made by people and not found" (Bleich 1978, 18).

From readers individually creating meaning from literary texts, Bleich then moves on to the view that, furthermore, in creating meaning, we make sense through our interactions with groups that share our social, cultural, educational, and ethical values. Wider and deeper knowledge is, therefore, created by human communities.

This idea of subjective criticism deals not only with different thoughts but with different kinds of thoughts. In this respect, many writers of the last century—who are labeled "modern"—produced works in which for the first time the subjective life of their characters was illuminated. As a result, these authors presented the subjective experience in language far different from any kind of previous language. James Joyce, for example, fine-tuned the "stream of consciousness" subjective experience in his experimental novels *A Portrait of the Artist as a Young Man* and *Ulysses,* and in the ultimate example of subjectivity in writing, *Finnegans Wake.* A preeminent example of the subjective experience in American literature is William Faulkner's novel *The Sound and the Fury,* in which characters in turn reveal themselves through their mental revelations, including the incredible but stunning rendering of the retarded Benjy's thoughts. The idea that characters' inner language is a legitimate kind of writing was acknowledged and utilized by many writers in the twentieth century.

Why is it important to study subjective experience? Because we now realize that every shred of subjective experience has meaning for us. The term "free association" was a cornerstone of Sigmund Freud's theories. It refers to the idea that as we reveal all of our subjectively perceived thoughts—often dredged up from below the level of consciousness—these thoughts have meaning for us and lead to profound insights into our personalities. To us, this idea of the nature of free association—that as we let words, feelings, and thoughts tumble freely from our minds, we learn about our inner selves—is crucial to self-understanding. It would appear, then, that there is no such thing as a non sequitur—a statement that does not follow logically from what preceded it—and that *all* statements, no matter how apparently unreasonable they may seem on the surface, are somehow meaningful. This expression of the nature of the subjective statement "became a widespread expression of the discovery of subjectivity as a fundamental and pervasive fact of the modern experience" (Bleich 1978, 36).

What does an acceptance of the subjective nature of reading literary texts indicate to us? If we read closed texts, whose meanings are readably observable, we have no problem with interpretation. But as we read complex and ambiguous texts, we are obliged to make all kinds of supplementary efforts to make the reading comprehensible. However, in most cases the authors provide us with enough background information that we can understand the particular cultural and historical setting in which the narrative unfolds. For example, an understanding of the medieval revenge tradition is necessary for a reading of *Hamlet,* but Shakespeare reveals enough of the traditional revenge background within the play for us to understand the custom. An understanding of whaling is necessary for us to understand Melville's *Moby Dick,* but Melville—to too great an extent, some believe—supplies us with this information through this open text. Sometimes, however, authors supply little of the necessary supplementary information, and we are obliged to turn to outside sources in order to read with full understanding sometimes exasperatingly open texts, such as Shirley Jackson's story "The Lottery" or J. D. Salinger's story "For Esmé, with Love and Squalor."

The Psychoanalytic Reader

We call Norman Holland's reader "psychoanalytic." As we examine Holland's background, we learn why this term is apt. Holland, former professor of English at the State University of New York (SUNY) at Buffalo, completed a program for nonmedical candidates at the Boston Psychoanalytical Institute and was founder and director of SUNY's Center for the Psychological Study of the Arts. Critic Jane Tompkins called him the "leading psychoanalytic interpreter of literary response" (Tompkins 1980, 274).

In a long, closely argued piece, entitled "UNITY IDENTITY TEXT SELF" (Holland 1975b), Holland explicates the major tenets of his theory of the psychoanalytic aspects of reader response, which is fully elucidated in his *Five Readers Reading* (Holland 1975a).

Holland distills his theory into the arcane phrase "Identity recreates itself," which we translate as "Every individual reads (and thus interprets) a literary text according to his or her unique personality," what Holland calls, in psychoanalytic terms, the person's "identity theme."

To Holland, the words in the title of the article, "UNITY IDENTITY TEXT SELF," and the spaces between the words suggest "the mysterious openness and receptivity of literature. Somehow all kinds of people from different eras and cultures can achieve and re-achieve a single literary work, replenishing it by infinitely various additions of subjective to objective" (Holland 1975b, 118. We have used the page numbers from Tompkins's *Reader-Response Criticism* [1980], in which the original Publication of the Modern Language Association [PMLA] article was reprinted).

For our purposes, though, what does this mean in ordinary language? Like all responsible intellectuals, Holland is scrupulous in defining his terms, most importantly the word "self." The term "self," we find, is a very old Anglo-Saxon word meaning the total, essential being of a single person. Its synonyms include "personality," "character," and "individuality." Holland, however, defines "self" as one's own person in relation to other persons but believes it to be more a commonsensical than a psychological term.

Although the word "identity" seems to be a more complex term than "self," psychologists have used the word in so many contexts that no clear meaning remains. Such words as "character," presently meaning a combination of distinctive features distinguishing a single person, or "personality," currently taken to mean a dynamic self that animates an individual person and makes his or her experience unique, serve as synonyms. In spite of the overlapping meanings of these terms relating to self, Holland prefers "identity" as his central, defining word, explaining his use of the term by these examples. For instance, when outstanding musicians play the same piece, we immediately recognize the identity of the performer. Likewise, when we meet persons we knew in childhood after an absence of many years, we may exclaim, "Why, you haven't changed a bit!" Of course, they have altered in many significant ways. They have become wrinkled, with graying hair and bodies thickened with age, but they nonetheless retain their immutable identity.

What does the idea of identity have to do with reading literature? For Holland—and for most other Reader Response theorists—everything. Here is how Holland describes his notion of identity:

> The unity we find in literary texts is impregnated with the identity that finds unity. This is simply to say that my reading of a certain literary work will differ from yours or his or hers. As readers, each of us will bring different kinds of external information to bear. Each will seek out the particular themes that concern him. Each will have different ways of making the text into an experience with a coherence and significance that satisfies. (Holland 1975b, 123)

If this is in fact how each of us reads literature, what process do we follow during the reading? What assumptions govern our actions? The overarching principle governing the psychoanalytic reading of a literary text is this: "Identity creates itself, or, to put it another way, style—in the sense of personal style—creates itself. That is, all of us, as we read, use the literary work to symbolize and finally to replicate ourselves. We work out through the text our own characteristic patterns of desire and adaptation" (Holland 1975b, 124).

Now, within this general, encompassing law, there are several related elements. First is the gnomic phrase, "Adaptations must be matched," meaning that to read a literary work successfully, we must adapt it to our personal identity. We find within the work what in our world we wish for or fear the most. Then we respond to the piece by calling up from our unconscious the characteristic ways we have developed for taming our deepest fears and approaching our overwhelming desires. For instance, virtually all of us have learned appropriate ways of dealing with authority figures, primarily our fathers or father figures. The authors have found that many people—those who later reported having been abused by their fathers—read Papa in "My Papa's Waltz," the provocatively open poem by Theodore Roethke, as an abusive father. Other readers, remembering only happy times with their fathers, see the coarse waltz as a joyous time. Several readers even recall dancing as small children around the kitchen floor with their feet on their father's shoes.

Now that we have adapted our characteristic strategies for dealing with our basic fears and desires aroused by a literary text, what happens next? Once we have matched our identity with the work, we receive pleasure form the fantasies we create, triggered by the work. For Holland, the matching of my identity to a work can be either tight or loose because no matter what fantasy is engendered, it is in reality created by the reader from the literary work to make explicit his or her psychological drives. This explains why, often to our amazement, readers of various personalities, of different ages, genders, and cultures, and from other historical periods can respond to the same literary work in similar ways. At the same time, the idea of an identity theme explains why a single person can enjoy a wide range of literary works, from the well-made novels of F. Scott Fitzgerald and Ernest Hemingway to the sprawling works of Fyodor Dostoyevsky. Holland explains the phenomenon in this way:

> The answer, I believe, is that different readers can all gain pleasure
> from the same fantasy and one reader can gain pleasure from many
> different fantasies because *all* readers create from the fantasy seem-
> ingly "in" the work fantasies to suit their several character structures.
> Each reader, in effect, re-creates the work in terms of his own identity
> theme. (Holland 1975b, 126)

A third element in this process is the fact that we have a gnawing need to arrive at some sort of general perception of the overall meaning of the work. We are not satisfied with our reading until we have arrived at a generalized meaning, what is traditionally called the "theme." States Holland, "Thus, we usually feel a need to transform raw fantasy into a total experience of esthetic, moral, intellectual, or social coherence and significance" (Holland 1975b, 126). It is important to note here the distinction between readers' finding a single, correct theme and each of us finding his or her own personally satisfying, individually created theme. In other words, we are driven to complete our reading of a worthwhile literary text by articulating our own version of its aesthetic or moral vision. It is something like saying to ourselves, "Okay, now I see what it's all about! And I feel pretty good about my interpretation."

If the process is accurately described, how do I go about reading as a psychoanalytic reader? What are the intellectual and intuitive skills I need to practice? This, the authors believe, is a simple list of Holland's methods: We compare our experiences to the experiences of the author. We bring personal associations to our reading. We place the text in a literary tradition. We treat the text as a puzzle or code and try to fit the parts of the puzzle together or break the code and try to decode it. And finally we try to fit all the parts into a satisfying, overall perception, combining feelings and thoughts. The aim of all these reading moves is to help us synthesize the experience of reading a text and reconstructing it as our own.

Fundamentally, as we read and respond to a worthwhile literary text through our subjective, personal identities, we by necessity become as creative in our responses as the author of the work was in creating the work. Holland explains: "Whenever, as a critic, I engage a writer or his work, I do so through my own identity theme. My act of perception is also an act of creation in which I partake of the artist's gift" (Holland 1975b, 130).

Instead of separating the work from the reader, Holland maintains that a reader, by matching his or her own personality with that of the author's and through reading and responding, creates a single, artistic work. By following the process described by Holland, we do away with "a dualism that has dominated systematic thought since Descartes: the belief that the reality and meaning of the external world exist alone, independent of the perceiving self, and that therefore true knowledge requires the splitting of the known from the knower" (Holland 1975b, 130).

In sum, argues Holland, we now recognize that as we read and respond to literature, we no longer think of ourselves as readers who are distinctly separate from a text. Rather, as we interpret the world around us—including literary texts—our interpretations become one with what we interpret. Our interpretations are determined by ourselves, by our identity themes.

The Interpretive Community Reader

We examine the ideas of the critic Stanley Fish as the last example of a Reader Response theorist dealing with the role of the reader. In his work, Fish stresses these ideas: that literary texts are inherently unstable and indeterminate, that meaning is found not in texts but within readers, and that meaning, however unreliable, is established to some degree by the norms of interpretive communities.

In his 1980 book *Is There a Text in This Class? The Authority of Interpretive Communities*—made up of a series of articles originally published in scholarly journals and of four essays revised from the John

Crowe Ransom Memorial Lectures, originally given at Kenyon College in April 1979—Fish examines and clarifies these principles.

First, his answer to the notorious question posed by the title of the book, Is there a text in this class? is an equivocal "No" and "Yes." No, there is not a text in this class if by "text" we mean a work that has a single, objective, unvarying meaning. But yes, there is a text if by "text" we mean "the structure of meaning that is obvious and inescapable from the perspective of whatever interpretive assumptions happen to be in force" (Fish 1980, vii). We take this statement to mean, yes, there is a text, but only in the sense that its meaning can be arrived at by a community of readers sharing the same traditions and cultural norms.

In his introduction to this book, "Introduction, or How I Stopped Worrying and Learned to Love Interpretation," Fish proclaims his manifesto toward reading literature. First, he disposes of the question of where meaning resides, in the text or within the reader. If meaning exists in the text, then the reader's job is limited simply to getting the sense of the work out. If, however,

> meaning develops, and if it develops in a dynamic relationship with the reader's expectations, projections, conclusions, judgments, and assumptions, and the assumptions, these activities (the things the reader does) are not merely instrumental, or mechanical, but essential, and the act of description must begin and end with them. . . . In this formulation, the reader's response is not *to* the meaning; it *is* the meaning. (Fish 1980, 2, 3)

Not only do readers establish meaning in literary texts, but they also decide what literature is, whether or not a text is literature. In other words, literature, argues Fish, is "a conventional category. What will, at any time, be recognized as literature is a function of a communal decision as to what will count as literature" (Fish 1980, 10). Literature, according to this position, is made up not of formal properties that signify it as literature. A text becomes literary because we agree that it is. "The conclusion," writes Fish, "is that while literature is still a category, it is an open category, not definable by fictionality, or by a disregard of propositional truth, or by a predominance of tropes and figures, but simply by what we decide to put into it. And the conclusion to that conclusion is that it is the reader who 'makes' literature" (Fish 1980, 11). Here, in this extended quote, we have a comprehensive statement of Fish's stance toward reading and interpreting literature:

> This [the idea that readers make literature] sounds like the rankest subjectivism, but it is qualified almost immediately when the reader is identified not as a free agent, making literature in any old way, but as a member of a community whose assumptions about literature determine the kind of attention he pays and thus the kind of literature "he" "makes." . . . Thus the act of recognizing literature is not constrained by something in the text, nor does it issue from an independent and arbitrary will [of a reader]; rather, it proceeds from a collective decision as to what will count as literature, a decision that will be in force only so long as a community of readers or believers continues to abide by it. (Fish 1980, 11)

In other words, there is no single, correct way of reading literary texts, just approaches that are sanctioned by interpretive communities.

We have available an account of one of these approaches: a report by the journalist Larissa MacFarquhar, for a piece in *The New Yorker,* of how Fish himself reads a complicated literary text. As MacFarquhar relates, Fish reads (in this case) a poem in this manner:

> along the line, one word at time, drastically slowing down the reading process in order to examine the frustrated expectations and tiny shifts in meaning that each word produced in the mind of the reader. (Later, he realized that he was not describing what took place in readers' minds so much as prescribing a method that would allow others to become as careful a reader as he.) (MacFarquhar 2001, 67–68)

But as Fish used these close reading techniques in reading certain difficult seventeenth-century English poems, he discovered that their effect on him was "self-consuming," in at least two senses. First, the texts "cannibalized" themselves as they initially set up expectations for interpretation and then, as he progressed in his reading, drastically altered his initial anticipations. Second, at the same time, the text of especially difficult works "consumed" him to the extent that he began to doubt his own judgment, and he finally "realized that his mind was not capable of discerning truth on its own—that he could see truth only through God" (quoted in MacFarquhar 2001, 68).

Such a mystical approach to reading dense and allusive literature has echoes of the medieval Scholastics' attitude toward interpreting Scripture and the most devoted New Critics' attitude toward literature. Such an approach to reading the ultimate open texts seems to us to be the most strenuous kind of wrestling with literature, employed by only the most talented, dedicated, and learned of readers.

As we ponder such a method of reading literature, however, we need to translate Fish's special vocabulary into ordinary language if we are to understand what he does. With sophisticated literary texts, we may say that as we read, we are constantly on the alert for the author to "hoodwink" us, to set us up for one interpretation and then abruptly jolt us out of our complacencies to look at the text in a totally different light. As experienced readers, we are constantly on guard for these setups. As we read this way, though, we find ourselves forced to look at what we read in a new light. For instance, in that gravest of stories, "A Good Man Is Hard to Find," by Flannery O'Connor, first-time readers are constantly fooled by the comic tone of the first part of the story. She sets us up for one kind of reading, but she disrupts our original mind-set as she moves to the inevitable but shocking ending. She forces the perceptive reader to ponder his or her anticipated interpretation by what we call "displaced perspective." We may start an open text from one point of view, but we are then surprised by a totally new and unexpected perspective.

As Fish describes his method of reading, he is at the same time working on the age-old epistemological question of where meaning is. As with other Reader Response theorists, Fish believes that since people always read literature from their own limited and idiosyncratic personalities—not from a divine omniscience—they will always read texts differently. It follows, then, that there is no possible way we can agree on an objective meaning in a text or decide that one interpretation is better than any other. As we might expect, such a radical position has upset a great many people, who refuse even to ponder such an argument.

But if it is true that texts of all kinds are written in symbols invented by humans and that it is impossible to point to one absolutely incontrovertible meaning for any text, why do we frequently agree on interpretations of certain works? Fish maintains that this agreement exists because we all belong to special groups that share the same social, cultural, educational, and ethical backgrounds. That is, we all belong to what are called "interpretative communities." Since for the most part we adhere to our beliefs unconsciously, we affirm them so strongly that we frequently fail to accept any beliefs outside those of our interpretive community. Are beliefs held by comparatively small groups maintained any less strongly than those held by large groups? No; "quite the reverse: beliefs are not objects we may take up, examine, and discard—they are the eyes through which we see. Realizing that we lack a godlike perspective on the world doesn't leave us without beliefs or principles of judgment; it leaves us exactly where we were before" (MacFarquhar 2001, 68)

But what about "misreadings" of literary texts in interpretive communities? Do students, even in rather homogeneous groups, always agree? Do they sometimes misread texts? Our experience with teaching literature has been that "misreadings" by students are virtually always surface-level "mistakes" and that as students discuss their readings in small groups and in classes as a whole, they help each other "correct" these inconsequential "misreadings." On the whole, students in interpretive communities, after responding and sharing their responses in groups, will agree on the deeper meanings of literary texts.

Principles of Reader Response Theory

Some of the Reader Response theorists are strange bedfellows, but all in all, they have contributed to a revolution in how we conceive the most basic questions concerning written language: the place of meaning in language, the gross differences between scientific and literary texts, how one reads literary texts, and the role of interpretive communities in reading literature. Here are some of the basic principles of Reader Response theory, as articulated by writers and theorists alike, in their own words:

1. "A text has no real existence until it is read" (Cuddon 1999, 726).
2. "The reader is an active reader in the creation of meaning" (Cuddon 1999, 726).
3. "The literary experience must be perceived as a *transaction* between the reader and the text" (Rosenblatt 1938, 35).
4. "But no one can read a poem for us. The reader of the poem must have the experience himself" (Rosenblatt 1938, 26–27).
5. "Critics and literary theorists, who have traditionally lavished attention on authors and texts, have only recently begun to recognize the reader" (Rosenblatt 1978, ix).
6. "The poem, then, must be thought of as an event in time. It is not an object or ideal entity. . . . The reader brings to the text his past experience and present personality. . . . he marshals his resources and crystallizes out of the stuff of memory, thought, and feeling a new order, a new experience, which he sees as the poem" (Rosenblatt 1978, 12).
7. "The reading of a text is an event occurring at a particular time in a particular environment at a particular moment in the life history of the reader" (Rosenblatt 1978, 20).

8. "The primary concern of the reader in 'efferent' reading is 'with what he will carry away from the reading,' the term 'efferent,' derived from the Latin 'efferre,' 'to carry away'" (Rosenblatt 1978, 24).

9. "In aesthetic reading, the reader's attention is centered directly on what he is living through during his particular text" (Rosenblatt 1978, 25).

10. "The reader is . . . immersed in a creative process that goes on largely below the threshold of awareness" (Rosenblatt 1978, 52).

11. "A text is meant to be an experience of transformation for its reader" (Eco 1994, 524).

12. "And I would define the poetic effect as the capacity that a text displays for continuing to generate different readings, without ever being completely consumed" (Eco 1994, 508).

13. "The reader should learn something either about the world or about language: this difference distinguishes various narrative poetics, but the point remains the same" (Eco 1994, 526).

14. "To understand a complex work of art, one must be something of an artist himself" (Gardner 1978, 8).

15. "All understanding is an articulation of intuition" (Gardner 1978, 152).

16. "Literary meaning is a function of the reader's response to a text and cannot be described accurately if the response is left out of the account" (Tompkins 1980, xiii).

17. "What began as a small shift of emphasis from the narrator implied by a literary work to the reader it implies ends by becoming an exchange of world views" (Tompkins 1980, x).

18. "Literature is not an object but an experience" (Tompkins 1980, xvii).

19. "If meaning is no longer a property of the text but a product of the reader's activity the question to answer is not 'what do poems mean?' or even 'what do poems do?' but 'how do readers make meaning?'" (Tompkins 1980, xvii).

20. "An individual's perceptions and judgments are a function of the assumptions shared by the groups [interpretive communities] he belongs to" (Tompkins 1980, xxi).

21. "The overall aim [of Reader Response criticism] is to provide a means of presenting literature in a way that will produce an internal motive for reading and thinking about literature. The motive is the awareness that readers can produce new understanding of oneself—not just a moral here and a message

there, but a genuinely new conception of one's values and tastes as well as one's prejudices and learning difficulties" (Bleich 1975, 3–4).

22. "Our initial and most important aim is to produce an *awareness* of one's own personality; the explanation of it comes later" (Bleich 1975, 5).

23. "Interpretation is a communal activity" (Bleich 1978, 79).

24. "Interpretation is always a group activity, since the individual interpreter is creating his statement in large part with an eye toward who is going to hear it. That is his community, whether it is of students, teachers, reviewers, or critics" (Bleich 1975, 94).

25. "Interpretation is a communal act, serving the collective subjectivity rather than an external absolute standard of truth" (Bleich 1975, 95).

26. "The New Critics had objected to confusing the poem with its results in order to separate literature from other kinds of discourse and to give criticism an objective basis. The later reader-response critics deny that criticism has such an objective basis because they deny the existence of objective texts and the possibility of objectivity altogether. . . . The net result of this epistemological revolution is to repoliticize literature and literary criticism. When discourse is responsible for reality and not merely a reflection of it, then whose discourse prevails makes all the difference" (Tompkins 1980, xxv).

READER RESPONSE: PRACTICE

The beauty of Classroom Reader Response is that it is unpredictable in what it may yield, given the unpredictable nature of children, adolescents, and people in general. The result of asking readers, particularly young readers, to express their thoughts and most importantly their feelings, are questions that are rarely expected. With Classroom Reader Response, literature can be used in a myriad of ways. In addition to learning skills involving grammar, spelling, and decoding, and such as characterization and metaphor, we see that literature's foremost role is to teach us about ourselves, life and our personal response to life.
(Catherine M., elementary school teacher)

In this quote, we have Catherine M.'s assessment of how well Classroom Reader Response works in her elementary school classroom as well as with her classmates, a group of some thirty graduate students who had just completed a course, "Reading and Responding to Literature, K–12" (kindergarten through twelfth grade). During the semester-long course, the students performed these activities: They read and discussed primary source statements on Reader Response theory; read primary sources dealing with various stances toward reading literature, such as the "psychological" stance, the "gender" stance, the "mythic" stance, the "personal intelligences" stance, and the "moral" stance; read and responded in writing to worthwhile adult and children's picture books, stories, and poems using Classroom Reader Response techniques and discussed in small groups and in the class as a whole their responses; and as final projects, reported on Classroom Reader Response activities engaged in by their elementary and secondary school students.

What did Catherine M. and her fellow in-service students find out about the effect of applying Classroom Reader Response methods in their classrooms?

First, they reported that the responses by children and adolescents were "unpredictable." Why was this so? We believe it is because students found confidence enough to come up with their own interpretations and not to worry about what their teachers thought their responses should be. What happened, then, was that students responded from their own personalities, coming up with rich, uninhibited interpretations. Even though each reaction was unpredictable and unique, the responses in general reflected a consensus by students about the overall significance of the texts. The primary aim of the Classroom Reader Response approach, the teachers in the in-service course accepted, is to help produce courageous readers, who feel free to present honest, unrestrained, personally satisfying interpretations of poems and stories.

As Catherine points out, schoolchildren—and her fellow graduate students—were emboldened after their initial readings to make intuitive, emotional responses to texts and then, on subsequent readings, to choose the details *they* deemed important for supporting their original responses. In other words, they were trained in classes to trust their first spontaneous experience with a text and then to use close reading techniques—calling up such literary elements as character, plot, theme, figurative language, irony, and ambiguity—to confirm their original sense of the meaning of a piece. In effect, Classroom Reader Response turns traditional criticism on its head. This is not a trivial point. With traditional literary interpretation—especially with New Criticism—we have been taught to deny our initial, emotional response and, rather, to go through a text, picking out details in an inductive, scientific manner in order to arrive at the inherent, objective theme. With Classroom Reader Response, we reverse these procedures. We maintain that reading a worthwhile literary text is first an emotional, aesthetic experience. If this is true, we should acknowledge the fact and allow our-selves—and our students—to express their initial responses, which are uniquely their own. Classroom Reader Response thus effectively removes the meaning from the text and places it where it belongs, in the hearts and minds of readers.

As they were reading in a Reader Response manner, students learned to trust their individual judgments about literature (forming such judgments, by the way, involves a very high-level intellectual skill called "comprehension"), and they were at the same time acquiring, perhaps unconsciously, a wide range of other language skills, such as an understanding of etymologies and denotative and connotative values of words, and an appreciation of how grammar and syntax contribute to meaning and how the author's "voice" determines meaning—high-level language and mental skills indeed.

As students share written responses in groups, listen to the responses of their peers, and comment pointedly on their classmates' responses, they are learning the social skills of listening and of speaking about their reactions to the responses—unlike in artificial exercises in listening and speaking—in small and large groups on matters of impor-tance to them. At another and even higher level of intelligence, over a fairly long time—which is necessary if we are to internalize important mental and emotional skills—they acquire what the cognitive psychol-ogist Howard Gardner calls the "personal intelligences," learning about one's own behavior (intrapersonal intelligence) and learning how to read the behaviors of others (interpersonal intelligences) (Gardner 1985). If using language to talk about language is metacognition, then mental activities such as these represent understanding *why* one uses language to talk about using language to respond in a certain way, what we might term "hyper-metacognition."

Embedded within Catherine's quote is a final observation we find significant. She reports that the Classroom Reader Response method yields unpredictable responses from persons of all ages: "children, ado-lescents, and people in general." We take this statement to mean that when individuals are free to make confident and spirited interpretations that are valuable to them—not to a teacher, textbook author, or univer-sity professor—they then become perceptive, sophisticated, and joyous readers of literature.

In this part of the chapter, we consider to what extent Reader Response theory has been adapted for practical classroom activities, discover some of the reasons why this promising model has not enjoyed a more widespread adoption, and describe approaches to teaching literature from a Reader Response orientation that have been successful, one with college and secondary students and another with elementary school children.

Why Reader Response Practice Has Evolved So Slowly

We believe there are three main reasons why college and university professors and schoolteachers do not teach literature by a Reader Response orientation. First, there is no generally accepted academic, theoretical Reader Response model. Second, few teachers in elementary and secondary schools or professors in colleges and universities have had training in Reader Response theory or practice. Third, it is difficult to find a fully developed pedagogical Reader Response model for teaching literature in schools; among other things, this means that there are few textbooks in elementary education with more than a passing reference to Reader Response and that state education English-language arts publications seldom base their K–12 curricula on Reader Response assumptions. It is no wonder, therefore, that schoolteachers are unsure how to teach children and preadolescents how to read literature from a Reader Response orientation.

From our experience and observation, we are convinced that the elementary, secondary, and college teachers we have taught, particularly in our full-semester course "Reading and Responding to Literature, K–12," have been able to use what we call "Classroom Reader Response" strategies in their classroom. They are pleasantly surprised to find that the strategies invigorate the classroom and that children learn how to read literature and at the same time are helped to become adept at the language skills of reading, writing, listening, and speaking (Blake 1989, 1991, 1996).

Lack of an Academic Theoretical Reader Response Model

Although most Reader Response theorists agree on a number of common principles, at present we have no consolidated position identified as a Reader Response theory. Writes Richard Beach,

> It is often assumed that reader-response criticism represents a relatively unified position. . . . However, writers who have been called "reader-response critics" embrace an extremely wide range of attitudes toward, and assumptions about, the roles of the reader, the text, and

the social/cultural context shaping the transaction between reader and text. (Beach 1993, 1–2)

The original Reader Response theories were pretty well accomplished in the United States during the 1970s and early 1980s. The literary theorists in research universities—where such theories are spawned—have gone on since then to produce one new critical theory after another. From Reader Response, the theorists have brought into being such significant theoretical edifices as linguistics-based structuralism, followed by its reaction, poststructuralism; semiotics and its ultimate reduction, deconstructionism; multiculturalism; feminism; and now the latest lit-crit flavor, postcolonialism. All the camps have no doubt contributed to our awareness of how to approach a literary text, but for our purposes, it would be unreal to expect such theories to contribute directly to our understanding of how persons—other than privileged students in the rarefied air of major research universities—read literature.

At Ivy League Columbia University, for instance, we observe that the often acrimonious debates among scholars lead to new ideas but seldom help with teaching students how to read literary texts in schools, junior colleges, colleges, and lesser-ranked universities. In a recent news feature story, Karen Arenson tells us, "As an academic discipline, English has been in a state of upheaval for decades. English departments across the country have been rocked by fierce arguments over how much emphasis to give to deconstructionism, feminism, postcolonialism, queer theory and other new schools of thought" (Arenson 2002, 321).

Obviously, there is no help here for the battered kids in New York City trying to pass the New York statewide exams reflecting the state's "Learning Standards for English Language Arts." To give us some idea of just how far removed such theoretical meanderings are from teaching practice, here is an account referring to a paper on postcolonial theory, given by Professor Gayatri Spivak, who is one of Columbia University's "Celebrity Scholars" and is recognized, we are told, as "one of the most famous practitioners of postcolonial studies, devoted to the culture of people of former colonies" (Smith 2002, A15). At a speech presented at the University of Pennsylvania, another Ivy League university, entitled "Moving Devi" (the talk was also a catalog essay for a museum exhibition of representations of Devi, the divine female principle in Hindu mythology), she was asked, "What does 'Moving Devi' mean?" This was her response: "The answer is a change in the relation of the subject who is writing from a place where Devi belongs as she slowly moves into the text of the museum. What I'm looking at here is that itinerary, not the nostalgic identarianism of the metropolitan migrant" (quoted in Smith 2002, A15).

Although the Oxford scholar Terry Eagleton has called her criticism "pretentiously opaque," he admits she is "among the most coruscatingly intelligent of all contemporary theorists whose insights can be idiosyncratic but rarely less than original." He continues, "She has probably done more long-term political good in pioneering feminist and post-colonial studies than almost any of her theoretical colleagues" (quoted in Smith 2002, A17).

Even though Professor Spivak's ideas appear "opaque" and "difficult," we need to accept—as Terry Eagleton believes—that she has contributed enormously to our overall understanding about reading literature. In a fresh exegesis of Charlotte Brontë's *Jane Eyre,* for instance, Professor Spivak disagreed with a previous reading, *The Madwoman in the Attic,* by Sandra M. Gilbert and Susan Bubar, in which the authors— in a feminist interpretation of nineteenth-century authors—labeled Rochester's insane wife Bertha as Jane's "dark double." In a penetrating critique of this position, Spivak remarked that it was pertinent that the authors had portrayed Bertha, a colonial Creole from Jamaica, as an "animal." Brontë herself had also used animal imagery to portray Rochester's wife. "'They [the authors] thought it was O.K. to represent her in those animalistic terms,' Ms. Spivak said. . . . 'It told us about the society when someone could present someone from the colonies as an animal. We are also marked by our time as she [Brontë] was by hers'" (quoted in Smith 2002, A17). Such an insight adds enormously to our capacity for reacting to literature from a global perspective and to developing postcolonialism as a bona fide stance within literary theory.

Not only do the vocal literary theorists in the top-drawer research universities offer little direct and immediate effect on Classroom Reader Response practice, we need also to remember that the "Celebrity Scholars" who promulgate new literary theories are few and far between even in the universities they represent. Many of their colleagues in English departments are traditionalists or conservatives. Again at Columbia University, the situation is described like this: "The divisions at Columbia were never neat or fixed, but the lineup often seemed to be men against women, old guard against new, liberals against conservatives, close readers of text against new-theory advocates and multiculturalists" (Arenson 2002, 32). From our experiences at the universities and colleges that we have attended and at which we have taught, although a few members of English departments wish to be known as feminists or postmodernists or multiculturalists, when they critique literature, they generally use close reading techniques—the heart of New Criticism. Invariably, they dismiss

Reader Response "criticism" as not even criticism but as the emotional ramblings of nonrigorous students and writers.

We can enjoy the shenanigans of literary theorists and snicker at their sometimes abstruse ideas, but we need to give them credit for creating new and ultimately influential concepts. Furthermore, we need to remember that the role of theorists is to spin original theories and to debate their validity in the intellectual marketplace. If certain theories are proved acceptable, then they gradually trickle down to less than top-rank research universities, to colleges, to secondary schools, and perhaps even to elementary schools. We owe a debt to original thinkers in the field of literary interpretation, for if it were not for their original ideas and formal discussions with their colleagues, we should never have any ideas to be translated into classroom practices.

Lack of Training for Schoolteachers in
Reader Response Practices

Why do English teachers not apply Reader Response theories in secondary school classes? Because they have not been trained to do so. Secondary school English teachers are trained to teach English not in departments of education but in university and college departments of English, and for the most part, the knowledge they have assimilated has been passed on by lecture. One of the authors recalls experiencing a large, graduate-level English class, "The American Novel"—held, significantly, in a "lecture hall" holding up to one hundred students. The renowned professor lectured for fifteen weeks on the lives of the novelists; examinations dealt exclusively with criticism of selected novels. In another course, "Spenser and His Predecessors," a highly respected professor used a teaching method dating back to medieval times: He read from his copy of *The Fairie Queene* while students followed along in their copies. The other author, while studying at the Sorbonne in Paris and attending classes in French literature, was taught solely by lectures on French novels and plays by *explication de texte*, a minute, exhaustive analysis of literary texts, the ultimate aim being to find the inherent "meaning"; this is, of course, the process we recognize as close reading. From all accounts, university and college teaching of English language and literature has not changed significantly over the years.

In all but intimate seminars with ten to fifteen students, university and college professors usually transmit their learning in one of three ways. First, they teach literature as history in such courses as "English Drama to 1642," "Chaucer," "Shakespeare's Tragedies," "Milton," "The Modern American Novel," and "Postmodern American Fiction." If college departments of English do have junior members teach acceptable methods of how to "criticize" literature in courses like "Introduction to Literature," they invariably pass on the system of New Criticism: close reading, inductive analysis, and finding the accepted meaning in a text. Professors who have earned the right by seniority and by extensive publications to teach "critical theory"—and who see themselves as belonging to a "school of criticism" such as Marxist criticism, deconstructionism, gender studies, multiculturalism, or postcolonialism studies, for example—lecture students on the most recent research on their favorite critical theory. We have found that most professors refuse to accept essay examinations or term papers based upon Reader Response assumptions—that is, including such features as intuitive personal responses, expression of emotion, or an interpretation not based upon an exhaustive account of what major critics have to say about a text.

The result of this kind of training for secondary school English teachers is that they naturally follow the practices they have experienced throughout undergraduate and graduate studies in English. Such a program of study—with few exceptions—simply does not include an understanding of Reader Response methods. As the researcher Richard Beach remarks, "New Criticism continues to influence undergraduate and high school literature instruction. Despite the dramatic shifts in interest in literary theory in the past thirty years, secondary and postsecondary teachers in general continue to employ methods reflecting New Critical orientation" (Beach 1993, 2). Beach refers to Arthur Applebee's nationwide survey of literature instructional practices in which Applebee, according to Beach, reported that "little has changed since a previous survey in the 1960s. Teachers continue to focus primarily on 'close reading' of literary texts," or students "focus on how the specific aspects of texts—setting, character, plot, language, and theme—fit together to form a coherent whole" (Beach 1993, 2).

Robert E. Probst, after having examined textbooks and curriculum guides, found that "New Critical and historical approaches to literature, neither of which have paid close attention to the problems and pleasures of the lonely reader, have dominated instruction not only in college but also in secondary schools" (Probst 1988, preface, no page). Such a situation in the secondary schools is unfortunate because although a relatively small number of privileged students in colleges and universities are familiar with New Critical methods, students in public schools represent the population as a whole and could profit from reading literature by Reader Response methods. "Yet it is in the secondary schools," notes Probst, "where the whole population is represented—not just the serious student of literature—that attention to the individual reader is most important" (Probst 1998, preface, no page). Probst asks why it is valuable for all students in public—and private— schools to learn how to read literature, and he answers, "Here the student can be led to organized and intelligent reflection on great issues of literature, which are also likely to be the great issues of life. Literature might serve them both to give pleasure and to sharpen understanding" (Probst 1988, preface, no page).

In another report, researcher Judith A. Langer notes that "although reader-based theory has received a good deal of pedagogical attention in recent years and teachers say they want their students to think as well as analyze and remember, a New Critical approach toward instruction still dominates" (Langer 1994, 2). Langer found the school English classroom in "conceptual disarray," for while students have internalized and follow a student-centered, process approach to writing, they must follow a text-centered New Critical approach to reading and "criticizing" literature. As a result of the New Critical approach to literature instruction, "literature lessons generally stress facts and 'correct' interpretations, and when student responses are sought, they are generally used at the beginning of lessons, for motivation. Then they get on with the 'real,' text-based lesson" (Langer 1994, 15–16).

As far as evaluating how well students are able to criticize literature, researchers find that most test questions treat knowing literature as getting the right answer. Alan Purves's favorite standardized test question is this: "Huck Finn is a good boy. True or False?" Neither in teaching nor in testing do students have much opportunity to share what they understand or to explain possibilities (quoted in Langer 1994, 16).

While academic theorists are not particularly concerned with creating models for teaching literature, or even with agreeing on what literary knowing is, the training in literature for prospective elementary schoolteachers is almost totally focused on studying children's literature and "reading." Even if college students in elementary education are introduced to teaching literature, literature is embedded within the reading program, in which little attention is afforded to teaching literature as literature. "In general," writes Sean Walmsley, a member of the National Center on Literature Teaching and Learning in a recent report on the contemporary state of elementary literature instruction, "The reading field has seen literature as the end purpose for learning how to read (i.e., what children do once they have mastered the basic reading skills" (Walmsley 1993, 509).

When students in elementary education do take courses in literature from English departments, they still receive little help in learning how to engage all the children they will be responsible for in reading and responding to literature. In fact, their instruction in literature may be harmful for that purpose. New Criticism, which carries the full weight of authority from college and university professors and of the secondary school English teachers they have prepared, teaches students to be objective, rational, inductive, detached, and scientific; it is a method particularly ill-suited for engrossing children and preadolescents in the joyous experience of reading and responding to literature.

Although elementary school teachers, particularly in the primary grades, use a great many trade picture storybooks, they use them to teach beginning reading. A few educators are concerned about this focus. As Alan Purves observes,

> Reader response approaches to teaching literature and the idea of the student-centered curriculum have not lived up to what I believe should be the balance of a response-centered literature curriculum: an inte-grated approach to the language arts. To that end I propose we think of the place of Literature in a literature program. A literature program should not be a reading program with trade books, which is currently the case in many elementary schools, nor should it be vehicle for "criti-cal thinking," which is the fashion in many secondary schools. It should have the elements of a Literature program. (Purves 1993, 356)

Walmsley remarks that elementary language arts programs have indeed been dominated by reading instruction, delivered through a commercial reading system. Even though more and more teachers use full-length children's picture books, for some time the literature pre-sented to children was made up of excerpts, frequently revised from the original texts to make the language simpler and the subject matter less controversial. When a researcher interviewed in depth a number of ele-mentary school teachers, remedial reading teachers, special education teachers, school librarians, and administrators, he found it difficult for teachers to articulate a purpose for studying literature other than it was "fun" or "it's for teaching reading skills." He discovered "little evidence of a coherent, articulated district philosophy, with respect to literature's role in the language arts program, across grades or across different lev-els of reading and writing ability" (Walmsley 1993, 510). The teachers, he reported, had virtually no idea of the "big picture" of literature instruc-tion: of how reading and literature are related, of the role of writing in lit-erature, or of a systematic set of methods for teaching literature. At the same time, teachers revealed they had little formal training in literature study, especially when compared to their extensive background in teaching reading. In sum, Walmsley concluded from the interviews that there was an absence of a philosophical underpinning for literature instruction (Walmsley 1993).

In another report, Judith Langer presented the results of a study into how children and their teachers understand literature from a Reader Response standpoint and related the strategies teachers used in their classrooms to teach literature. Langer, like Walmsley, found that elementary school teachers were "unclear" about how to teach literature even by "traditional" methods, but they were also unable to explain what Reader Response to literature meant to them. For this researcher,

> the field [literature instruction in elementary grades] has not provided
> adequate guidelines or strategies to allow teachers to build "new
> bones"—internalized routines and options to take the place of plot
> summaries and leading questions guiding students toward predeter-
> mined interpretations—new bones that can guide their moment-to-
> moment decision-making as the they plan for and interest students.
> (Langer 1994, 204)

Lack of a Reader Response Pedagogical Model for Teaching Literature in the Schools

If the model of Reader Response for teaching literature to all school-children and adolescents—not just to an elite few in college preparatory classes, colleges, and universities—shows so much promise, then why has the translation of its principles not taken place in classrooms? Why has a generally agreed upon pedagogical model not been put in place for elementary, middle, and secondary schools? We think there are at least three related reasons. First, for elementary school teachers, teaching beginning reading is viewed as more urgent than teaching literature, while in secondary schools, teaching writing has received a greater emphasis than has teaching literature by any other method than the "traditional" one. Second, the texts for in-service elementary and secondary teachers—with few exceptions—do not reflect Reader Response. And third, if we search in the publications by state education departments for evidence of curricula based upon Reader Response theoretical assumptions, we will be, for the most part, disappointed. For instance, despite an attempt by the California Department of Education in the mid-1980s to implement a literature-centered Reader Response curriculum, most of the present-day state education department English/language arts frameworks and content standards we have examined focus on teaching reading and relegate teaching literature to a less than prominent role.

First, although contemporary theory on writing and on teaching writing has had a far-reaching influence on the development of a practical model for teaching writing in elementary and secondary schools, few models have been developed for teaching literature. The task of teaching writing in schools was plainly deemed a priority. Programs to develop writing skills were simply more important than were systematic literature programs. For a period of time, beginning in the 1960s and during the 1970s and 1980s, a number of influential theoretical works and research reports were generated on the nature of writing—on how professional writers actually compose and how schoolchildren and adolescents write effective compositions—and on teaching writing. Particularly influential were the works of Donald Murray (1968), James Moffett (1968), James Britton et al. (1975), Peter Elbow (1973), Donald Graves (1983), and Lucy Calkins (1983). The writings from theorists like these were translated into practice in numerous professional articles, textbooks, and state education publications, expressing in ordinary language the results of theories and research reports on the "composing process" and on "process writing." With respect to teaching literature, though, "reader-response theories may have had less influence on practice because [with few exceptions] there was little systematic attempt to translate theory into practice" (Beach 1993, 3).

At the same time that there were few models for Reader Response practices in the schools, literary theorists from English departments in research universities—where theoretical models are spawned—showed little interest in determining how all the children enrolled in public and private schools could read literature from a Reader Response reference point. If there is no academic theoretical Reader Response model from the research universities, then it is highly unlikely that educational theorists would develop their own brand of Reader Response. If there is no theory, how can practice follow?

Because of the lack of theoretical models, few education textbook writers reflected Reader Response methods. At the secondary school level, Richard Beach and James Marshall's *Teaching Literature in the Secondary School* (1991), an exception to the rule, is a comprehensive literature text that includes examples of teaching methods and student activities—"illustrating the application of theory to practice"—written for secondary school English teachers. The text is aimed at teachers who "are looking for alternative approaches to the reading of literature—approaches that will take account of new developments in literary theory and reading research, while remaining sensitive to the realities of classroom life" (Beach and Marshall 1991, ix).

The presence of textbooks for elementary school teachers is another matter. For the most part, students in elementary education receive preparation in the field of reading—New York State, for instance, requires two full-semester courses in reading, and Maryland requires four three-semester-hour courses, one of which may be a one-semester course in "Children's Literature." Most elementary school teachers also take a course—or part of a course—in "language arts."

If prospective elementary school teachers do have a course in "literature," it is a course on children's literature, entitled something like "Introduction to Children's Literature." One highly successful children's literature text, *Through the Eyes of a Child,* states its purpose thus:

> The text is intended for any adult who is interested in evaluating, selecting, and sharing children's literature. Its focus and organization are designed for children's literature classes taught in the departments of English, Education, and Library Science. *Through the Eyes of a Child* is written in the hope that adults who work with children and literature will discover and share with children the enchantment in books and will help foster a lifelong appreciation for literature and a respect for our literary heritage. It is my hope that my own love for literature and enthusiasm for books will be transmitted to the readers of this text. (Norton 1991, xi)

This compendium of children's literature—with its wide range of topics, several bibliographies, and numerous black-and-white and many attractive four-color illustrations from children's books—is aimed at adults for the purpose of selecting and evaluating children's literature. As is common with such a text, the focus is on instilling in its readers a "love for literature" and, it is assumed, on enabling them to pass on the love to elementary schoolchildren. There is no mention in the text of how to teach literature by a Reader Response approach or, for that matter, by any other approach. If prospective elementary school teachers are seeking methods for teaching literature to children, they cannot expect to find them here.

Another place we might look for a theoretically based Reader Response model for teaching literature in the schools is in state education departments' publications on "English-Language Arts Frameworks" or "Content Standards." It is instructive to examine the progress of such a model: In 1987, the California State Education Department published a literature-centered *English–Language Arts Framework for California Public Schools Kindergarten through Grade Twelve* (hereafter *English–Language Arts Framework*), explicitly based upon Reader Response assumptions. Then, in reaction to the literature-based curriculum—because the 1987 *English–Language Arts Framework* took the full blame for the claim that a majority of California children were failing to learn how to read—the Education Department published a heavily phonics-based statewide system of teaching what it called "English/Language Arts."

What precisely was the *English–Language Arts Framework*, the literature-based program of 1987 officially adopted by the California State Board of Education? The curriculum was received by the schools of California, and because California had the largest number of students of any state in the country, it exerted a great deal of influence throughout the country as an official or quasi-official document. The publication was "a systematic literature program with a meaning-centered approach based upon intensive reading, writing, speaking, and listening." The *English–Language Arts Framework*, moreover, was a "literature-based program that encourages and exposes all students, including those whose primary language is not English, to significant literary works" (*English–Language Arts Framework* 1987, 3). A "meaning-centered approach" to teaching literature is in opposition to a "skill-based program that uses brief, unfocused narratives and work sheets lacking meaningful content or that are constructed to teach independent skills in isolation" (*English–Language Arts Framework* 1987, 3). The effective English/language arts program thus introduces students to many different styles, cultures, points of view, and a "range of modes from fiction and drama through poetry and essays and speeches. It prepares them for understanding ideas and expressing themselves effectively about important human issues" (*English–Language Arts Framework* 1987, 17). In conclusion, the *English–Language Arts Framework* writers give this reason for reading literature:

> Direct teaching of literature helps students move into, through, and beyond the literary work to a new understanding of themselves and the world around them. Teachers who evoke a desire to read literature by asking provocative questions, providing interesting background information, or structuring oral activities enable students to explore the work in depth, ask important questions, and explore the possibilities for learning in the work, and connect the meaning of the work to the world and their own lives. (*English–Language Arts Framework* 1987, 17)

In the section "Emphasizing Significant Literary Works" from an accompanying 1987 *English–Language Arts Model Curriculum Guide: Kindergarten through Eight* (hereafter *Curriculum Guide*), the writers argue that "teachers use literature as a basis for integrating instruction in the language arts and as a means for helping students improve their skills in thinking, listening, speaking, reading, and writing" (*Curriculum Guide* 1987, vii). A bold and noble objective; let us see how explicitly the authors follow the lead of Reader Response.

The authors of the *Curriculum Guide* use this stark quote from a lecture by Louise Rosenblatt, "Reading is a transaction between a reader and a text," in a sidebar and then describe their version of Rosenblatt's transactional theory of Reader response:

> Reading literature involves an interaction between reader and text. Students respond to what they read first in personal terms, emotionally and intellectually. They express their response to what they have read through a variety of means, and as ideas are shared among students, they refine and revise their views, returning to the printed or spoken text to verify, question, or modify responses. Ultimately, each student's response to a work of literature is a blend of universal understanding and personal views. (*Curriculum Guide* 1987, 6)

Now, with this *English–Language Arts Framework* and the supplementary *Curriculum Guide,* we have evidence of some pretty basic Reader Response notions underlying the California publications. This is heady stuff, perhaps too new and exotic for teachers with no formal background in literature or in Reader Response theory. The elementary teachers then faced the major problem of converting these abstract declarations into pragmatic classroom strategies while at the same time carrying on instruction with upward of thirty kids in elementary school classrooms.

From the general pronouncements in the 1987 *English–Language Arts Framework* and in the 1987 *Curriculum Guide,* it is little wonder that elementary school teachers had so many and varied perceptions about what Reader Response and "literature-base reading instruction" were and about how effective methods were to be derived from these starkly simple theoretical statements. Although the underlying principles of Reader Response were present—along with descriptions of appropriate classroom approaches—the statements were so totally unfamiliar that it is surprising how successfully classroom teachers translated the guidelines of the *English–Language Arts Framework* and the *Curriculum Guide,* often in most conscientious and admirable ways, into a wide variety of classroom practices.

What happened to the Reader Response, literature-based reading instruction movement in California? For many children across the country, and especially for children in the state of California, the literature-centered approach to reading failed to teach a majority of children how to read. In *Every Child a Reader: The Report of the California Reading Task Force* of 1995 (hereafter *Every Child a Reader*), we are told in no uncertain terms, "There is a crisis in California that demands our immediate attention. National and state reports indicate that a majority of California's children cannot read at basic levels. The reading failure begins in the early grades and has a harmful effect for a lifetime" (*Every Child a Reader* 1995, 1).

The Reading Task Force, formed to find out why so many children in California were not learning to read, studied research reports and listened to testimony from various experts in the field of reading—none, by the way, from literature—"about what works in effective, comprehensive reading programs" (*Every Child a Reader* 1995, 2). In effect, the task force found that the 1987 *English–Language Arts Framework* "did not present a comprehensive and balanced reading program and gave insufficient attention to a systematic skills instruction program" (*Every Child a Reader* 1995, 2). As a consequence, "many language arts programs have shifted too far away from direct skills instruction." What was needed, the authors argued, was a balanced and comprehensive reading program with these components:

1. a strong literature, language, and comprehension program that includes a balance of oral and written language;
2. an organized, explicit skills program that includes phonemic awareness (sounds in words), phonics, and decoding skills to address the needs of the emergent reader;
3. ongoing diagnosis that informs teaching and assessment that ensures accountability; and
4. a powerful early intervention program that provides individual tutoring for children at risk of reading failure. (*Every Child a Reader* 1995, 2)

From this and other publications, we learn that California has done an about-face in its focus, turning from a literature-based approach to a reading-research mandate for teaching reading, especially in the primary grades and for children who have difficulty with beginning reading.

In order to understand this radical change in policy, we turn to the *English–Language Arts Framework Content Standards for California*

Public Schools Kindergarten through Grade Twelve (hereafter *Content Standards*), published in 1998. What is strikingly apparent is that the major emphasis in English/language arts is on reading. The *Content Standards* are divided into four categories: Reading, Writing, Written and Oral English Language Conventions ("The standards for written and oral English language conventions have been placed between those for writing and for listening and speaking because these conventions are essential to both sets of skills" [*Content Standards* 1998, 4]), and Listening and Speaking. The classification of literature, labeled "3.0 Literary Response and Analysis," falls in the general category of Reading. The other subtopics under Reading are "1.0 Word Analysis, Fluency, and Systematic Vocabulary Development" and "2.0 Reading Comprehension." In the early grades, children "listen and respond to stories." In later grades, students "read and respond" to literature, chiefly "analyzing" works of literature. We note that the content of literature study—what students need to acquire—is drawn entirely from New Criticism, except that the term "New Criticism" is not used to describe the procedures of literary analysis. We can only assume that New Critical assumptions are so deeply embedded in the school culture that the name of the approach need not be specified. Any reference to Reader Response is noticeably absent.

When we examine the "Selected References"—upon which we might assume the *Content Standards* are based—we find five items: an *Introduction to Logic* (Copi and Cohen 1990); a *Literary Dictionary* (Harris and Hodges 1995); two California State Education Department publications, *Recommended Literature: Grades Nine through Twelve* and *Recommended Readings in Literature: Kindergarten through Grade Eight;* and the *Merriam-Webster's Collegiate Dictionary.* Terms in the "Glossary" are mainly related to reading, such as "alphabetic principle," "decoding," and "phoneme"; to oral discourse, such as "appeal to reason"; and to traditional grammar, such as "compound sentence." Terms referring to literature—such as "archetypal criticism," "archetype," "climax," "denouement," "literary analysis" ("The study of a literary work by a critic, student, or scholar; a careful, detailed reading and report thereof"), "literary criticism" ("The analysis and judgment of works of literature. The body of principles by which the work of writers is judged"), "metaphor," and "onomatopoeia"—all relate to a traditional view of literature instruction, with nary a hint of any contact with recent theory and practice in modern literature study.

In the 1999 *Reading/Language Arts Framework for California Public Schools Kindergarten through Grade Twelve* (hereafter *Reading/Language Arts Framework*), we find the emphasis overwhelmingly on teaching kids to read. In the preface, we are informed that "they [students] must be able to read all forms of text fluently and independently, communicate effectively and creatively in oral and written form, and comprehend and deliver complex forms of discourse." This 1999 *Reading/Language Arts Framework* replaces the 1987 *English–Language Arts Framework* (which is literature-based and Reader-Response oriented); it "relies heavily on the converging research base in beginning reading" (*Reading/Language Arts Framework* 1999, viii). We see evidence of the focus on reading in *Reading/Language Arts Framework* from several sources. The principal writers of the new *Reading/Language Arts Framework* were college professors at the University of Oregon, but we are not told their academic departments, whether they were from an education department or an English department. We may assume they were experts in "reading." Members of the committees "responsible for overseeing the development of the framework" of the *Reading/Language Arts Framework* were almost entirely public school people. California Department of Education staff members also contributed to the *Reading/Language Arts Framework*.

The materials in the "Works Cited" and "Additional References" sections are chiefly reports of empirical research on beginning reading. There are no citations of works on literature study from academics. Such people obviously were not consulted. And as we examine the "Glossary of Selected Terms" —which should reflect the emphasis in *Reading/Language Arts Framework*—we find these "literary" terms: "literary analysis" ("The study or examination of a literary work or author"), "literary criticism" ("The result of literary analysis; a judgment or evaluation of a work a body of literature"), "narrative," "story frame/map," and "story grammar." That is (apparently) all elementary school teachers need to know about literature. As we look at "Appendix A: Matrix for the English–Language Arts Content Standards," we see under "Literary Response and Analysis" three categories: "Structural Features of Literature," "Narrative Analysis of Grade-Level–Appropriate Text," and "Literary Criticism."

It is clear that what California did was change from a literature-based program for teaching reading to commercial reading programs based primarily on teaching reading through direct, systematic instruction in "phonics." In Diana Jean Schemo's recent feature article in the *New York Times*, significantly entitled "California Leads Chorus of Sounded-Out Syllables," we have one account of reading instruction in Los Angeles, the second largest school district in the country after New York City. We learn that after having dropped phonics instruction for a literature-based reading program in 1987, California "is returning to basic phonics in a big way" (Schemo 2002, A9).

Why did California drop its literature-centered reading program? It seems that the California Board of Education was dismayed when it was notified in the mid-1990s that the reading scores of elementary school students had sunk to nearly the worst in the country: "'In California, 56 percent of our children were reading below a basic level,' reported Marion Joseph, a member of the State Board of Education." Not only were poor children and those from bilingual families not learning how to read well, but children from families with college-educated parents also scored low on reading tests. "'Forty-nine percent of our kids whose parents were college graduates were below basic. This is not about poverty or class or race,' said Ms. Joseph. 'It's about curriculum'" (Schemo 2002, A9). As Joseph reported, the board replaced the previous "literature-based/whole language" beginning reading approach with a "systematic phonics" method because board members like Joseph argued that the alternative "'whole language instruction left too much to each teacher's ability and imagination, with resulting gaps in children's preparation in reading'" (Schemo 2002, A9).

As evidence of the success of a phonics-based approach to teaching beginning reading, we are told that in Los Angeles, where the poorest reading scores were reported, two years after "systematic phonics" was adopted, first-grade reading scores climbed from the 42nd percentile to the 56th percentile of scores reported throughout the nation. Second-grade scores rose from the 32nd to the 37th percentile. However, at the same time, even for Los Angeles students in classes in which students had not received direct instruction in phonics, the scores for students rose by 10–20 percent. There seem to be other factors besides phonics instruction responsible for the dramatic rise in reading scores.

It may be that literature-based beginning reading instruction and phonics instruction are not necessarily antagonistic but, in reality, share many features. For instance, in the original California reading program, children practiced reading expository texts as well as literature in their quest to acquire comprehension skills. And contrary to some statements about the literature-centered approach that children read literature without ever learning how letters represent English sounds, children in the literature-based reading programs *did* learn sound-symbol correspondences, but rather than studying the sounds of letters in English through isolated drills in phonics, children learned about English letter sounds implicitly, as they read whole books from "real" authors rather than basal readers or excerpts from books created by committees of "reading experts."

Another factor possibly contributing to the recent rise in children's reading scores is the fact that "as the poorest performing schools picked up phonics, the school system also invested heavily in teacher training, with frequent assessment to diagnose weaknesses in students" (Schemo 2002, A9). Still another factor may be that federal money originally allocated for unskilled paraprofessionals had gone to pay for 271 especially trained "literacy coaches" in the year 2001, with 150 more coaches being added in 2002.

CLASSROOM READER RESPONSE: PRACTICAL MODELS

Although the application of Reader Response to classroom practices has been evolving slowly and has had some setbacks—witness the situation in California—there have been a number of reports of successful uses of Reader Response approaches in individual classes and a few accounts of systematic models for school use.

There are several collections of edited essays dealing with applying Reader Response theory in individual classrooms. Here are some worth examining: Ben F. Nelms's *Literature in the Classroom* (1988); Robert W. Blake's *Reading, Writing, and Interpreting Literature* (1989) and *Literature as a Way of Knowing* (1991); Nicholas J. Karolides's *Reader Response in the Classroom* (1992); and Joyce Many and Carole Cox's *Reader Stance and Literary Understanding* (1992).

One of the most impressive programs is that of David Bleich, as reported in his important little book *Readings and Feelings: An Introduction to Subjective Criticism* (1975). Bleich's model for teaching literature springs from his theoretical position, which he calls "subjective criticism," a theory he discusses in detail in his academic book entitled, fittingly enough, *Subjective Criticism* (1978).

Bleich's pedagogical plan is based upon the assumptions that all interpretation is subjective, that feeling precedes knowledge, and that knowledge is achieved only because of a passion to discover and know. His purpose, he states, is to enlarge the range of vision of ordinary persons by including a subjective basis for reading and judging literature. He is careful to point out that by embracing a subjective basis for reading literature, he is at the same time including, not dismissing, close, precise reading. His aim is for students to gain new perceptions of themselves, to acquire new ideas of their own values, tastes, and prejudices. Ultimately for Bleich, "the role of personality in response [to literature] is the most fundamental act of criticism" (Bleich 1975, 4).

Using a model based on these presumptions, Bleich followed a course of study over a semester with privileged university students, requiring them to read worthwhile stories, poems, and novels; to write responses; and to discuss their written reactions in these four sequential stages:

1. *Thoughts and feelings.* In this initial stage, the students, through reading and discussion, explore the nature of their feelings. They are asked to express feelings and relate experiences they have had of which literary works reminded them.
2. *Feelings about literature.* At this stage, students learn to respond in several ways. They relate what literary works essentially mean to them, an act of "perceiving" the work. They also respond to works by making pointedly "emotional" remarks, an "affective response." And finally, they respond by an "associative response," in which students relate incidents in their lives, triggered by works of literature, as a means for understanding the texts. This response is the most complex, but it is the most useful for students' self-understanding because they rework poems and stories according to their own personalities.
3. *Deciding on literary importance.* At this level, students determine the meaning for themselves of works by pointing out the most important *word,* most important *passage,* and most important *aspect* and then explaining why they made their choices. By these exercises, the students learn about the relation of intellectual judgment to an initial emotional response.
4. *Interpretation as a communal act.* At the final stage in their development, students learn, by discussing their responses in small groups and in the class as a whole, that interpretation is a social act, a communal experience. As they discuss their explanations, they learn that interpretation, rather than being a quest for an eternal, absolute conclusion, is the result of arriving at an overall consensus about a work, based upon the shared values and attitudes of the group. Most significantly, as they share their expressions of what literary texts mean to them, students have their responses validated by others and become comfortable with communal interpretation.

The systematic, classroom-tested program moves from basic, low-level, and often unconscious feeling activities to high-level, sophisticated emotional and intellectual experiences, invariably culminating in new insights for students into their capacities for feeling and thinking and leading finally to recognition of the subtle ways their responses to literary texts are dependent upon their individual personalities. Although such a method is not simple and requires discipline, concentration, honesty, and a willingness to participate in group activities, Bleich feels that students come away from such a rigorous course of study with the palpable feeling—a surprise to most students—that "reading a book or a poem can have some very important connection with the things that most concern and occupy them" (Bleich 1975, 6).

Here we would like to present the results of a program using many of the features of Bleich's approach, modified for use with secondary and elementary students as well as with college students, that we call "Classroom Reader Response."

Assumptions Underlying Classroom Reader Response

Because Classroom Reader Response is so radically different from the traditional, objective approach to criticizing literature, the authors believe it is necessary first to state the assumptions underlying Classroom Reader Response before we discuss examples of practical activities.

1. *Primary emphasis on the reader's response to a text.* With this method, the emphasis is not solely on one's examination of a text as a text but, rather, is principally on the reader's response to the text. The work itself, of course, is not insignificant, for we all know that Mark Twain's *Huckleberry Finn* is in a different category from the yellow pages of a telephone book. The practical result of this assumption, though, is that each reader is recognized as existing uniquely—as a result of many factors, such as age, gender, education, experiences, culture, race, and so forth—and that the reader's response will be a direct result of a mysterious combination of these factors.

2. *Reader creates personal meaning.* Rather than finding someone else's meaning—whether it is the teacher's or that of the teacher's previous professors or the meaning declared over years and formalized within some canon—the reader creates his or her own meaning of the text. The implication of this assumptions is that the reader is literally creative, and, as a result, with confidence, eventually becomes a "courageous" reader, trusting himself or herself to create rich, satisfying responses to literature.

3. *Feelings are allowed.* Since readers' initial responses to worthwhile pieces of literature are emotional, readers are "allowed," even encouraged, to respond emotionally. With Classroom Reader Response, feelings are okay. Related to the notion of feelings being all right, readers admit their feelings for a piece because it is through emotions that readers enter into a work.

4. *Memories and associations are encouraged.* When readers permit memories evoked by a literary piece to arise from their unconscious, when they accept associations related to these experiences, to other works of literature, and even to movies, television shows, and popular songs, they are able in a powerfully significant way to relate literature to their own lives. Those who read a literary piece from a traditional stance, our experience has shown, seldom see a poem or story as being relevant to their lives. This is not a trivial point. Literature is a special way of knowing only if one accepts the fact that it *is* a special way of knowing, only if the reader lets the piece release deep personal memories and associations. We have found that allowing memories to surface through and from a reading and making available one's response to trusted readers is the single most potent way for readers to perceive literature as a special way of knowing.

5. *Intuition invoked.* After readers have allowed themselves to become emotionally involved in a piece, have let themselves experience the piece through memories and associations, they learn to trust themselves to give an immediate, intuitive reaction to the piece. The authors have found that when we ask readers of any age to take a few minutes to write out immediate responses, that primary reaction is invariably the one they stick to. What remains for the readers is to find out why they responded in the way they did and to justify their responses.

6. *Close reading techniques used to substantiate initial responses.* Only after readers have gained enough confidence in themselves to give beginning responses do they then move to close reading techniques in order to justify their original responses. With objective criticism, readers traditionally make an educated guess at the correct interpretation of a piece only after having collected evidence by a systematic, step-by-step gathering of details. In the Classroom Reader Response approach, though, readers use close reading techniques to discover why they responded the way they did.

7. *Sharing reader responses with others in a learning community.* The assumption that reading and responding to literature is essentially a social event, that it occurs within a learning community, is the bedrock upon which Classroom Reader Response rests. When readers share their literary responses with others (especially with fellow readers under the guidance of trained and sensitive teachers), their responses are validated. Such common experiences often offer varying viewpoints that contribute to deepening and widening responses, while, at the same time, sharing responses helps to correct surface-level misreading.

On a higher level, though, sharing responses within a learning community is a natural way for readers to become acculturated, to participate in the ways of living accepted by a culture. Since worthwhile literary works imply personal and social codes of behavior, reading and responding to literature within a learning community make the members aware of the mostly unwritten codes of personal, social, and moral behavior endorsed by a culture.

8. *Readers come to understand responses as reflections of their distinct personalities.* As readers become increasingly sophisticated in Classroom Reading Response, they are able to understand how their particular responses are a direct result of the factors of their unique personalities.

These are the classroom activities the authors have found useful in teaching people of all ages and all aptitudes how to read and respond to generally acclaimed literary works.

Classroom Reader Response Program for Secondary Students

First, we discuss the activities we devised for high school students and undergraduate English majors to follow as they are asked to respond to Robert Beloof's poem "A Spring Night," chosen especially to evoke responses by adolescents and young adults.

His son meant something that he couldn't name.
He had his picture in his wallet,
but never remembered taking out the wallet
for anything but cash, or an address, or a name.

He could have hated him, but didn't
even though the boy reminded him
how stuck he was because of him.
He could have loved him, too, but didn't.

When Mr. Cuff came home at night
there was reading, or sitting on the stoop till dark,
watching the dead-end street he lived on fade to dark,
so they didn't talk together much at night.

Sitting as usual this April evening
watching an impassively dying sun,
he became aware that hesitantly his son
was coming to him out of the evening.

They sat awhile together, then quietly
the boy asked him, "Do you really like boys?
I'd just like to know that, if you really like boys."
Mr. Cuff was stunned. The sun set quietly.

Communication was a rusted hinge to Cuff.
He sought some way convincingly to say
"There's just the word I've wanted long to say
but couldn't say." "Like is the word," thought Cuff.

"I'm damned," said Mr. Cuff under his breath.
Finally the boy shuffled off. Cuff went to bed.
"What's that you're mumbling over there in bed?"
Asked Mrs. Cuff in the dark. Cuff lay still as death.

1. *Initial response.* We gave this task for students to become used to responding intuitively and without inhibitions to a literary work. The initial response is a crucial feature of Classroom Reader Response. With it, we want to wean students away from the idea that they need to approach a literary text in a New Critical, scientific, rational way, collecting evidence from a text in order to find its correct meaning. Rather, we want them to learn to trust their immediate, intuitive responses to literary texts and then to choose significant evidence in the works to substantiate their personal interpretations. We continually stress that they should trust their own interpretations—not those of a critic or teacher—so that in any response, from the simplest to the most sophisticated, they start with an intuitive sense of what the work means to them. In sum, our aim is to help students trust their responses, to become courageous readers.

> In a short paragraph, write out what ——— (poem, story, novel) means essentially *to you.* Don't worry about what anybody else thinks it means, even your teacher. Also, at this time, don't worry about spelling, punctuation, or other writing errors. And don't worry about getting the "right" meaning. We really want to know what *you* believe the piece means. Write as quickly as you can about your feelings and thoughts without stopping to think about them too much.

Here is what some high school sophomores, untrained in Classroom Reader Response, wrote after first reading "A Spring Night":

> MELISSA: "I thought this was a sad poem about a father who either couldn't or didn't want to see his son. (If there's a will, there's a way.)"
>   ROBBIE: "I liked this poem because it showed how a father feels when not able to see his son. Or didn't want to."

2. *Feeling response.* This is what Bleich calls the "affective" response, but we have chosen the word "feeling" because it appears to

be more easily accepted and understood by students and teachers. Since most school assignments deal primarily with intellectual tasks, we want students to realize that with Classroom Reader Response, feelings are okay. Not only will the students not be penalized for expressing feelings, but, in fact, they will be lauded for relating their feelings to overall interpretations.

Here's the task we set for students to become comfortable with making known their feelings and relating them to their perception of a literary work:

> As you read this poem (or story), how did you feel? Jot down in a few sentences what your feelings were. Here are some samples of the kinds of sentences you might use to show you're writing a feeling response.
> I felt (sad, happy, disgusted, bored) as I read this poem (or story).
> I (laughed out loud, cried, felt sad) as I read this poem (or story).

Here are some examples of simple "feeling" responses by high school sophomores, new to Cleassroom Reader Response assumptions and methods:

> KIM: "The poem started out sad, and I expected it to wind up happy, when the way I see it, it remained sad. I really don't care for the poem. Sorry."
> KATHY: "I found the poem being sad."
> MIKE: "My response to the poem is that it was dull. Cuff is a very withdrawn man he doesn't care. I think he was trying to communicate with his son and be a friend to him. He wanted someone to talk to."
> CHRIS: "It's rather depressing but was easy to read. The father hardly ever thought about his son. He didn't really have any feelings for him. Eventually he realized he liked him."

3. *Memory response.* With this task, we ask students to let their reading bring memories and associations triggered by the piece, which, in turn, illuminate for them the meaning of the poem or story. We find this task to be the most powerful one for allowing students to relate literature to their lives.

Here is the task we use to help students see how their own experiences are related to feelings, images, or events evoked by a poem or a story:

> What memories come to mind as you read this poem (story)? Don't worry about what the recollections are, how far-fetched they may seem

to you at this time. Your memories are a valuable part of reading literature because they help you understand the poem (or story). Here are
some sample sentences you might use in your memory response.

This poem (story) reminds me of a time when ———.

This *word*, this *line*, this *part* brought back memories of ———.

Here is an initial memory response by a high school sophomore,
again, a student just being introduced to Classroom Reader Response
approaches:

DIANE: "I really didn't understand it at all. What I did understand I liked
because I could relate to it with our relationship with my father. Sometimes it feels like my own father resents me but we still get along."

And finally here are the memory responses to the poem by two
college undergraduate English majors, both experienced in Classroom
Reader Response activities. It is important to note that the heart of all
responses—whether they be feeling, memory, or any other—is the initial, intuitive response.

DONNA: "During my first reading of 'A Spring Night' I was reminded of
my relationship with my father, the man whom I call 'dad' is really my
step-father. He married my mom and adopted me when I was seven
years old, yet I feel I barely know him. He never made the effort to get
close to me, for which I no longer blame myself, as he is the same way
with his three other daughters by his first marriage. He doesn't communicate well with his family, which I think is a major problem for Mr.
Cuff. 'Communication was a rusted thing to Cuff.' Not only with his
son, who must be very confused where his father is concerned, but also
with his wife, who he refuses to confide in, despite his feelings of frus-
tration and loneliness."

ROBIN: "After reading and pondering the poem 'Spring Night,' I could
not help but be reminded of the classic folk song, 'Cat's in the Cradle.'
The son relates the trials a father has in expressing his love for a child,
and the ambiguous feelings and attitudes he has toward his son. Eventually, the man realizes that his son, grown, is just like him. I really felt
or sensed this ambiguous, ambivalent attitude Mr. Cuff had for his son
in 'Spring Night.' Mr. Cuff not only suffers the inability to express emotions to his child, he also is unsure of his feelings toward his son. This is
a highly tragic element of the poem, a father's lack of love for his own
flesh and blood.

"Unfortunately I think this is a common attitude today and so many innocent, helpless children suffer emotional scars by feeling unloved and insecure in this troubled world. Obviously, Mr. Cuff's son, young and innocent, is aware of his father's lack of emotional ties to him. How tragic and sad. And yet, I almost felt a hint of sadness for Mr. Cuff. Perhaps he, like his father before him, is incapable of loving because he has never been loved. And saddened because of the oppressive trapped feeling he has toward his child. It is quite clear that Mr. Cuff blames his situation and stagnant life on the birth of his child, this is highly selfish but yet also common in our world. But I sensed that Mr. Cuff saw himself in his child and he likes him. Like himself, Mr. Cuff was unable to hate or love himself and his child. I also felt a sense of deep-seated emotion for the child. Mr. Cuff 'lay still as death' after his son finalizes his belief that his father doesn't love him. It is as if the son, knowing he is unloved, will reject his father and Mr. Cuff lies still as death because a living part of him has just died. Perhaps Mr. Cuff does love his son but is unable to recognize or acknowledge this emotion. This really created a sense of the 'typical' dysfunctional family in today's society. The inability to loves oneself and each other."

We think that the first question here might be: How well did the college students Donna and Robin fulfill the requirement for using a memory response to read and respond to a poem, "A Spring Night." We need to remember that after some experience with Classroom Reader Response, students very naturally become comfortable with recognizing *their own* first, sharp insight into the poem. After this act, they are asked to relate memories triggered by the poem and to tell how the memories helped them confirm their original insight.

As a dutiful student, Donna first read the poem about the relationships among a boy, Mr. Cuff, and Mrs. Cuff. Their relationships reminded her of her own relationship with her stepfather, a man who "never made the effort to get close" to her. She interprets the poem as expressing the fact that "he doesn't communicate well with his family, which I think is a major problem for Mr. Cuff." We note that here Donna chooses to quote the one line "Communication was a rusted thing [hinge] to Cuff." To her, in this short, uninhibited response, this line appears as the most important one. She substitutes the word "thing" for the original word "hinge," thus missing the apt metaphor of a rusty hinge, but to our way of thinking, she still pinpoints the most important line in the poem. And finally, she picks up on the fact that Mr. Cuff's inability to show affection extends to his wife as well.

Now to Robin's memory response to the poem. After she has read and pondered the poem, she makes the marvelous leap from the poem to a "classic folk song, 'Cat's in the Cradle.'" Is this a valid allusion, even though it is not a literary one? Of course, and it is a wonderfully appropriate one at that. (By the way, why is the song a "classic"? Because it is a classic for her and for the members of her generation. The allusion is an example of an act of communal interpretation.)

The poem reminds Robin of the song because both deal with a father's inability to show love for a child. She states she "really felt or sensed" the "ambivalent" attitude Cuff felt for his son—an appropriate feeling indicator—and she interprets the father's coldness as a "highly tragic element of the poem, a father's lack of love for his own flesh and blood."

Now Robin moves outward from the poem itself, from the specifics of the father in "Cat's in the Cradle" and Mr. Cuff in "A Spring Night" to the wider world, and makes a general statement about the inability of some fathers to show love for their children: "Unfortunately I think this is a common attitude today," she tells us, and she adds that such a situation is "tragic and sad." However, though, she also "almost felt a hint of sadness for Mr. Cuff" and remarks that it is possible that the son, "knowing he is unloved, will reject his father," and that "Mr. Cuff lies still as death because a living part of him has just died." Robin, however, offers a reason for this unhappy family: "Perhaps Mr. Cuff does love his son but is unable to recognize or acknowledge this emotion." And finally Robin makes her final general statement: The poem "really created a sense of the 'typical' dysfunctional family in today's society. The inability to love oneself and each other."

It seems that Robin has met the requirements for a successful memory response to the poem "A Spring Night," but on the whole we ask ourselves whether her response was an example of successful traditional criticism. First of all, in this memory response, she misses the relation of the structure of the poem to its overall meaning. The rhyme scheme has in each stanza not rhyming words but repeated words, and each stanza is complete unto itself, giving the impression of halting, repetitious language devoid of fresh words, perhaps reflecting Cuff's lack of communication. She also misses the images "dead-end street" and "impassively dying sun" and the pun in the sentence "The sun set quietly," and she fails to note the significance of Cuff's pronouncement "I'm damned" and of the last statement, "Cuff lay still as death." And finally, Robin might have related the poem's ironic title—"A Spring Night," reminding us of the advent of spring, bringing with it a renewal of life and hope—to the somber tone of the poem.

We need to remember that Robin's initial intuitive reaction was just that, an immediate, unmediated response. From our experience, after rereadings and discussions with other students, she would probably pick up several of those elements of the text that we have mentioned, helping her verify her initial statement of meaning. Was her response successful? From our way of thinking, you bet it was.

Classroom Reader Response Program for Elementary Students

But how does Classroom Reader Response work in the elementary school classroom? Here we show how a first-grade group of children read, discussed, and wrote about a delightful children's picture book (Blake 1996). In April, the teacher, Mrs. Mary C. Kelly, invites four of her independent readers to take part in an informal experiment with beginning Classroom Reader Response as they read and discuss Nancy White Carlstrom's picture book *Jesse Bear, What Will You Wear?* (1989), which recounts one day in the life of a preschooler, Jesse Bear.

For their first reading of the book, Mrs. Kelly has the children sit together in a circle and asks the children to read their books silently. Then they all read the book together out loud, and when they are finished, they talk in the group about their initial impression of the book, why they like it.

> KRYSTEN: "The whole book rhymes and I think it is neat."
>
> JOLENE: "I like Jesse because he was a bear and because my sister's name is Jesse."
>
> LINDSAY: "I read the book before and after and I think it is funny."
>
> BRYAN (in a low voice; he is intimidated by these articulate girls): "I think the book is good."

Now Mrs. Kelly asks for volunteers to retell the story.
"I will," says Jolene as she raises her hand.
"Okay. Go ahead," prompts Mrs. Kelly.
"Jesse Bear had dirt on his shirt and ants in his pants."
"Would you like Jesse as a friend?" asks Mrs. Kelly.
"I would love that."
"Why?"
"Because he looks so cuddly and cute."
Bryan pipes up, "I would like him for a friend because Jesse has neat toys."

"I'm almost like Jesse Bear," adds Krysten. "I get up, get dressed, play outside, have lunch, play some more, have dinner, take a bath, put on my pj's, and then go to bed."

All the children agree they are somewhat like Jesse Bear. Krysten even goes so far as to identify with him, seeing no difference between a little girl and a bear cub.

For the next step in the Classroom Reader Response process, the children are asked to go back to their seats and write a response to the book. They are also encouraged to illustrate their responses. What follow are the teacher's directions, descriptions of the children's drawings, and a verbatim account of what they wrote:

> KRYSTEN (Krysten draws a picture of Jesse Bear in his red shirt and jockey pants with blue stars): "I't all rime's. And I't says in the morning at nigte in the after noon. And Jesse Bear rime's with is clothes like with noon at nigte in the morning. And I like this story very much I injoy this book."
>
> LINDSAY (at the top of her paper, she draws and colors a picture of Jesse's dirty shirt and a picture of Jesse with his red shirt and his blue pants): "The book was good. Because Jesse Bear was funny. He said I'll wear my blue pens and my red shirt. Then at noon he said I'll wear my blue pj's. At night I wear white pj's with peanda [panda] bears on it."
>
> BRYAN (Bryan's picture shows a brown Jesse, looking somewhat like a happy seal, reclining in an immense expanse of blue water in an old-fashioned claw-footed bathtub): "I like Jesse Bear because I like the part when he's in the tub and it tells all of the times in a day and it is a very good book and there is very good carters [characters]."
>
> JOLENE (Jolene's illustrations in purple, green, and red include Jesse at the breakfast table, Jesse reading, and Jesse in bed): "The book has bears in it. It had singing in it. There was a mama bear a papa bear in it and a little bear. Jesse was dreminge. Jesse was taking a bath. He had a pipe [to blow bubbles with in the bathtub]. He had sors [stars] on in the morning. He had a tesrt [tee shirt] on in the morning."

In summary, the elementary school children illustrated these elements of Classroom Reader Response:

1. *Children experience worthwhile literature in a number of ways.*
   They read books by themselves, they read books chorally, and they have books read to them. As they perceive literary texts in several different ways, they feel comfortable with entering into them, with first experiencing them emotionally, rather than using literary texts as a means for testing reading skills.

2. *After having "experienced" a literary text, children make an initial, intuitive response to a work.* A person's first, uninhibited response invariably remains, even after extended discussion, the right one for that person.
3. *Children commonly retell a story to fix the sequence of events in their minds, to come to an understanding of plot (i.e., what happens in a story).* Although some teachers insist that children go beyond the simple recounting of plot, an ordering of the events of a story is not always a simple task. Even though the events in books for children are usually presented in simple chronological order, the plot lines in complex stories may be very puzzling, especially in books where stories within stories and flashbacks interrupt the forward movement of the narrative. Even with Classroom Reader Response, then, children need to understand the idea of narrative events and make explicit their comprehension of how plot contributes to the overall meaning of a story, of "what happens."
4. *Children use close reading techniques to find specific details on their own, to support their initial responses.* Rather than filling in blanks in texts and in workbook sheets with single words or phrases, they identify concrete details with special meaning *for them,* choosing examples with a minimum of teacher direction, thus creating their own personal meaning for a literary text.
5. *Children allow feelings to arise and make use of personal memories triggered by the piece to assist them in relating the text to their lives.* Building upon one's feelings in order to understand a text is the "feeling response." Using memories and associations for connecting with a text is the "memory response." Bleich, of course, calls these activities, respectively, the "affective" and "associative" responses.
6. *Children, at almost all ages, are able to write out responses to literary texts if they are allowed to follow their own voices.* Children need to be constantly nudged, coaxed, and prompted to create their *own* responses, without worrying about what the teacher "wants" or what they may think the "correct" meaning should be. Furthermore, *at this initial stage,* children need to be reassured constantly that it is all right to write freely, not threatened with such surface concerns such as correct spelling, punctuation, capitalization, or standard usage. All in all, they need to relinquish any uneasiness they may harbor about what others may think about their uncensored, spontaneous reactions.

7. *Children are able to create their own interpretations of literary texts, if we who read their written responses have the stance of Classroom Reader Response teachers and are perceptive enough to translate what they write into our grown-up terms (such as "theme").* Moreover, we need to explore further how children arrive at "themes" for literary texts. Articulating "theme," which signifies an individual's overall understanding, is another essential element of Classroom Reader Response. There is a commonly held belief that young children cannot generalize about stories or poems until they reach adolescence, that they are unable to identify themes in literary texts. We have not found this to be true. Real children reading and talking about what a worthwhile book means to them have no trouble revealing, in their own words, what the book's essential meaning is to them, its "theme," if you will. As they express their idea of a text's "theme," they reveal a refined knowledge of the elements of narration even if they cannot express this understanding in adult terms.

The following chart summarizes—in an admittedly simplified fashion—the elements of Classroom Reader Response, contrasted with the salient features of traditional literature instruction.

Traditional	*Classroom Reader Response*
1. The teacher emphasizes the text primarily.	1. Although a worthwhile text is necessary, the primary emphasis is on the child's oral or written response to that text.
2. The teacher guides the child to find the "correct" meaning within the text.	2. The child creates her own personal meaning for the text, with the sophisticated help of a specially trained and sympathetic teacher.
3. The teacher directs the child to answer specific comprehension questions about such elements of a literary text as setting, plot, characters, and theme.	3. The child gives an initial response to a literary piece and then uses her knowledge about literary elements to support her interpretation.
4. Emotions and personal opinions are not emphasized, since the traditional method is essentially objective, detached, inductive, and scientific.	4. Feelings, memories, associations, and intuition (perceptions arrived at without rational thought) are not only allowed but form the core of Classroom Reader Response.

Traditional	Classroom Reader Response
5. The child typically shares her responses with the teacher only.	5. The child shares her responses with other children in small groups and in the whole learning community. Each child thus sees an individual response grow, becoming enriched and validated by the responses from her peers.

SUMMARY

We are now witnessing the slow evolution of a new dominant model for reading and teaching literature, Classroom Reader Response. Over the past century, we have moved from an emphasis on "appreciating" writers of literary texts (Old Criticism) to an emphasis on "criticizing and judging texts" (New Criticism) to an emphasis on "reading and responding" to literary texts (Reader Response), as a means for readers to learn about themselves and to understand the culture in which they find themselves. Perhaps most notably, we are giving literature back to the people, where it originated in oral epics, legends, folktales, and plays, listened to and watched by all. We are, in the best sense of the word, "democratizing" literature.

Why is this movement toward a new way of perceiving literature so glacially slow? One reason may be that in academic circles, there has been no generally agreed upon model for all students, in elementary and secondary schools as well as in colleges and universities. Another reason, therefore, is that since there is no academic, theoretical model, secondary school English teachers, who have been trained in literature instruction in college and university English departments, have had little exposure to Reader Response theory or practice. Furthermore, elementary school teachers, who seldom have an English collegiate major or courses in literature instruction, not only do not study Reader Response but seldom have instruction in any other school of literary theory. A third reason may be that few pedagogical leaders have created models of literature instruction directly applicable in classrooms.

If this is so, then why are there no pedagogical Reader Response models? There may be several reasons for this lack. First of all, the aim of the elementary school is primarily to teach children how to read and only secondarily to teach them how to read literature as literature. As a result, the primary focus in teacher education programs for prospective elementary school teachers is on study in the field of reading. As a result of this emphasis on reading, elementary education college students usually complete a course in children's literature as their sole course in literature instruction, and they may take a course—or a part of a course—in language arts. Almost never do prospective elementary education teachers have instruction in teaching literature, unless they take courses offered by English departments.

We might look for help for teaching literature by studying the English/language arts frameworks and content standards of state education curriculum publications. We note that the 1987 *English–Language Arts Framework for California Public Schools Kindergarten through Grade Twelve* represented a "systematic literature program with a meaning-centered approach for all students" constructed explicitly on a Reader Response foundation. For many reasons, however, the K–12 program failed to teach a majority of California children to read, and therefore subsequent publications, *English–Language Arts Content Standards for California Public Schools Kindergarten through Grade Twelve* (1998) and *Reading/Language Arts Framework for California Public Schools Kindergarten through Grade Twelve* (1999), overturned the 1987 *English–Language Arts Framework* and mandated a new reading curriculum, relying "heavily on the converging research base in beginning reading."

There have been, however, many edited books giving examples of isolated successful classroom practices based upon authentic Reader Response theory from kindergarten through college levels, and we find a few examples of fully developed models for use in college and lower-school classrooms, the Classroom Reader Response approach. In classrooms using this method, children, adolescents, and adults learn to make initial, intuitive, and emotional responses to worthwhile literary texts and to have faith in their responses. They then use close reading techniques to support their primary responses. The chief aim of such an approach is to encourage all students not to rely on authoritative statements of meaning from teachers or from writers of textbooks but to trust their own responses, becoming courageous readers. The emphasis of the Classroom Reader Response system is to move away from an interest in what the author meant by his text—authorial intent—and away from an emphasis on the inherent meaning of a text (generally known only to a teacher or professor) toward an emphasis on each individual student's creation of a highly personal meaning. At the highest mental and emotional levels, rather than learning how to criticize and judge literature, students learn how to read and respond to worthwhile literature as a means to learning about themselves and at the same time understanding their place in the culture in which they find themselves.

REFERENCES

Arenson, Karen W. 2002. "Columbia Soothes the Dogs of War in Its English Department." *New York Times,* March 17, 321.

Beach, Richard. 1993. *A Teacher's Introduction to Reader-Response Theories.* Urbana, IL: National Council of Teachers of English.

Beach, Richard, and James Marshall. 1991. *Teaching Literature in the Secondary School.* Orlando, FL: Harcourt Brace Jovanovich.

Beloof, Richard. 1965. "A Spring Night." In *Poems and Poets,* ed. David Aloian. New York: McGraw-Hill.

Blake, Robert W. 1996. "Reader Response: Toward an Evolving Model for Teaching Literature in the Elementary Grades." *Language and Literacy Spectrum* 6 (Spring): 39–44.

———, ed. 1991. *Literature as a Way of Knowing: Critical Thinking and Moral Reasoning through Literature.* Albany: New York State English Council.

———, ed. 1989. *Reading, Writing, and Interpreting Literature: Pedagogy, Positions, and Research.* Urbana, IL: National Council of Teachers of English.

Blake, Robert W., and Anna Lunn. 1986. "Responding to Poetry: High School Students Read Poetry." *English Journal* 75, no. 2 (February): 68–73.

Bleich, David. 1978. *Subjective Criticism.* Baltimore: Johns Hopkins University Press.

———. 1975. *Readings and Feelings. An Introduction to Subjective Criticism.* Urbana, IL: National Council of Teachers of English.

Britton, James, et al. 1975. *The Development of Writing Abilities (11–18).* London: Macmillan Education.

Byrd, Max. 2002. "The Great American Sermon." Review of *Lincoln's Greatest Speech: The Second Inaugural,* by Ronald C. White. *New York Times Book Review,* February 10, 12, 13.

Calkins, Lucy McCormack. 1983. *The Art of Teaching Writing.* Portsmouth, NH: Heinemann.

Copi, Irving M., and Carl Cohen. 1990. *Introduction to Logic.* 8th ed. New York: Macmillan.

Cuddon, J. A. 1999. *The Penguin Dictionary of Literary Terms and Literary Theory.* Revised by C. E. Preston. New York: Penguin Books, Penguin Putnam.

Eco, Umberto. 1994. "The Author's Postscript." In *The Name of the Rose.* San Diego, CA: Harcourt Brace.

———. 1979. *The Role of the Reader: Explorations in the Semiotics of Texts.* Bloomington: Indiana University Press.

Elbow, Peter. 1973. *Writing without Teachers.* New York: Oxford University Press.

English-Language Arts Content Standards for California Public Schools Kindergarten through Grade Twelve. 1998. Sacramento: California Department of Education.

English-Language Arts Framework for California Public Schools Kindergarten through Grade Twelve. 1987. Sacramento: California State Education Department.

English-Language Arts Model Curriculum Guide Kindergarten through Eight. 1987. Sacramento: California State Education Department.

Every Child a Reader: The Report of the California Reading Task Force. 1995. Sacramento: California Department of Education.

Fish, Stanley. 1980. *Is There a Text in This Class? The Authority of Interpretive Communities.* Cambridge, MA: Harvard University Press.

Gardner, Howard. 1985. *Frames of Mind: The Theory of Multiple Intelligences.* New York: Basic Books.

Gardner, John. 1978. *On Moral Fiction.* New York: Basic Books.

Graves, Donald. 1983. *Writing: Teachers and Children at Work.* Exeter, NH: Heinemann.

Harris, Theodore L., and Richard E. Hodges, eds. 1995. *The Literary Dictionary: The Vocabulary of Reading and Writing.* Newark, DE: International Reading Association.

Holland, Norman. 1975a. *Five Readers Reading.* New Haven: Yale University Press.

———. 1975b. "Unity Identity Text Self." *Publication of the Modern Language Association (PMLA)* 90 (1975): 813–822. Reprinted in *Reader-Response Criticism: From Formalism to Post-Structuralism,* ed. Jane P. Tompkins. Baltimore: Johns Hopkins University Press, 1980.

Iser, Wolfgang. 1978. *The Act of Reading. A Theory of the Aesthetic Response.* Baltimore: Johns Hopkins University Press.

Karolides, Nicholas J., ed. 1992. *Reader Response in the Classroom: Evoking and Interpreting Meaning in Literature.* White Plains, NY: Longman Publishing Group.

Langer, Judith A. 1994a. "Reader-Based Literature Instruction." In *Literature Instruction: Practice and Policy,* ed. James Flood and Judith A. Langer. New York: Scholastic.

———. 1994b. "Focus on Research: A Reader-Response Approach to Reading Literature." *Language Arts* 71: 203–211.

MacFarquhar, Larissa. 2001. "The Dean's List: The Enfant Terrible of English Lit Grows Up." *The New Yorker,* June 11, 62–71.

Many, Joyce, and Carole Cox, eds. 1992. *Reader Stance and Literary Understanding: Exploring the Theories, Research, and Practice.* Norwood, NJ: Ablex Publishing Corporation.

Moffett, James. 1968. *Teaching the Universe of Discourse.* Boston: Houghton Mifflin.

Murray, Donald M. 1968. *A Writer Teaches Writing: A Practical Method of Teaching Composition.* Boston: Houghton Mifflin.

Nelms, Ben F., ed. 1988. *Literature in the Classroom: Readers, Texts, and Contexts.* Urbana, IL: National Council of Teachers of English.

Norton, Donna E. 1991. *Through the Eyes of a Child: An Introduction to Children's Literature.* 3rd ed. New York: Macmillan.

Poulet, Georges. 1970. "Criticism and the Experience of Interiority." In *The Structuralist Controversy: The Languages of Criticism and the Sciences of Man,* ed. Richard Macksey and Eugenio Donato. Baltimore: Johns Hopkins University Press.

Probst, Robert E. 1988. *Response and Analysis: Teaching Literature in Junior and Senior High School.* Portsmouth, NH: Boynton/Cook Publishers.

Purves, Alan C. 1993. "Toward a Reevaluation of Reader Response and School Literature." *Language Arts* 70 (September): 348–361.

Reading/Language Arts Framework for California Public Schools Kindergarten through Grade Twelve. 1999. Sacramento: California Department of Education.

Rosenblatt, Louise M. 1978. *The Reader, the Text, the Poem: The Transactional Theory of the Literary Work.* Carbondale: Southern Illinois University Press.

———. 1938. *Literature as Exploration.* New York: Noble and Noble Publishers, Inc. Revised edition, 1968.

Schemo, Diana Jean. 2002. "California Leads Chorus of Sounded-Out Syllables." *New York Times,* February 9, A9.

Smith, Dinitia. 2002. "Creating a Stir Wherever She Goes." *New York Times,* February 9, A15, A17.

Squire, James R. 1994. "Research in Reader Response: Naturally Interdisciplinary." In *Theoretical Models and Processes of Reading,* ed. Robert S. Ruddell, Martha Rapp Ruddell, and Harry Singer, 4th ed. Newark, DE: International Reading Association.

Tompkins, Jane P., ed. 1980. *Reader-Response Criticism: From Formalism to Post-Structuralism.* Baltimore: Johns Hopkins University Press.

Walmsley, Sean A. 1993. "Reflections on the State of Elementary Literature Instruction." *Language Arts* 69: 508–514.

White, Ronald C. 2002. *Lincoln's Greatest Speech: The Second Inaugural.* New York: Simon and Schuster.

Wimsatt, W. K. Jr., and Monroe C. Beardsley. 1954. *The Verbal Icon: Studies in the Meaning of Poetry.* Lexington: University of Kentucky Press.

Chapter Nine

❧ Literacy among Diverse Learners

Say the word "diversity" in today's society and it will undoubtedly stir controversy. Mention the words "literate" or "literacy" in the same breath, and it will assuredly cause a commotion. "Those people don't want to learn English" or "Why waste our tax dollars on kids whose families are here illegally?" are fairly typical of the comments we hear when we talk with both teachers and noneducators alike. In fact, it seems to us that the sentiments of the United States in the twenty-first century mirror the feelings the United States held in the twentieth century, especially at the *turn* of each of the centuries, when immigrants were entering the country at unprecedented rates. And many of the issues remain the same: discrimination, fear, hatred, and a strong belief that "our" money should not be used to educate "those" children.

And yet no matter how similar these sentiments may be, there are striking differences in the expectations that we in the twenty-first century have of and for a literate society. That is, unlike the society of 1900, for example, today's society demands that we prepare all students to be fully literate in order to compete and succeed in a technological, print-oriented culture. This is reflected in our schools and in our understandings of precisely how to help these students to become successful members of such a society.

Diverse learners are the fastest growing group of students in our public schools across the country. As a result, both urban and rural school districts alike find themselves, under federal law, obligated to set up English as a second language (ESL) programs as numbers of immigrant students continue to add to or fill classrooms. Questions about "multiculturalism" or "educating for a diverse society" have become commonplace in teachers' lounges and in local parent-teacher association (PTA) meetings. No one in the United States is untouched by the great richness, and the great complexity, of educating diverse students.

Who are today's diverse learners? What do we mean by "diverse" and "diversity"? How do diverse students' acquisition of language and literacy differ from their "mainstream" counterparts' acquisition of the same skills? What are some of the underlying theories on diverse learners and reading, for example? And what kinds of techniques can we use in the classroom to help these students become fully participating members of a literate society?

These are some of the questions that we will answer in this chapter. We will first define and describe who today's diverse students are by providing vivid scenes of the lives of two such students. Second, we will briefly review the underlying theories of second language acquisition and move into an explanation of the major theories of second language learners and reading or literacy. Third, we will provide concrete examples from actual classrooms on how to include diverse learners in the classroom's literacy processes and practices. And last, we will review the major challenges facing diverse learners in the twenty-first century, discussing ideas, for example, on "local literacies" and "standards and the diverse learner." Overall, however, this chapter will highlight how truly successful diverse learners can be as they strive to become literacy learners.

WHO ARE TODAY'S DIVERSE LEARNERS?

Made up of members of multiple interpretive communities, any group of literacy learners is always "diverse." Here, however, we use the word "diverse" to refer to students who are culturally different from "mainstream" students. Diverse students include those who come from other countries, those who speak languages other than English at home, and those who by virtue of their socioeconomic status, for example, are also often deemed culturally different. These diverse learners' voices have often been silenced (Blake 1995a, 1995b, 1997), and yet when they are heard, they are vibrant reflections of their distinct experiences and perceptions of the world. Note that the term "diverse" is often widely used to represent students who have "special needs" or who are "gifted and talented." Although we agree that both these groups are indeed "diverse," and as a consequence provide an added richness and diversity to our classrooms, we have chosen here to focus on what we consider the most common group labeled "diverse" in schools across our country: English language learners (ELLs). In the section "Classroom Examples" below, however, you will learn about a classroom of kids with special needs who are also ELLs—doubly diverse, perhaps, or in the words of William Ayers, "multiply marginalized" (1997).

Within the broad definition we use here of "diverse," the group of diverse students called ESL learners—or as they are more commonly labeled today, ELLs—constitutes the fastest growing population in public schools across the country. In California, for example, students whose native language is a language other than English represent the majority of school-aged children in public schools. In New York City—the country's largest district—more than fifty different languages can be heard at any one time, including Bengali, Chinese, French Creole, Russian, Spanish, Vietnamese, and Urdu. There are now at least four languages other than English that are spoken regularly in the United States by more than one million people: Spanish, French, German, and Italian. Soon, demographers predict, ELLs will become the majority population among school-aged children in what are perhaps less obvious places, such as Hartford, Connecticut; Rochester, New York; Houston, Texas; and St. Paul, Minnesota. By midcentury, Latinos will constitute well over 30 percent of *all* the public school student population.

ELLs can be defined as "students whose first language or home language is not English and [who] are learning English as a second language, primarily in school." Additional challenges face these diverse students, however, both in and out of school. First, on average, ELLs begin their U.S. school career already significantly behind their English-speaking counterparts. Second, ELLs are not just learning language per se; they are learning to become literate both in language and in subject areas, such as math and science. Third, ELLs often struggle with issues of identity and self-worth as they work both to maintain their home language, customs, and traditions and to learn to adjust to life in American schools and in American culture in general. And finally, diverse learners like ELLs are often discriminated against and assumed to be less intelligent simply because they come from another country or speak another language. Unfortunately, in too many classrooms, uncertified or unsympathetic teachers are unable or unwilling to help these students achieve the literacy skills necessary for them to be successful both in and out of school. In fact, as Linda Harklau, a well-known researcher on the effects of tracking and ESL students, tells us, "[There is] little support for students' linguistic needs . . . little recognition of fostering of linguistic and ethnic diversity in the school at large and a strong tendency to confound bilingualism with academic deficiency" (1999, 56).

TWO SCENARIOS: ENGLISH LANGUAGE LEARNERS IN DIVERSE SETTINGS

Before we turn to a brief review of the major theories that help us work with diverse learners in the classroom, we introduce to you two of our ESL students: Terrell and Rolando.

We meet Terrell, a seventeen-year-old Spanish speaker whose parents were biracial (thereby giving him the dark complexion that he refers to below), in a jail classroom, and we meet Rolando, an elementary-age student from Mexico, in the migrant camp where he and his family worked and lived. (Each scenario is based on field notes written by us as researchers.)

A Jail Classroom

Terrell and I [Brett Elizabeth Blake] were talking about career choices. Terrell was excited about continuing his education at the local community college when he got out of jail, although he feared that there wasn't much available for kids "like him." I met Terrell the first day I came to the jail. He was standing in front of one of the classrooms, talking to the teacher, and when I came in, he moved immediately toward me with his hand out for me to shake. Quite frankly, I was taken aback. I certainly didn't expect "these" kids to have the wherewithal to walk right up to an adult (a white adult) extend his hand, and introduce himself. If I had closed my eyes, Terrell and I could have been playing out this scene in one of the affluent white schools nearby, where this kind of behavior, I thought, probably occurred on a regular basis.

Terrell had learned to play the game, a game he knew was a prerequisite for his attempts at entering mainstream society: to have successfully engaged with schooled literacy practices to receive his GED degree; to have learned to speak to adults (teachers, guards) as politely and deferentially as possible; and even to try out the use of what mainstream society might describe as impeccable manners in welcoming a newcomer, like me, into the classroom. Prison personnel would say that they had rehabilitated Terrell; that the change that manifested itself both in his behavior and in his schoolwork was reflective of an effective prison program designed to do just that. And there was tangible proof, too: Terrell, they pointed out, began to write about his experience of finding "truth," something he could not have done without having come to jail in the first place. In one of his final essays for his GED teacher, indeed, Terrell writes:

I am most proud of getting a chance to learn more and coming to reality and finding out the truth about life.

If I wouldn't have never came to jail, I would never found out [*sic*] the quality of life.

And about school, one thing I'm proud of is taking my GED test and I feel real good to know that I accomplished one of my goals.

Another thing I was proud to find out was knowledge is infinite.

Despite these outward appearances, however, Terrell was still acutely aware of who he was and how he would be received as he left the jail, GED in hand, to attend classes at the local community college. When I pressed him, privately, to tell me more about his career aspirations, he was quick to list off any number of jobs that he, as a biracial male, would have difficulty getting. "Can't be a lawyer if you're a nigger" was not only a matter-of-fact statement; to Terrell, it was simply a statement of truth.

A Migrant Camp

Colleen's friend diligently stops the van at the stop sign. I turn my head both ways and for a moment I wonder why she bothers to stop. We are so far out in the country all I can see is fields; no houses, no cars, no people. Colleen, an ESL teacher, continues to talk to me, describing in quick sentences the conditions of the migrant camp I am about to visit for the first time. "It's better that we have [my] children with us, that way we're less of a threat and no one will run." "Yesterday," she continues, "the border patrol raided the camp with their sirens roaring and guns pulled." Colleen has helped create a frightening image in my mind: young children barefooted and staring, mothers and fathers confused and exhausted, being "ticketed" and told, in English, that they must leave the country by a certain date.

The camp, indeed, is a frightening place to a first-time visitor like myself; mingled with the smell of garbage that has carefully been placed in black bags in a bin, overflowing, not having been picked up in weeks, is the acid-chemical smell of the portable toilets, perhaps, too, overflowing, not having been emptied for the same amount of time. And yet the camp seems also a warm place; a place that also smells of food cooking; a place that, today, abounds with sounds of laughter and music and of children playing as mothers and fathers return from fourteen-hour-long days in the field to their "homes"— cinder-block barracks with a communal kitchen area—ready to share the evening meal. Colleen finds Rolando, the child she has come to see, and speaking in Spanish asks him to please come back to summer school. He smiles; they talk some more; she gives him a bag of clothes, pats him on the shoulder; and we leave. We begin the long drive back in silence; I don't even notice the stop sign this time, my head remains low and bowed. Somehow the ritual of glancing side-to-side has become far less important.

As our descriptions indicate, diverse students come in all shapes and sizes and are found in a variety of classrooms or classroom-like settings throughout the United States. And there are so many more scenarios we have not described here: Bosnian students from war-torn villages learning in rural America; Russian children sponsored by a local synagogue learning in suburban America; Haitian teenagers working and learning in after-school programs in urban community-outreach programs and centers. Given the huge increase in the numbers of immigrant students (the *New York Times* magazine section reported on September 17, 2000, that fifteen new immigrants per hour settle in New York City alone), as well as the variety and mobility of these diverse learners, most teachers throughout their careers will be asked to teach and work with diverse learners as they engage in literacy learning.

WHERE DO I BEGIN?

Teaching literacy skills to diverse learners is not an easy task, and most teachers report to us that they feel ill-equipped, adding, "We just don't know where to begin!" In our experience as teachers of literacy and of working with ESL students, we believe one must begin with a basic understanding of how children learn languages and of how they develop literacy skills in both their native language and in the target language, in this case, English.

Second Language Acquisition Theories

There are three major theories to explain how a child learns a second language. (These theories need to be modified slightly when we are talking about adults, but here we will focus on children from birth to twelve years of age.) First, behavioralists believe that language is learned solely by imitation and rote memorization. In other words, children are "empty vessels" into which language is poured. Although behavioralist theory can account for some of a child's early acquisition, it cannot, for example, account for the creative, ingenuous phrases we hear coming out of children's mouths every day: "longcut" to match "shortcut"; "touchup" instead of "touchdown"; "new lady" as the opposite to "old lady"; "goed" instead of "went"; and so on. The examples are countless, showing that in learning language, children create, construct, and play with language all the time; in the cases just given, no one would ever suspect that the child had heard those words before. If language were learned only by imitation, then children would have *had* to have heard those constructions before, because they would just be mimicking the adults around them.

The creation of language is the central focus of the second major theory of second language acquisition: the innatist position. The innatist theory (attributed to the seminal work of Noam Chomsky) posits that all human beings are capable of creating an infinite number of phrases in an infinite number of languages. Chomsky (1957) hypothesized that humans are hardwired with something like a "black box" (formally termed the "language acquisition device" or "LAD," a system used by the brain that is prewired for linguistic analysis) in their brains that gives them the ability to infinitely create and use language. However, innatists believe that at about puberty the brain literally hardens, or "lateralizes," so that learning a language becomes less natural and fraught with many more challenges.

The third major theory can be called the social interactionist position. A social interactionist views the "communicative give and take of natural conversation between native and non-native speakers as the crucial element of the language acquisition process" (Peregoy and Boyle 2001, 45). The focus here is on learners' social interactions, the subsequent ways ELLs adjust their language to be better understood, and the ways native English speakers modify their speech to try to make themselves better understood. Meaning is constantly negotiated and refined. On this theory, language cannot be learned in isolation or without this dialogic interplay of words, phrases, and certainly, meaning.

Missing from these three theories, however, is an emphasis on the sociocultural/political nature of language and its uses, a view that makes more complex the other three, by acknowledging the fact that language is not only inherently social but also, inextricably, cultural and political. By that we mean that language is never neutral: Which language a student speaks and how that language (or home country) is viewed politically, culturally, or economically may affect the way the student wants (and is expected) to engage in language and literacy learning. Language is expressed in a wide range of contexts and experiences, contexts that are always present and always changing. And it is important to note that these contexts may differ from our perception that Standard English is the only acceptable dialect of English in which to communicate, orally and in writing, and in which to participate in American schools and society. We must take care to remember that Standard English is but one way of seeing and expressing oneself in this global society in which we all live.

Reading and Second Language

Children who are learning to become literate in English face a dual task: Besides the characteristics of written language, they have to learn an unfamiliar language, one that in large part refers to an unfamiliar cultural background. In fact, the written system in which these students' home language, culture, and identity is embedded may not even be one that uses an alphabetic script (see chapter 3 for a review and a fuller discussion of the advent and importance of an alphabetic script). For example, students may read Chinese symbols that represent whole words, or they may read, as many do in the Middle East, from bottom to top and from right to left, using an alphabet markedly different from the Greek alphabet.

But this is only part of the challenge. The students' background knowledge, or schema (schema, or background knowledge, refers to a learner's familiarity with a topic, including its content and its cultural implications, as well as the structure of a particular text), may be so different from that of their English-speaking counterparts that language transfer (the ability to extrapolate rules, skills, general knowledge, and cultural information from one language to another) in reading can be hindered. For example, the source of students' problems in reading is often not that they cannot read a particular passage, using decoding skills, but that they find it difficult to make a connection to the sociocultural context in which all words, and hence all stories and informational texts, are embedded. Furthermore, on a metacognitive level, where students are asked to make interpretations of text, their understandings of particular words, phrases, and whole stories are often predicated upon the sociocultural contexts in which they have developed different interpretations of what we might consider "basic" knowledge. For example, in some countries, "The Three Little Pigs" is considered vulgar and thus not worthy of the "American" interpretation, which may include lessons on greed, friendship, and the value of hard work, that is, the Protestant work ethic.

Most newer research on second language learning and literacy, however, focuses on the "substantial similarities between the strategies employed in first language learning and those in second language learning" and the "home-school" connection between expectations of schooled literacy and various types of literacies and literacy practices in diverse homes around the country (Verhoeven 1999). That is, if a diverse student's literacy practices at home match those at school (such as story time and an abundance of print materials and "book talks" and discussions), then strategies similar to those used to teach mainstream learners to read—such as simple decoding, decoding by analogy, blending, and structural analysis (such as compounding or working with prefixes and suffixes)—can be used fairly effectively. It is generally agreed that literacy exposure and development in the first language is a predictor of a diverse student's ability to become a literacy learner in the second language.

Knowing all this, however, teachers still ask us, "But where do I begin?" In the next section of this chapter, we help answer that all-important question first, by outlining some basic assumptions about literacy and diverse learners and offering general suggestions for implementing these assumptions, and second, by providing some concrete examples of how successful diverse learners can be with language and literacy learning, given the right tools from which to work and to learn.

LITERACY AND DIVERSE LEARNERS

Five Assumptions

1. All students, even students with severe disabilities, such as mental retardation, have the ability to learn and develop with language (although, as is the case, for example, of a child with a severe disability, the level of language and literacy achieved may vary). Human beings are unique in this respect.
2. No language is inferior to another, and no matter what language children speak at home, they can develop literacy skills in English given the right tools and encouragement from their teachers.
3. All students have a rich background or schema from which to engage in literacy practices. All students have something to say about their lives and their experiences, so begin your literacy work with those experiences. Choose books and topics that are related to students' lives. Encourage your students to write about their families or their native lands (see Blake 1997).
4. Beginning students engage best with literacy activities that are context-embedded. Provide your diverse learners with real audiences and with hands-on materials they can hold, taste, and smell. Give them tactile opportunities from which to create.
5. All students like to have fun with literacy. Although many states are implementing statewide assessments and higher standards (see, especially, accounts on New York State), take the time to remind children that reading and writing are fun!

Classroom Examples

An Urban Fourth-Grade ESL Classroom

In urban classrooms around the country, classes are full of students from all over the world, and many teachers have had to retrain themselves to understand their students' literacy needs, as they themselves struggle to understand what works best with such a diverse population.

We spent a lot of time in one classroom working with the teacher as he moved his primary focus and classroom time toward an emphasis almost exclusively on literacy-building activities, such as process writing, Reader Response, and literature circles. We watched as ESL students began to internalize the rules of peer writing conferences, including critical and positive feedback to their own peers in English, and became more comfortable and prolific with English literacy skills and activities. One such peer conference between two ESL students sounded like this (the conference was on a piece Jesus had just completed on the "Ninja Turtles"):

> MANUEL: "Why did he have to fight him?"
>
> JESUS: "'Cause he wanted to kill 'im."
>
> MANUEL: "No, but then, why did he want . . .? Why did you say, 'Let's fight?' Why did he say that?"
>
> JESUS: "He didn't say that!"
>
> MANUEL: "Says he did!"
>
> JESUS: "Nooooo!"
>
> MANUEL: "Right here! He says right here [pointing to Jesus's draft]. 'And they said first they got Shredder, you've got to fight him.' Why's he got to fight him?"
>
> JESUS: "Because!"
>
> MANUEL: "Because he don't have to!"

As a result of these two ESL students talking and sharing ideas (and yes, even debating!) in what is called a "peer conference," they actually became more engaged, and therefore more competent, confident, and better readers and writers in English. The teacher reported (to us) in subsequent visits that his ESL students, regardless of native-language background, engaged in reading and writing activities much more prolifically and that they actually enjoyed conferencing and sharing their pieces in front of the class. Even the students who began their literacy journeys in Spanish in his class moved into English, comfortably and easily over time as he provided more opportunities for them to display their knowledge in either language!

There are many more classrooms in our country where ELLs and other diverse students are struggling to become literate in English. One of these classrooms can be found in a smaller urban setting than the one we just visited. But here, students grapple not only with the too-frequent urban issues of poverty and lack of opportunity but also with special needs and with having to learn English.

Mrs. Kuhn's Urban Adolescent Classroom: ELLs and Special Needs

In New York State, a special needs "Option III" classroom is in many ways a last resort for students to remain in public school. It is here that one full-time teacher and one full-time aide work with only six students, students who are among the most challenged, both emotionally and educationally. (Technically, the criteria for placement in an Option III classroom are these: a 50 percent discrepancy between a student's cognitive abilities or IQ test scores and his or her actual achievement, or extreme socio-emotional difficulties.) One can also find here ESL students who have either been misplaced, misdiagnosed, or simply misunderstood because of their (and their parents') lack of English literacy skills. (Note that this is not to say that some ESL students are not, indeed, in need of special education services; they are, but historically ESL students, like African American students, have been placed disproportionately in classrooms for students with special needs.)

Mrs. Stephanie Kuhn, a teacher we worked with over many years, struggled with her students and their literacy skills. All six of her students had been tested at the first- or second-grade reading/writing level, and as a result, both she and the students became very frustrated when her lessons turned toward language arts. And yet Mrs. Kuhn believed that her students could and would read and write. Despite all the research she had read telling her that ESL students with special needs found reading and writing extremely difficult—that even choosing a topic for them was so terribly challenging they would give up—she persisted.

"Failure," she reported, "is ingrained in their school career. The fear associated with reading and writing can paralyze these young learners. If that is not the direct result, then they turn toward acting out in order to hide their perceived academic inadequacies."

Arnella entered Mrs. Kuhn's classroom with serious management needs. Her repertoire of bizarre behavior included making disruptive noises, tipping over chairs, slamming doors during class, and lunging toward staff members with pencils. Arnella's gaze shifted constantly:

side to side, up and down, but never eye to eye. When she spoke, she was barely audible; her voice was comparable to a young child's whisper.

For the first six months Arnella was in Mrs. Kuhn's classroom, she always needed a physical prompt to engage her in any classroom activity or dialogue. Mrs. Kuhn touched her often, on the shoulder or the elbow, while repeatedly using verbal reinforcement to help her stay on task. After months of working together, however, Arnella still responded to Mrs. Kuhn with, "I don't know."

And yet when Mrs. Kuhn introduced a unit on poetry that included physical activities such as a walk outside to gather ideas, Arnella became particularly intrigued. Here is her first attempt at writing haiku (all the students' pieces are presented in their original, unedited forms except where meaning would be lost):

> I have a snowball
> It is part of nature
> It snows all Winter

Because this haiku was one of Arnella's first attempts at writing anything, particularly anything "positive," Mrs. Kuhn was very excited. She reported that through this poem, Arnella had truly begun to "move beyond her rage—away from a [suspected] abusive childhood, toward a pleasant experience that allowed her to recognize nature and walk through it as a participant observer." And so Mrs. Kuhn persisted, and Arnella continued to discover her voice through poetry. The following diamanté poem (a poem whose structure subtly introduces and incorporates grammar conventions), prompted both by another walk outside and by sculpting clay into shapes, was Arnella's favorite:

> Basket
> orange yellow
> carring holding stuff making
> fruit candy clothes food
> sleeping keeping using
> purple soft
> bed

It was with this poem that Arnella exclaimed, "I like to go outside and walk around [because] finding stuff and writing is easy." Indeed, through poetry, Arnella's language skills became evident as she learned to express a voice, her voice that had been silenced and hidden for so long.

Josh had a history of difficulty in school. He had repeated kindergarten and first grade. He was socially promoted in fourth grade and fifth grade only because of his age and size. Josh's parents refused to consider a special needs classroom for him until he began acting out as a fifth grader. Instead, his parents moved him in and out of four different schools searching for another solution. By the time he was finally referred for special services, his skills were measured at a first-grade level, and he experienced extreme difficulties with any reading or writing. By the time he reached Mrs. Kuhn's room in the seventh grade, his skills had only slightly improved.

Mrs. Kuhn reports that in Josh, she saw a "hopeless" child whose feelings of despair contributed to his need to threaten and control others. She initially tried to "hook" him with many different prompts and rewards, including giving him computer time, time to read sports magazines, and such special privileges as eating lunch with her in the classroom. Nothing seemed to work, however, and Josh continued to respond to Mrs. Kuhn both orally and in writing like this:

> School is but [butt] work is but [butt] because we do to muck work
> in class. I will have Gym all day we will play basketball in Gym all
> day.

Although Josh's work deteriorated on many levels, he too seemed to respond to Mrs. Kuhn's introduction of poetry into the classroom. Like Arnella, Josh wrote a poem immediately after returning from the class walk:

> Stick
> It dropped from a tree
> And fell to the ground
> I found it outside
> In some leaves
> There it was
> On the ground
> Where I saw it
> I picked it up
> It is rough
> It was alive
> Now it is dead
> The wind came by
> And killed it

Mrs. Kuhn initially viewed this poem as simply an expression of Josh's anger, but at the same time, it made her feel hopeful, for she believed she had found a safe avenue in which Josh could express his voice, whether it be angry, sad, or joyful. Interestingly, as Josh continued to write poetry, his anger seemed to turn inward, and he began to write more about himself and his love of sports. Here are two of his favorite diamanté poems:

> Me
> Restless Tired
> Running Playing Hanging
> Ball Book Hall Shoes
> Rapping Shopping Reading
> Big Bad
> Me

and

> Ball
> Oval Big
> Throwing Running Kicking
> Football Basketball Baseball Soccer Ball
> Bouncing Passing Shooting
> Round Hard
> Rock

Cognizant of his love of sports and of talking about himself, Mrs. Kuhn continued to push Josh to write. And as she continued to push him, she continued to see a marked change in Josh's attitude and behavior. She remarked that

> Josh had had a fear of written language. He was a helpless reader with few word attack strategies and he didn't have a good recall of sight words. . . . it was just jumble to him. However, poetry was him. There really was not a lot of jumble because it was about his thoughts and feelings. He became the expert. . . . he was in control of his learning for once.

The students in both the urban ESL classroom and in Mrs. Kuhn's ESL and special needs classroom, we think, show how motivated, engaged, and thereby successful diverse learners can be as participants in literacy learning, given the right tools and the right opportunities by their teachers.

In the urban classroom, for example, the teacher not only refocused his entire morning routine on literacy, thereby helping students to create and use language for real purposes and for real audiences, but he also created an accepting environment, where he, as the leader and role model, encouraged the use of language in a variety of forms, including in students' native languages, in a variety of genres, and on various topics, such as action heroes, sports figures, and even gang violence. Mrs. Kuhn, in turn, because of her strong belief that all children can learn, worked hard to provide context-embedded activities (here, tactile activities, such as a walk outside to pick up and feel rocks and leaves) so that her students, too, could find some measure of success in literacy activities in the classroom. And in doing so, both teachers clearly showed that they believed in the assumptions of literacy and language learning presented above that presume all children can engage in literacy practices using their rich background knowledges, in context-embedded and fun ways.

STANDARDS AND ACCOUNTABILITY:
ROLE OF SCHOOL VERSUS "LOCAL LITERACIES"

Major challenges remain for teaching literacy among diverse learners, however.

As the twenty-first century unfolds, so does the debate on assessment, accountability, and standards for both teachers and students in public and private education across the United States. In fact, high achievement on "large-scale" and "high-stakes" testing has become synomonous with the notion of "success." Such large-scale assessments become a matter of "life or death" for students—affecting whether they have a chance to enter the college of their choice, for example—as well as having important implications for how we, as educators, teach and evaluate all our students, particularly regarding their language and literacy growth. These standardized statewide (for example, in New York State) tests, along with a push toward national mandatory testing, have critical implications for diverse students, including consequences that may lead them to "failure" and to dropping out of school altogether (Blake 1995).

The major problem with using high-stakes assessment tools as a way to gauge diverse learners' language and literacy development is that these assessments cannot capture their diverse abilities, learning styles, and hence, knowledge in English. Simply put, standardized tests are "based on the norms of native English speakers and therefore may be culturally biased" (Fraser 2000, 28). Indeed, according to Kathleen Fraser, "expected prior knowledge" on cultural life in America is by itself enough to become a "deadly pitfall" for all but the most acculturated English language learner (Fraser 2000, 28).

In other words, these tests cannot measure the kinds of language and literacy development that are going on in the teachers' classrooms that we presented here. Large-scale literacy assessments are meant to capture "schooled literacy" practices (Blake 2001; Street 1995), that is, the ability to recall facts and details of text, the ability to use schema to connect to content, the ability to reproduce writing in scripted ways without mechanical errors, and of course, the ability to do all this in Standard American English.

In contrast, standardized measures of language and literacy growth are *not* meant to capture "local literacy" practices (Blake 2001; Street 1995), that is, the ability to write freely as a system of expression, the ability to write for real purposes and for real audiences, the ability to make interpretations of text that draw on diverse students' schemas and background experiences, the ability to allow for language to flow fluidly even if it contains errors, and the ability to do this in one or perhaps two languages. And thus, such large-scale measures of literacy achievement are not effective in documenting diverse students' abilities in their English language learning.

Alternative assessment among ELLs remains the most powerful way we can document and highlight a student's development in language and learning over time (see Goodman, Goodman, and Hood 1989; Weiner and Cohen 2002). Large-scale tests simply lack the breadth and depth required to truly make visible the knowledge and experience that our diverse ELLs bring to school. We believe, therefore, that alternative assessments, such as portfolio assessment, need to be introduced or to be allowed to continue in our classrooms amid (and despite) new standards and high-stakes tests.

SUMMARY AND IMPLICATIONS

The challenges of educating diverse students in twenty-first-century America are much more complex than simply providing a classroom, teachers, and tests. In today's world, we must also educate society as a whole about diversity, about the potential richness it can add to our lives, about the increased understandings we can uncover as we listen to different voices, and certainly about our own lives as fellow human beings engaged in literacy and language learning in our own varied, yet daily, interactions with each other and the world.

Literacy learning is a complex act in itself. But it is neither so complex nor so "protected" that it is reserved solely for English speakers or gifted children, for example. Literacy learning, especially literacy learning that recognizes the local literacies of diverse learners—students who speak other languages at home, who have special needs, or who come from urban areas where poverty abounds while opportunity falters—should be universally offered and accepted. It should not be seen as a gift from one culture or society to another; it should be seen not as a privilege but as a right of all students; it should be seen as an exchange and understanding of many texts, of many voices, of multiple and varied literacies.

We have seen in this chapter that given the right tools and attitudes (primarily by the teachers of diverse students, but certainly also by administrators, parents, and community), all diverse learners can develop language and literacy, even if it appears to be in small ways. Getting diverse learners hooked on the joy of reading and writing, we believe, is the primary and crucial first step in helping them begin a journey of literacy learning. And this requires patient, understanding, forward-thinking teachers who know that language, and hence literacy, is best learned in context-embedded ways that draw on the rich schemas of all students, and who strongly believe that all diverse students can and will learn in the safe and positive environments they provide in their classrooms.

REFERENCES

Ayers, William. 1997. *A Kind and Just Parent: The Children of Juvenile Court.* Boston: Beacon Press.

Blake, Brett, Elizabeth. 2001. "Fruit of the Devil: Writing and English-Language Learners." *Language Arts* 78: 435–441.

———. 1997. *She Say, He Say: Urban Girls Write Their Lives.* Albany: State University of New York Press.

———. 1995a. "Broken Silences: Writing and the Construction of 'Cultural Texts' by Urban, Pre-adolescent Girls." *Journal of Educational Thought* 29: 165–180.

———. 1995b. "Doing Number 5: From Process to Cultural Texts in an Urban Classroom." *Language Arts* 72: 396–404.

Chomsky, Noam. 1957. *Syntactic Structures.* Mouton: The Hague.

Faltis, Christian J., and Paula Wolfe, eds. 1999. *So Much to Say: Adolescents, Bilingualism, and ESL in the Secondary School*. New York: Teachers College Press.

Fraser, Kathleen. 2000. "A Reflection of What People Want out of Testing." *The State Education Standard*: 27–30.

Galdone, Paul. 1984. *The Three Little Pigs*. New York: Clarion.

Goodman, Kenneth S., Yetta M. Goodman, and Wendy J. Hood. 1989. *The Whole Language Evaluation Book*. Portsmouth, NH: Heinemann.

Harklau, L. 1999. "The ESL Student Learning in Secondary School." In *So Much to Say: Adolescents, Bilingualism, and ESL in the Secondary School*, ed. Christian J. Faltis and Paula Wolfe. New York: Teachers College Press.

Long, Michael A., and Patricia L. Porter. 1985. "Groupwork, Interlanguage Talk, and Second Language Acquisition." *TESOL Quarterly* 19: 207–227.

Peregoy, Suzanne F., and Owen F. Boyle. 2001. *Reading, Writing, and Learning in ESL: A Resource Book for K–12 Teachers*. New York: Longman.

Sadovnik, Alan R., Peter W. Cookson, and Susan F. Semel. 1994. *Exploring Education: An Introduction to the Foundations of Education*. Boston: Allyn and Bacon.

Street, Brian V. 1995. *Social Literacies: Critical Approaches to Literacy in Development, Ethnography, and Education*. London: Longman.

Verhoeven, Ludo. 1999. "Second Language Reading." In *Literacy: An International Handbook*, ed. Daniel A. Wagner, Richard L Venezky, and Brian V. Street. Boulder, CO: Westview Press.

Weiner, Robert, and Judith Cohen. 2002. *Literacy Portfolios: Using Assessment to Guide Instruction*. 2nd ed. Upper Saddle River, NJ: Merrill/Prentice Hall.

Chapter Ten

⬤⟜ Organizations and Educational Associations

The following list provides brief information on some of the organizations and educational associations that have a direct interest in literacy and literacy learning as a broad category. Because literacy is currently a major concern of both our national and state governments, general information on literacy, including state standards and assessments, can also be found at each of the fifty states' education Websites. Check links through your state's government or education Webpages.

ORGANIZATIONS

American Federation of Teachers (AFT)
555 New Jersey Ave., NW
Washington, DC 20001
(202) 879-4400
http://www.aft.org

One of the largest teachers' unions in the United States, the AFT is a good source for information on a broad array of topics, including guidelines and expectations for teachers of literacy and related policies.

American Literacy Council
148 West 117th St.
New York, NY 10026
(800) 781-9985
http://www.americanliteracy.com/

The American Literacy Council provides resources and assistance to persons and organizations involved in promoting literacy in the United States.

The Barbara Bush Foundation for Family Literacy
1201 15th St. NW
Suite 420

Washington, DC 20005
(202) 955-6183
Fax: (202) 955-54924
http://www.barbarabushfoundation.com

The foundation is dedicated to establishing literacy as a value in every family in America. It provides publications for parents about how to foster literacy and literacy practices with their children.

Beginning with Books
5920 Kirkwood St.
Pittsburgh, PA 15206
(412) 361-8560
http://www.beginningwithbooks.org

Beginning with Books focuses on increasing the number of children who are lifelong readers through programs for low-income families.

BlakeCo International
New York City area:
15 Dunwood Rd.
Port Washington, NY 11050
e-mail: adolescentdr@aol.com or bobbillydumpling@aol.com

This educational consulting group provides consulting, workshops, and advocacy for both public and private schools and agencies in language and literacy learning, particularly in urban and other "challenged" settings.

BookPALS
www.bookpals.net (This main site will direct you to a list of state-by-state local sites.)
Ellen Nathan, National Coordinator
e-mail: Enathan@bookpals.net

"Performing Artists for Literacy in Schools." Professional actors read aloud to children at public elementary schools, provide workshops in theater and art and connect them to literacy activities, and promote reading and writing in general. BookPALS also provides recommended reading lists.

California Literacy, Inc.
2028 East Villa St.
Pasadena, CA 91107-2379

(626) 395-9989 or (800) 894-READ
e-mail: office@caliteracy.org
www.caliteracy.org

Founded in 1956, the nation's largest and oldest statewide volunteer literacy organization establishes literacy programs and supports them through tutor training, consulting, and ongoing education. California Literacy is also involved in designing and supporting programs for students with learning disabilities.

Center for the Improvement of Early Reading Achievement (CIERA)
University of Michigan School of Education
Rm. 1600 SEB
610 E University Ave.
Ann Arbor, MI 48109-1259
(734) 647-6940
Fax: (734) 615-4858
http://www.ciera.org/

CIERA is a national center for research on early reading and literacy, supported under the Federal Educational Research and Development Center program. The center provides free research articles as well as for-sale publications on a wide range of literacy topics.

The Children's Book Council
12 W 37th St., 2nd floor
New York, NY 10018-7480
(212) 966-1990
Fax: (212) 966-2073
http://www.cbcbooks.org

A nonprofit trade association, the Children's Book Council's membership publishes and packages test booklets to measure literacy achievement, as well as promoting the enjoyment of literacy by sponsoring National Children's Book Week and National Children's Poetry Week, nationwide, each year.

Children's Literature for Children
104 Madison Ave.
Peachtree City, GA 30269
http://www.childrensliterature.org/

This not-for-profit organization is dedicated to bringing children and books together by implementing and supporting teaching programs in elementary schools serving disadvantaged children, as well as providing books and literacy experiences to hospitalized and house-bound children.

Coalition for Essential Schools (CES)
1814 Franklin St.
Suite 700
Oakland, CA 94612
(510) 433-1451
Fax: (510) 433-1455
http://www.essentialschools.org

The CES is a national network of schools and regional centers and a national office where teachers work to perfect their craft of teaching literacy toward the goal of national school reform.

Ezra Jack Keats Foundation
Dr. Martin Pope, President
http://www.ezra-jack-keats.org

Ezra Jack Keats, a well-known children's author who died in 1983, directed that all royalties from sales of his books be used to support programs focused on literacy and literacy development among children. These programs include storytelling in public libraries and sponsorship of a UNICEF award for best book illustrator.

First Book National Book Bank
1319 F Street NW
Suite 1000
Washington, DC 20004-1155
(202) 393-1222
e-mail: staff@firstbook.org
bookbank.firstbook.org

First Book National Book Bank is the first centralized system enabling publishers to donate large quantities of books to the nonprofit sector for distribution to children from low-income families participating in community-wide programs.

International Book Project, Inc.
Van Meter Building
1440 Delaware Ave.

Lexington, KY 40505
(888) 999-BOOK

The International Book Project promotes global friendship and world literacy through book distribution projects.

Literacy Volunteers of America
P.O. Box 6506
Syracuse, NY 13217
(315) 472-0001
Fax: (315) 472-0002
http://www.literacyvolunteers.org

This nonprofit educational organization provides training, technical assistance, and community and program support to literacy programs. Most larger communities have a local branch. The main Website can be searched by town or county name to find local branches.

National Institute for Literacy
1775 I Street NW
Suite 730
Washington, DC 20006
(202) 233-2025
http://www.nifl.gov/

This federal organization strives to ensure that all Americans with literacy needs have access to services that can help them gain the basic skills necessary for success. It shares information about literacy and supports the development of high-quality literacy services.

National Jewish Coalition for Literacy
Susan Neiman Ferency, Director
P.O. Box 202
Accord, MA 02018
(781) 925-9545
http://www.njcl.net

The National Jewish Coalition for Literacy is the Jewish community's vehicle for participation in childhood literacy initiatives. The coalition encourages local participation where literacy efforts are needed.

National Right to Read Foundation (NRRF)
P.O. Box 490

The Plains, VA 20198
http://www.nrrf.org

The goal of the NRRF is to improve literacy nationwide through phonics and good literature.

Read In Foundation
6043 Channel Dr.
Riverbank, CA 96367
http:\\www.readin.org
(209) 869-3945
Jane Coffey, President and Founder
e-mail jane@readin.org

The foundation promotes global literacy and the use of telecommunications technology in education. It sponsors an annual project connecting authors and kids through chat rooms with an underlying focus on developing strong reading skills.

Readers & Writers
PEN American Center
568 Broadway
New York, NY 10012-3225
(212) 334-1660
Fax: (212) 334-2181
http://www.pen.org/readers/info/program.html

Readers & Writers uses literature to promote literacy by sending writers and their books to schools, prisons, community groups, and other organizations nationwide.

Reading Is Fundamental (RIF)
1825 Connecticut Ave. NW
Suite 400
Washington, DC 20009
(206) 673-0020
(877) RIF-READ
http://www.rif.org

Founded in 1966, RIF develops and delivers children's and family literacy programs that help prepare children for reading success.

Student Coalition for Action in Literacy Education (SCALE)
208 N. Columbia St.

University of North Carolina at Chapel Hill
CB #3505
Chapel Hill, NC 27599
(919) 962-1542
http://www.readwriteact.org/

This national organization supports campus-based literacy programs across the country. College students serve as literacy tutors or teachers in their communities. SCALE provides a full range of technical assistance in this endeavor.

EDUCATIONAL ASSOCIATIONS

Educational associations are usually made up of teachers, professors, and administrators in a particular field or area of study, but most are concerned with education in general, particularly in the literacy development of all students, in all content areas, at all levels. Educational associations are often wonderful sources of position papers and the latest research. Educational associations often have local affiliates as well as national organizations.

American Educational Research Association (AERA)
1230 17th St. NW
Washington, DC 20036
(202) 223-9485
http://www.AERA.net

The AERA promotes educational research and its practical application. It is concerned with the improvement of the educational process and the literacy process worldwide.

International Reading Association (IRA)
800 Barksdale Rd.
P.O. Box 8139
Newark, DE 19714-8139
(302) 731-1600
Fax: (302) 731-1057
http://www.reading.org/

The IRA promotes literacy worldwide through publications, conferences, community activities, international projects, resources, advocacy, and professional development.

National Council of Teachers of English (NCTE)
1111 W. Kenyon Rd.
Urbana, IL 61801-1096
(800) 369-6283
Fax: (217) 328-9645
http://www.ncte.org/

Since 1911, NCTE has provided a forum for educators to deal with all issues related to the development and improvement of the teaching of English, the language arts, and literacy.

Each state has an NCTE affiliate. Some of the larger NCTE affiliates are

California Association of Teachers of English (CATE)
http://www.cateweb.org

Florida Council of Teachers of English
http://www.fcte.org

Illinois
http://www4.district125.k12.il.us/CA/IATEpages/

Maryland Council of Teachers of English Language Arts (MCTELA)
http://www.mctela.org

New England Association of Teachers of English (NEATE)
http://www.neate.org

The New York State English Council (NYSEC)
http://www.nysecteach.org

Teachers of English to Speakers of Other Languages (TESOL)
700 S. Washington St.
Suite 200
Alexandria, VA 22314
(703) 836-0774
http://www.tesol.org
e-mail: info@tesol.org

This organization is dedicated to the education of English language learners in the United States and around the world. Its goal is to foster effective communication and literacy skills in diverse settings while respecting individual language rights.

Chapter Eleven

✎ Selected Print and Nonprint Resources

The works listed in this chapter are divided into two categories. The first lists both popular and scholarly books, articles, conference presentations, and other studies that deal with the topic of literacy in its broadest sense. The list is unannotated, but many of these resources deal with the controversial nature of literacy, including literacy and politics, literacy and ethnicity, and notions of "whose literacy?" We include these selections to present a balanced portrait of the nature of literacy education today.

The second section contains nonprint resources such as Websites and Internet research sites that include lesson plans, teaching resources, and research, including articles from the ERIC database and various professional organizations and publishers.

PRINT SOURCES

Ayers, W. *A Kind and Just Parent: The Children of Juvenile Court.* Boston: Beacon Press, 1997.

Bailey, R. **"Literacy in English: An International Perspective."** In *Literacy for Life,* ed. R. Bailey and R. Fosheim. New York: MLA, 1983.

Bhola, H. S. *Campaigning for Literacy.* Paris: UNESCO, 1984.

Blake, B. E. **"Broken Silences: Writing and the Construction of 'Cultural Texts' by Urban, Preadolescent Girls."** *Journal of Educational Thought* 29 (1995): 165–180.

Blake, B. E. **"'Critical' Reader Response in an Urban Classroom: Creating Cultural Texts to Engage Diverse Readers."** *Theory into Practice* 37, no. 3 (1998): 238–243.

Blake, B. E. *A Culture of Refusal: The Lives and Literacies of Out-of-School Adolescents.* New York: Peter Lang, forthcoming.

Blake, B. E. **"Doing Number 5: From Process to Cultural Texts in an Urban Writing Classroom."** *Language Arts* 72 (1995): 396–404.

Blake, B. E. **"Fruit of the Devil: Writing and English Language Learners."** *Language Arts* 78, no. 5 (2001): 435–441.

Blake, B. E. *She Say, He Say: Urban Girls Write Their Lives.* Albany: State University of New York Press, 1997.

Blake, B. E. **"Using Portfolios with English Language Learners."** In *Literacy Portfolios,* ed. R. Weiner and J. Cohen. Upper Saddle River, NJ: Merrill/Prentice Hall, 2002.

Blake, R. W. *Reader Response: Toward an Evolving Model for Teaching Literature in the Elementary Grades. Language and Literacy Spectrum* 6 (1996): 39–44.

Blake, R. W. *Whole Language: Positions and Pedagogy.* Urbana, IL: NCTE, 1990.

Brandt, D. *Literacy as Involvement: The Acts of Writers, Readers, and Texts.* Carbondale: Southern Illinois University Press, 1990.

Friere, P. *Literacy: Reading the Word and the World.* Boston: Bergin and Garvey, 1987.

Heath, S. B. *Ways with Words.* Cambridge: Cambridge University Press, 1983.

Hoggart, R. *The Uses of Literacy.* London: Penguin, 1957.

McLaren, P. **"Culture or Canon? Critical Pedagogy and the Politics of Literacy."** *Harvard Educational Review* 58 (1988).

Mercer, N., ed. *Language and Literacy from an Educational Perspective.* Milton Keynes: Open University Press, 1988.

Olson, D., N. Torrance, and A. Hildyard, eds. *Literacy, Language, and Learning: The Nature and Consequences of Reading and Writing.* Cambridge: Cambridge University Press, 1985.

Ong, W. *Orality and Literacy.* London: Methuen, 1982.

Rodby, J. *Appropriating Literacy: Writing and Reading in English as a Second Language.* Portsmouth, NH: Boynton/Cook/Heinemann, 1992.

Scollon, R., and S. Scollon. *Narrative, Literacy, and Face in Interethnic Communication.* Norwood, NJ: Ablex, 1981.

Scribner, S., and M. Cole. *The Psychology of Literacy.* Cambridge, MA: Harvard University Press, 1981.

Smith, F. *Joining the Literacy Club.* Victoria, Alberta: ABEL Press, 1984.

Street, B., ed. *Cross-Cultural Approaches to Literacy.* Cambridge: Cambridge University Press, 1993.

Street, B. *Literacy in Theory and Practice.* Cambridge: Cambridge University Press, 1984.

Street, B. *Social Literacies: Critical Approaches to Literacy in Development, Ethnography, and Education.* London: Longman, 1995.

Stuckey, E. *The Violence of Literacy.* Portsmouth, NH: Boynton/Cook, 1991.

Wagner, D. *The Future of Literacy in a Changing World.* Oxford: Pergamon Press, 1987.

Wagner, D., ed. *Literacy and Ethnicity: International Journal of the Sociology of Language,* 42.

Weiner, R., and J. Cohen. *Literacy Portfolios.* Upper Saddle River, NJ: Merrill/Prentice Hall, 2002.

Weinstein, G. **"Literacy and Second Language Acquisition: Issues and Perspectives."** *TESOL Quarterly* 18 (1984): 471–484.

Willinsky, J. *The New Literacy: Redefining Reading and Writing in the Schools.* New York: Routledge, 1990.

NONPRINT SOURCES

The resources listed in this section have been compiled and edited from George Suttle's Website "Reading and Language Arts Resources on the Internet." The full, annotated, text version of his Website can be found at http://GeorgeSuttle.com/presentations/MSRC/index.shtml.

George Suttle encourages the use of this Website for educational purposes and welcomes any comments, suggestions, and questions. He can be reached directly at George@GeorgeSuttle.com.

General Interest

Children's Book Council's Teacher and Librarian Page
http://www.cbcbooks.org/.

Offers links to a variety of bibliographies, brochures, and handouts geared toward teachers and librarians.

Children's Literacy Development with Suggestions for Parental Involvement
http://eric.indiana.edu/www/indexdb.html

An ERIC Reading, English, and Communication digest, a project of the U.S. Department of Education with funding from the Library of Education.

Choose the Right Book for Kids
http://www.members.aol.com/ivonavon/booklis.htm

A set of links to bibliographies of the "best" books for children.

Let's Read!
http://www.ed.gov/pubs/parents/LearnPtnrs/read.html

Advice from the U.S. Department of Education for parents on how to read to their children. Includes reading activities and resources for beginning to advanced young readers.

Multicultural Resources for Children
http://falcon.jmu.edu/~ramseyil/multipub.htm

Offers a series of bibliographies on books about different ethnic and cultural groups as well as links to other sites.

Ten Ways to Help Your Children Become Lifelong Readers
http://www.naeyc.org/

A handy set of suggestions and ideas; ideal for sharing with parents.

What Do You Know about Reading to Your Child?
http://www.babycenter.com/calculator/6512.html/

A ten-question self-quiz to "test" parents on how much they know about the power of reading to children. Includes related topics, including tips on writing.

Lesson Plans and Teaching Resources

Classroom Material
http://www.sonoma.edu/CThink/K12/k12class/trc.nclk

The Center for Critical Thinking has created a wealth of information including instructional guides and lesson plans to help educators.

Enhancing Student Literacy in Secondary Schools
http://www.bced.gov.bc.ca/irp/ela1112/tpc/toc.htm

Provided by the Curriculum and Resources Branch of the British Columbia Ministry of Education, this is an in-service resource guide.

Exemplary Sample Lesson Plans
http://eric.indiana.edu/www/indexbs.html

Links to sample lesson plans found in books available from the ERIC bookstore.

Literacy Research

Center for the Improvement of Early Reading Achievement
http://www.ciera.org/

Most of the center's publications are for sale, but they do provide some free research articles.

ERIC Clearinghouse on Reading, English, and Communication
http://eric.indiana.edu/www/indexdb.html

Almost no one has time to keep abreast of all the research being done in literacy. The digest summaries published by the ERIC Clearinghouse offer both general awareness and guides to further research.

How Now Brown Cow: Phoneme Awareness Activities for Collaborative Classrooms
http://www.ldonline.org/ld_indepth/teaching_techniques/cld_howno
w.html

This article presents a set of developmental phoneme awareness training activities that the special educator can use at the K–1 levels.

Learning to Read: Resources for Language Arts and Reading Research
http://www.toread.com/

The purpose of this Webpage is to improve the quality of reading instruction through the study of the reading process and teaching techniques.

1–2–3 Reading Road
http://www.thinkquest.org

Developed as a "ThinkQuest" project, this Website provides a multimedia experience to enable young children to practice the basic skills necessary for reading success. The site supports parents and teachers by providing additional teaching methods, games, and activities.

The Politics of Reading Research and Practice
http://ed-web3.educ.msu.edu/pearson/ppt/polit/index.htm

A research paper by renowned literacy scholar P. David Pearson of the Center for the Study of Professional Development at Michigan State University.

Preventing Reading Difficulties in Young Children
http://www.nap.edu/readingroom/books/prdyc/

This highly acclaimed study synthesizes the research on early reading development and makes practical, commonsensical recommendations.

Reading Online: An Electronic Journal of the International Reading Association
http://www.readingonline.org/

This peer-reviewed on-line journal for literacy educators includes fulltext research articles and offers on-line forums for readers to react and interact.

Stony Brook Reading and Language Project
http://www.read+lang.sbs.sunysb.edu/

Grover Whitehust provides this introductory page for the SUNY, Stony Brook project. From the introduction, one can proceed to pages on the project itself or to a list of papers and publications.

Teaching Ideas: Reading
http://www.ncte.org/teach/read.html

The National Council of Teachers of English Website contains a variety of short essays and excerpts from its publications.

⬤⬥ Index

Achilles, 53, 55, 58, 109
Active reader, 168–170
Adams, Marilyn, 31
Aesthetic knowing, 110–111, 121. *See also* Literary knowing, Narrative thought
creating knowledge, 111
Aesthetic reading, 161, 162–164
Affective Fallacy, 139, 159
Age of Criticism, 135, 137
Alphabets, 25. *See also* Greek alphabet, Scripts
acoustic and visual qualities, 41–42
Cyrillic, 27, 29, 41
and diacritical marks, 43
imperfections, 44, 46, 48
as instruments of acoustic recognition, 44–45, 48
and meaning, 38, 47–48
modifications of, 43–44
and new way of thinking, 60–61
and non-original sounds, 44
Roman, 26, 27, 29, 41, 45
vs. syllabaries, 40–41
Ambrose, 80
American Educational Research Association, 245
American Federation of Teachers, 239
American Literacy Council, 239
Angers, University of, 88, 89
Anglo-Saxons and language, 3–4, 26–27
Antigone, 109
Antigone, 52, 127
Appalachia, 2

Applebee, Arthur, 143, 189
Aquinas, Thomas, 66, 89
Arabic, 41
Arabic numerals, 28, 97
Aramaic, 41
Arenson, Karen, 186
Aristotle, 62
Articulators, 34
Asides, 97
Associations, 245–246
Augustine, Saint, 27, 80
Autonomous literacy, 19–21

Bacon, Francis, 67
Baker, Nicholson, 65
Balzac, Honoré de, 134
The Barbara Bush Foundation for Family Literacy, 239–240
Basic Education for All, 3
Beach, Richard, 143–144, 185–186, 189, 193–194
Beardsley, Monroe C., 29–30, 139, 159
Beginning to Read: Thinking and Learning, 31
Beginning with Books, 240
Beloof, Robert, 205–206
Beloved, 158, 170
Beowulf, 27
Bible, 27
Gutenberg, 28
Bibliography, 247–249
Bilingualism, 5, 6–7, 18
Blackmur, R. P., 137–138
Blake, Brett Elizabeth, 224
Blake, Robert, 164–165
Blake, William, 141

BlakeCo International, 240
Bleich, David, 170–171, 201–203
Bobrick, Benson, 69–70
BookPALS, 240
Brontë, Charlotte, 187
Brooks, Cleanth, 135, 141, 147–149,
    152–153
  criticisms of, 149–152
Browne, Thomas, 67
Bruner, Jerome, 103–104, 111–114,
    121
Bubar, Susan, 187
Byrd, Max, 163

California, 192–193, 194–201, 216
  non-English native languages
    among students, 223
California Literacy, Inc., 240–241
Cambridge University, 89. *See also*
    Richards, I. A., reading study
Canadian Francophone movement,
    6
Canterbury Tales, 136
Carlstrom, Nancy White, 211–212
"The Cask of Amontillado," 145
Cathedral of Notre Dame, 86
"The Cave," 119
"Celebrity Scholars," 186–188
Censorship, 91
Center for the Improvement of Early
    Reading Achievement, 241
Chall, Jeanne, 32
Charles of France, 98
Charles V, King of France, 93–94
Chaucer, Geoffrey, 136
Chekhov, Anton, 117–118, 121
Cherokee syllabary, 29
Children, 63
The Children's Book Council, 241
Children's Literature for Children,
    242–242
China, 6, 36
Cicero, 98
The Civil War, 119
Classroom instruction, 143–145

  Brooks and Warren on, 147–152
  comprehension, 146–147
  short-answer questions, 146
  trivialization of New Criticism
    principles, 146–147
Classroom Reader Response, 17,
    215. *See also* Reader
    Response
  application in schools (Bleich
    method), 201–203
  and close reading, 204, 213, 216
  contrasted with traditional
    approach, 214–215
  emphasis on reader's response to
    text, 203
  encouragement of memories and
    associations, 204
  experiencing literature in a
    number of ways, 212
  feeling response, 206–207, 213,
    216
  and feelings, 203
  initial response, 206, 216
  and intuition, 204, 213, 216
  memory response, 207–211, 213
  program for elementary
    students, 211–215
  program for secondary students,
    205–211
  reader understanding of
    responses as reflections of
    personalities, 205
  reader-created meaning, 203
  results, 182–185
  retelling a story, 213
  sharing with others, 204–205
  slow development of, 215
  students' interpretations, 214,
    216–217
  underlying assumptions, 203–205
  writing responses, 213
Close reading, 29, 134, 135, 143,
    153–154, 187
  defined, 136
CNN, 64

Coalition for Essential Schools, 242
Cognition, 103, 121. *See also*
    Aesthetic knowing, Literary
    knowing, Narrative thought,
    Paradigmatic thought,
    Personal intelligences,
    Rational knowing
  irreducibility of paradigmatic
    and narrative, 103, 113–114,
    121–122
  multiple intelligences, 114
Coles, Robert, 118–119, 121, 127
Columbia University, 186–188
Community programs, 7
Computer literacy, 9, 14–15, 16
Computers, 64
Connell, Richard, 145
Consonants, 34, 35
Content Standards. See English–
    Language Arts Framework
    Content Standards for
    California Public Schools
    Kindergarten through Grade
    Twelve
Conventional orthography, 37
Craft literacy, 37–38, 62–63
The Crawl (televised print
    information), 64
Criticism, 133–134. *See also* New
    Criticism; Reader Response;
    Richards, I. A., reading study
Cuba, 6, 8
Cuddon, J. A., 136, 157
"Cultural book(s)," 109
Cultured literacy, 10
Cursive, 85, 92
  cursive formata (*lettre batarde* or
    hybrida), 96, 97
Cyril, Saint, 27

Dante, 96
Dark Ages, 26
Data storage, 64–65
De officiis, 98
Death of a Salesman, 54, 158

"The Death of the Hired Man," 112
Deconstructionism, 186
Democracy, 63
  and King James Bible, 69–70
Descartes, René, 68
Developing countries, 2–3, 7–8
The Diary of Anne Frank, 170
Dickinson, Emily, 137–138
Diverse learners, 221–222, 236–237.
    See also English as a second
    language, English language
    learners
  all students have ability to learn
    and develop, 229
  assumptions, 229
  defined, 222
  schema (background
    knowledge), 228–229
Divine Comedy, 96
Document knowledge, 14, 17
Double Fold: Libraries and the
    Assault on Paper, 65
Douglass, Frederick, 163

Eagleton, Terry, 125–126, 127, 187
Eco, Umberto, 85, 149, 170
Education, 63
  after development of word-
    separated text, 86, 101
Educational associations, 245–246
Efferent reading, 161, 162–164
Egypt, ancient, 25, 36
  papyrus, 46–47
Eisner, Elliot, 110, 114, 121
ELLs. *See* English language learners
Emerson, Ralph Waldo, 136
England. *See also* Great Britain
  French and Anglo-Saxon
    languages, 3–4
English as a second language, 221
  adolescent classroom example,
    231–235
  elementary classroom example,
    230–231
  and poetry, 232, 233–234

English language
    and King James Bible, 68–69
    phonemes and script, 38–39
    and Roman alphabet, 45
    Standard English, 227
English language learners, 222–223
    assumptions, 229
    challenges faced, 223
    defined, 223
    examples, 223–226
    and reading, 228–229
    schema (background
        knowledge), 228–229
    second language acquisition
        theories, 226–227
    and standardized testing,
        235–236
English–Language Arts Framework
    Content Standards for
    California Public Schools
    Kindergarten through Grade
    Twelve, 197–198, 216
English–Language Arts Framework
    for California Public Schools
    Kindergarten through Grade
    Twelve, 195–197, 199, 216
ESL. *See* English as a second
    language
Etruscans, 26
Every Child a Reader: The Report of
    the California Reading Task
    Force, 197
"Every Good Boy Does Fine," 164
Explication de texte, 134, 135, 136,
    188
Exposition, 104, 106–107
    panda example, 104–105
Ezra Jack Keats Foundation, 242

Faulkner, William, 172
Feminism, 186–187
Financial News Network, 64
Finnegans Wake, 171–172
First Book National Book Bank, 242
Fish, Stanley, 176–180

Flaubert, Gustave, 134
Flesch, Rudolph, 30
Foote, Shelby, 119
"For Esmé, with Love and Squalor,"
    172
Formalists, 135
Fox News, 64
Frames of Mind: The Theory of
    Multiple Intelligences, 114
Frank, Anne, 170
Free association, 172
Freud, Sigmund, 172
Frost, Robert, 112, 161–162
Functional illiteracy, 2, 15, 22
Functional literacy
    and age, 12–13
    defined, 11–12

Gaelic, 4–5
Galileo, 67, 68
Gandhi, Mahatma, 116
Gardner, Howard, 114–117, 121
Gilbert, Sandra M., 187
Glyphs, 36
"A Good Man Is Hard to Find," 179
The Grapes of Wrath, 158
Graphemes, 37
Great Britain, 63, 69–70. *See also*
    England
Greece, ancient, 8–9, 25–26. *See also*
    Poetry (Greek epics)
    alphabet. *See* Greek alphabet
    golden age, 26
    periods of literacy, 26
    and the psyche, 57
    shift from poetic to prosaic
        language, 51, 56, 70
    writing surfaces, 46–47
Greek alphabet, 25, 26, 27, 29
    as alphabetic script, 37, 41
    and Athenian dialect, 45
    and inflection, 75
    as last important step in history
        of writing, 33
    and new way of thinking, 60–61

and prose, 56, 70
and vowels and consonants, 35, 41
and writing of oral literature, 62
Gregory of Tours, 82–83
Gutenberg, Johannes, 28, 70

Halliday, M. A. K., 30
Hamlet, 111, 113, 134, 150, 170, 172
Hardy, Thomas, 113
Harklau, Linda, 223
Havelock, Eric, 8–9, 67
    "cultural book" concept, 109
Hawthorne, Nathaniel, 170
Hebrew, 41
    and English language, 68–69
Hector, 54, 58, 109
Hermeneutics, 58, 67
Herodotus, 46
Hieroglyphics, 36
High-stakes testing, 235–236
Histoire ancienne jusqu'à César, 92
Holland, Norman, 173–176
Homer, 52–53, 109–110, 111, 113.
        See also Poetry (Greek epics)
Huckleberry Finn, 134, 190
Hugo, Victor, 134

Iliad, 52, 53, 61, 109, 111, 150
Illiteracy, 22
    defining, 11
    developing countries, 2–3
    functional, 2, 15, 22
    industrialized countries, 2, 3
    pejorative connotation, 8, 9
The Imitation of Christ, 98
Imitation theory, 226–227
Immigration, 221
India, 36
Inflection, 74–75
Innatist theory, 227
Intellectual knowing. *See* Rational
        knowing
Intentional Fallacy, 139–140

International Book Project, Inc., 242–243
International Reading Association, 245
Interpersonal intelligence, 115–116, 121
Interpretive community reader, 176–180
Intrapersonal intelligence, 115, 121
Intuition
    and Classroom Reader Response, 204, 213, 216
    and New Criticism, 150
    and Reader Response, 165, 166, 168
Iraq, 36
Ireland
    and Gaelic, 4–5
    and word-separated text, 27
*Is There a Text in This Class? The
        Authority of Interpretive
        Communities,* 176–177
Iser, Wolfgang, 168–170
"It Bids Pretty Fair," 161–162

Jackson, Shirley, 145, 172
Jane Eyre, 187
Jesse Bear, What Will You Wear?, 211–212
John II, King of France, 94
Joyce, James, 111, 113, 171–172
"Just before the War with the
        Eskimos," 146

Kelly, Mary C., 211
Kilborn, Peter, 2
King James Bible, 68–69
    and popular government, 69–70
King, Martin Luther Jr., 116
Knowing. *See* Aesthetic knowing,
        Literary knowing, Narrative
        thought, Paradigmatic
        thought, Personal
        intelligences, Rational
        knowing

Kuhn, Stephanie, 231–235

Langer, Judith A., 190, 192
Language
    literacy and opacity of, 51
    Plato's prosaic approach, 51, 56,
        70
    prosaic vs. poetic, 55, 70
Languages
    equality of, 229
    innatist theory, 227
    learning by imitation, 226–227
    non-English native languages
        among students, 223
    numbers of, 35
    second language acquisition
        theories, 226–227
    social interactionist theory, 227
    sociocultural/political nature,
        227
Large-scale testing, 235–236
Latin
    and inflection, 74–75
    throughout Europe, 84
Latinos, 223
"The Laughing Man," 146
Lawrence, D. H., 126
Lecture method, 86
Lesson plans (websites), 250–251
Libraries, 65
    changes due to word-separated
        texts, 89–90
    and Charles V, 94
    medieval, 86–87
Lincoln, Abraham, 116
Lincoln's Greatest Speech, 163
Linguistics-based structuralism, 186
Literacy
    advanced or high, 10, 16
    autonomous, 19–21
    basic, 16
    changing demands, 17–18
    and the community, 7
    context-embedded activities, 229
    craft, 37–38, 62–63

    cultured, 10
    defined, 8, 10–11
    defining, 1, 3
    developing countries, 7–8
    and economic well-being, 6
    and fun, 229
    functional, 11–13, 15
    high-quantity vs. high-quality
        education, 21–22
    historical spread of, 35
    importance of, 1
    and the individual, 5
    and language, 51
    local, 236, 237
    "many literacies" concept, 19, 21,
        22
    measuring, 15, 19, 22–23
    minimal, 15–16
    musical, 67
    and national economic
        development, 7–8
    and national policy, 15
    nonfunctional, 11–12
    and nonnative speakers, 18
    numerate, 13–14, 17
    and political stability, 6–7
    pragmatic, 10
    and reading, 73
    recitation, 26
    required, 16
    research (websites), 251–252
    scriptorial, 26
    semiliteracy, 26
    skills, 13–15
    and society, 6
    types of programs, 1–2
    and women, 6
Literacy Volunteers of America, 21,
    243
Literary knowing, 103–104, 108–109,
    121–122, 127. *See also*
    Aesthetic knowing, Narrative
    thought, Rational knowing
    and personal intelligences,
    116–117

and rational knowing, 117–119,
120–121
Literature, 17
democratization of reading of,
125–126
determination by reader, 177–178
as transaction, 160–161, 196
Literature as Exploration, 160–161
Litteratus, 9, 10
Local literacy, 236, 237
Logico-mathematical knowing. *See*
Rational knowing
"The Lottery," 145, 172
Louis, Saint, 92
Louis XI, King of France, 98
Lunn, Anna, 164–165
Luther, Martin, 66, 68

Macbeth, 134
MacFarquhar, Larissa, 178
Madame Bovary, 134
The Madwoman in the Attic, 187
Malcolm, Janet, 117–118, 121
Mansel, Jean, 98
Marshall, James, 193–194
Mayor, Federico, 1, 3
Meaning, 125–126, 133, 142, 149,
151–152
and being, 140
reader as agent in creation of,
157–158
and subjectivity, 171
Melville, Herman, 172
Mesopotamia, 25, 36
Metacognition, 57
Metalinguistics, 57
Methodius, Saint, 27
Mexico, 36
Miller, Arthur, 54, 158
Les Misérables, 134
Moby Dick, 163, 172
Morrison, Toni, 158, 170
"The Most Dangerous Game," 145
MSNBC, 64
Multiculturalism, 186

Multiple intelligences, 114
Multiply marginalized students, 222
Musical literacy, 67
Musical notation, 29
"My Papa's Waltz," 174–175

The Name of the Rose, 85, 149, 170
Narration, 104, 107–108
panda example, 105–106
Narrative thought, 103–104,
111–113, 121
National Council of Teachers of
English, 246
National Institute for Literacy, 243
National Jewish Coalition for
Literacy, 243
National Right to Read Foundation,
243–244
Neo-Thomists, 135
New Criticism, 29–30, 126
and Affective Fallacy, 139, 142,
159
and author's intention, 149
and classroom instruction,
143–152
and close reading, 135, 136, 143,
153–154
and emotion, 139, 159
growing up to level of a poem,
150–151
and Intentional Fallacy, 139–140,
142
and intuition, 150
and John Crowe Ransom,
137–138
literature as literature, 142
and meaning, 142, 149, 151–152
and meaning vs. being, 140
and old criticism, 141, 152
organic unity, 142, 154
principles, 142–143
proponents of, 135
scientific approach, 140,
142–143, 147, 154
and secondary schools, 189–190

New Criticism, *continued*
  text as text, 140, 142, 149,
    151–152, 153
  as theology, 135, 136–137
  and universities, 187–188, 189,
    190–191
  and university professors, 140–141
  and "untouchable flower"
    syndrome, 150
The New Criticism, 137
New York City, 223
New York State, Option III
  classrooms, 231–235
NFE. *See* Nonformal education
NGOs. *See* Nongovernmental
  organizations
"Ninja Turtles," 230
Nonformal education, 5
Nongovernmental organizations, 7
Nonliteracy, 8–9, 22
North Semitic tribes and languages,
  41, 43–44
Numeracy, 13–14, 17, 67

O'Connor, Flannery, 179
Odysseus, 109
Odyssey, 52, 109, 111
Oedipus Rex, 52, 111, 127
Olmecs, 36
Olson, David R., 20–21, 51
Ontological criticism, 138
Organizations, 239–245
Oxford University, 89
Ozick, Cynthia, 135–136

Page format. *See* Text format
Papyrus, 46–47
Paradigmatic thought, 103–104,
  111–112, 121. *See also*
  Rational knowing
  and categorization and
    conceptualization, 112
Parchment, 46
  advantage of sheets, 85, 86
Paris, University of, 86

Pecia system, 88, 100
Peer conferences, 230
*Penguin Dictionary of Literary Terms
  and Literary Theory,* 136
Le Père Goriot, 134
Pericles, 60
Periodic sentences, 75, 79–80
Persian, 41
Personal intelligences, 114–115, 121.
  See also Interpersonal
    intelligence, Intrapersonal
    intelligence
  and literary knowing, 116–117
Philosophers, 59–60
Phoenicians, 41
Phonemes, 37, 47–48
Phonics method, 30
Piaget, Jean, 113, 114–115
Plato, 51, 56, 109–110, 114, 119
  and categorization of knowledge,
    62
  and concept of "philosopher," 60
  and theory of forms, 58–59, 110
Poe, Edgar Allan, 145
The Poetics, 62
Poetry. *See also* New Criticism
  in ESL teaching, 232, 233–234
Poetry (Greek epics), 52
  didactic purpose, 52, 109
  dreamlike quality, 53, 55
  and *ethos* (private law), 53–54
  mnemonic devices, 53, 109
  narrative and characters, 53,
    54–55
  and *nomos* (public law), 53–54
Points of articulation, 35
Political bureaucracies, 65–66
*A Portrait of the Artist as a Young
  Man,* 111, 171–172
Postcolonialism, 186–187
Poststructuralism, 186
Poulet, Georges, 166-1–68
*Practical Criticism: A Study of
  Literary Judgment,* 29, 128,
    137, 160

Pragmatic literacy, 10
Preliteracy, 8, 22
"Pretty Mouth and Green My Eyes,"
    146
Print resources, 247–249
Printing, 28–29, 62, 100–101
    and communications systems,
        63–64
    consequences, 63–70
    and data collection, 64
    and family life (socialization of
        children), 63
    and King James Bible, 68–69
    and literacy, 46–47
    and political bureaucracies,
        65–66
    and Protestant Reformation, 66,
        99
    and science, 66–68
Probst, Robert E., 189–190
Process writing, 16
Prose
    and abstraction, 56, 58–60
    and Greek alphabet, 56, 70
    and Plato, 51, 56, 70
Protestant Reformation, 66, 99
Psyche, 57
    and thought, 57–58
Psychoanalytic reader, 173–176
Punctuation, 90
Purves, Alan, 146, 190, 191

Quires, 85, 86

Ransom, John Crowe, 29–30, 135,
    137–138, 139, 140
Rational knowing, 103–104,
    109–110, 121–122, 127. *See
    also* Literary knowing,
    Paradigmatic thought
    discovering knowledge, 111
    and literary knowing, 117–119,
        120–121
Read In Foundation, 244

Reader Response, 30, 126. *See also*
    Classroom Reader Response
    and the active reader, 168–170
    aesthetic reading, 161, 162–164
    and aesthetic response, 169
    and California, 192–193, 194–201,
        216
    and closed text, 170
    and concretization, 169–170
    and cultural codes, 170
    defined, 159
    determination of literature by
        reader, 177–178
    efferent reading, 161, 162–164
    and elementary schools, 192–201
    and emotion, 158
    and fantasy, 175
    focus on reader, 158–159, 162
    and I. A. Richards, 128
    and identity, 173–176
    interiorization, 166–167, 168
    and the interpretive community
        reader, 176–180
    and intuition, 165, 166, 168
    lack of academic theoretical
        model, 185–188, 215
    lack of pedagogical model for
        teaching literature in
        schools, 192–201, 215–216
    lack of training for
        schoolteachers in its
        practices, 188–192, 215
    literature as transaction, 160–161,
        196
    and Louise M. Rosenblatt,
        160–161, 165–166
    and meaning, 157–158, 177, 179
    and open text, 170
    principles, 180–182
    and the psychoanalytic reader,
        173–176
    reading process, 164–166
    and the semiotic reader, 170
    subjective criticism, 170–172, 201

Reader Response, *continued*
　and the subjective reader, 170–172
　and the submissive reader,
　　166–168
　and text, 177
　and theme, 175
The Reader, the Text, the Poem, 161
Readers & Writers, 244
Reading, 13, 17
　aesthetic, 161, 162–164
　in ancient times, 46–47
　democratization of
　　interpretation, 125–126
　of different types of material,
　　73–74
　early systematic instruction
　　programs, 40, 48
　efferent, 161, 162–164
　and English language learners,
　　228–229
　and inflection, 74–75
　and laypersons, 91–92, 93–97
　and literacy, 73
　medieval expansion of, 100
　multiple-stage theories, 31–32
　and nobility, 93–97
　one-stage teaching models, 29,
　　30–31
　phonics teaching method, 30
　psycholinguistic approach, 30–31
　schema theory, 31
　silent, 83–84, 88, 90–92, 94, 98
　and standardized spelling, 76
　and syntax, 74
　and text format, 74, 75–76, 82
　and thinking, 61–62
　two-stage teaching model, 29
　and underlying text structures, 31
　and vocabulary, 75
　"whole language" movement,
　　30–31
　and word-separated text, 76,
　　83–84
　and writing system, 76–78

Reading Is Fundamental, 244
Reading/Language Arts Framework
　for California Public Schools
　Kindergarten through Grade
　Twelve, 198–199, 216
Readings and Feelings: An
　Introduction to Subjective
　Criticism, 201–203
Reference texts, 89, 94–95
Renaissance, 28
　and word-separated text, 96
The Republic, 51, 56, 109–110
Richards, I. A., reading study, 29,
　　128–129, 137, 160
　difficulties of criticism, 130–131,
　　132, 133, 139
　elite study group, 128–129, 132
　and meaning, 133
　and nature of criticism, 133–134
　and psychology, 130, 132, 140
　"statements" and "mental
　　operations," 129–130
"The Rocking Horse Winner," 126
Roethke, Theodore, 174–175
Rolando, 225
The Role of the Reader: Explorations
　in the Semiotics of Texts, 170
Roman du Lancelot, 92
Rome, ancient, 26
　and Greek alphabet, 45, 62
Roosevelt, Eleanor, 116
Rosenblatt, Louise M., 160–164,
　　165–166, 196
Royal Society of London, 68
Rubricators, 90
Rumelhart, D. E., 31
Runic script, 26, 27

Saenger, Paul, 73
Salinger, J. D., 146, 172
Sandburg, Carl, 163
The Scarlet Letter, 134
Schaller, George, 107–108, 112
　passage by, 105–106

Schema (background knowledge),
    228–229
Schema theory, 31
Schemo, Diana Jean, 199
Science, 66–68
Scientific knowing. *See* Rational
    knowing
Scribes, 88
    addition of punctuation, 90
    increased rapidity of copying,
        100
    and *scriptura continua,* 97
    and vernacular languages, 92–93
Scripts. *See also* Alphabets, Cursive,
    Textualis
    alphabetic, 37
    and ambiguity, 39, 40, 44, 48
    efficiency, 38–40, 48
    exhaustiveness, 38–39, 40, 48
    imperfections of, 43–44
    and learning to read, 76–78
    logographic, 36, 40–41, 43, 47
    North Semitic, 43–44
    qualitative aspects, 38
    quantitative aspects, 37–38
    and recognition of sounds, 39
    small size, 39, 40, 48
    syllabic, 36. 40–41, 43, 47
    vocalized and unvocalized, 41–42
Scriptura continua, 27
    in contemporary "hard" writing
        systems, 76–77
    and Italian scribes, 97
    and ocular regressions, 79
    and periodic sentences, 79–80
    persistence of, 80–81
    and *praelectio,* 80, 82
    reading out loud, 78, 79
    reading process, 78–79
    and vowels, 80
Scripture, 66–68
"Sea Lullaby," 152
Semiotic reader, 170
Semiotics, 186

Sequoyah, 29
Shakespeare, William, 111, 113, 170,
    172
    study of, 134–135
Silent reading, 83–84, 88, 91–92, 94
    and independent or dissident
        thought, 90–91, 98, 100
    and spiritual life, 98–99
    and university life, 88
Slavonic, 27
"Slouching toward Bethlehem," 150
Smith, Frank, 30
Social interactionist theory, 227
Social literacies, 21
Socrates, 56
    dialectic method, 57–58
Sophocles, 111
Sorbonne, 86–87, 89–90, 188
The Sound and the Fury, 172
Southern Agrarians, 135
Soviet Union, 4, 6
Speech
    characteristics and mechanisms
        of, 34–35
    and writing, 33–34
Spelling, 76, 92–93, 99–100
Spivak, Gayatri, 186–187
Sprat, Thomas, 68
"A Spring Night," 205–206
Spurgeon, F. E., 113
Squire, James, 128
Stages of Reading Development, 32
Standard English, 227
Standardized tests, 235–236
Stationers, 88
Steinbeck, John, 158
Street, Brian, 21
Structuralism, 186
Student Coalition for Action in
        Literacy Education, 244–245
Subjective criticism, 170–172,
        201–203
Subjective Criticism, 170–171
Subjective reader, 170–172

Submissive reader, 166–168
Summa Theologica, 66
Sweden, 6
Syllabaries, 36
   vs. alphabets, 40–41
   Cherokee, 29
Syntax, 74

Tanzania, 8
Tatarstan, 4
Tate, Allen, 135
Teachers of English to Speakers of
   Other Languages, 246
*Teaching Literature in the Secondary
   School,* 193–194
Teaching resources (websites),
   250–251
Television news, 64
Terrell, 224–225
Text
   closed, 170
   open, 170
   in potentia, 157
   Stanley Fish on, 177
   as text, 140, 142, 149, 151–152,
     153
Text format, 74, 75–76, 82, 99
   and advantage of parchment
     sheets, 85, 86
   capitals, 87, 97
   dashes, 97
   development of chapters and
     other subdivisions, 87
   diagrams, 87
   glosses, 87
   illustrations, 95
   medieval developments, 87–88
   paragraph marks, 87
   parentheses, 97
   and silent reading, 88
   and vernacular books, 94–95
Textualis, 84, 85, 95–96, 97
*Theoretical Models and Processes of
   Reading,* 31
Theory, 126–127

Thomas à Kempis, 98
Thought, 57–58. *See also* Aesthetic
   knowing, Literary knowing,
   Narrative thought,
   Paradigmatic thought,
   Personal intelligences,
   Rational knowing
"The Three Little Pigs," 228
Through the Eyes of a Child, 194
Tompkins, Jane, 159
   on Georges Poulet's views, 166
   on Norman Holland, 173
   on Wolfgang Iser's theory,
     169–170
Trilling, Lionel, 135

Ulysses, 111, 171–172
Understanding Poetry, 141, 147–153
*Understanding Reading: A
   Psycholinguistic Analysis of
   Reading and Learning to
   Read,* 30
UNESCO, 2–3, 8
   on age and literacy, 12
   on functional literacy, 11
   on minimal and functional
     literacy, 15
UNICEF, 8
United Nations Children's Fund. *See*
   UNICEF
United Nations Educational,
   Scientific, and Cultural
   Organization. *See* UNESCO
United States, 63. *See also*
   Appalachia
   use of Spanish, 6–7
U.S. Census Bureau, 12
U.S. Office of Education, 12
"Untouchable flower" syndrome,
   150

The Verbal Icon, 139
Vernacular texts, 92–93, 94–95,
   97–98, 99, 100
   and spiritual life, 98

Vie de Christ, 98
Vivas, Eliseo, 135
Vowels, 34, 35

Wagoner, David, 164
Walmsley, Sean, 190, 191–192
Warren, Austin, 29–30
Warren, Robert Penn, 141, 147–149,
    152–153
  criticisms of, 149–152
Waxed tablets, 47
WCEFA. *See* World Conference on
    Education for All
Websites
  general, 249–250
  lesson plans and teaching
      resources, 250–251
  literacy research, 251–252
Wellek, René, 29–30
White, Ronald C., 163
Whitehead, Alfred North, 110–111
"Whole language" movement, 30–31
Why Johnny Can't Read, 30
Wide as the Waters, 69–70
William the Conqueror, 3–4
Wimsatt, W. K. Jr., 29–30, 139, 159
Word-separated text, 27, 28, 76. *See
    also Scriptura continua*
  before development of vowels, 80
  changes spawned by, 84

importance of, 81–82
and reading silently, 83–84, 88
reintroduction of by Irish scribes,
    83
and Renaissance, 96
spread throughout Europe, 83–84
and writing, 85
The World Book Encyclopedia,
    106–107
  passage from, 104–105
World Conference on Education for
    All, 5
Writing, 13, 16–17
  alphabetic, 37
  emphasis on teaching of,
      192–193
  logographic, 25, 36, 40–41, 43, 47
  origins, 36
  and speech, 33–34
  syllabic, 36, 40–41, 43, 47
  as technology of the intellect, 61
  as tentative structure of
      language, 61–62
  and word-separated text, 85
Wylie, Elinor, 152

Yeats, William Butler, 150
"Young Goodman Brown," 170

Zimbabwe, 8

◆◇ About the Authors

Brett Elizabeth Blake is an associate professor and coordinator of the Graduate Adolescent Education Programs at St. John's University in New York. Dr. Blake has written extensively about the challenges urban adolescents face in their literacy learning, including a book from SUNY Press, *She Say, He Say: Urban Girls Write Their Lives* (1997), and a forthcoming book from Peter Lang Publishing, entitled *A Culture of Refusal: The Lives and Literacies of Out-of-School Adolescents.* Dr. Blake continues her work in the public schools as a consultant with the Educational Alliance at Brown University's field office in New York City, where she, teachers, and students seek ways in which literacy learning can be rewarding, successful, and equitable for all.

Robert W. Blake is emeritus professor of Education and Human Development at the State University of New York College at Brockport, where he was director of the undergraduate and graduate programs in English Education and English as a Second Language. His latest books are *Literature as a Way of Knowing: Critical Thinking and Moral Reasoning through Literature* and *Whole Language: Explorations and Applications.* He lives in Brockport with his wife and cat.